Additional Praise for
Augustine's Theology of Preaching

"Augustine is one of the great Christian preachers, and his sermons show him at home with his people and perceptively engaged with human life from many angles. Dr. Sanlon has not only brought Augustine's preaching to life and given a rich, nuanced account of its core teaching on a range of topics; he has also thought deeply about its relevance today and shows how we too can benefit from engaging with him."

David F. Ford
University of Cambridge

"Augustine is known today as great theologian and church leader but in his own day he would have placed his calling to preach at the very heart of his ministry. Yet so often scholars have neglected this area of his life, with the result that our understanding of him is somewhat truncated. In this important study, Peter Sanlon redresses this imbalance by placing Augustine the preacher at the center. This is a book which not only enriches our scholarly understanding of Augustine but which will also be a delight for those called to preach the Word today."

Carl R. Trueman
Westminster Theological Seminary

AUGUSTINE'S THEOLOGY OF PREACHING

AUGUSTINE'S THEOLOGY OF PREACHING

PETER T. SANLON

Fortress Press
Minneapolis

AUGUSTINE'S THEOLOGY OF PREACHING

Scripture quotations are from the New Revised Standard Version Bible, copyright © 1989 by the Division of Christian Education of the National Council of the Churches of Christ in the USA. Used by permission. All rights reserved.

Cover design: Laurie Ingram

Library of Congress Cataloging-in-Publication Data

Print ISBN: 978-1-4514-8278-2

eBook ISBN: 978-1-4514-8760-2

The paper used in this publication meets the minimum requirements of American National Standard for Information Sciences — Permanence of Paper for Printed Library Materials, ANSI Z329.48-1984.

Manufactured in the U.S.A.

This book was produced using PressBooks.com, and PDF rendering was done by PrinceXML.

In Memory of Calvin Sanlon
Dormiens natus est, in Christo natus est
August 1, 2009

Jesus said, "Suffer the little children to come unto me, and forbid them
not: for of such is the kingdom of God."
Mark 10:14

CONTENTS

Acknowledgements

I have accumulated many debts of gratitude in the course of this project. Professor David Ford was a generous doctoral supervisor, always happy to discuss theological matters when countless other responsibilities called for his attention. The staff and students of Ridley Hall were patient with their longest serving student, who too often was late for an appointment or meeting due to tracking down yet another reference in Augustine's works. My wife Susanna has been a great encouragement through the years and has been a constant source of joy and perspective.

I am very thankful to the Rt. Rev. and Rt. Hon. Dr. Richard Chartres for his generosity in funding this research from the James Taylor Fund. It is no small achievement that the Church of England can demonstrate its support for theological education by equipping some of its clergy through ordination training which includes doctoral study. I am also grateful to the Latimer Trust for their grant.

Many groups have invited me to speak to them on the topic of Augustine's preaching in recent years. These have all been a great encouragement to me as I have sought to integrate academic and pastoral ministries. In addition to various Cambridge churches, I was thankful for invitations to speak at L'Abri, Hampshire; Trinity Episcopal Church, Dallas, USA; Wycliffe Hall, Oxford; Oak Hill College, London and the European Leadership Forum, Hungary.

I have learned an immense amount from my sustained engagement with Augustine. Augustine's frequent meditation on 1 Cor. 13:12 led him to sense that our knowledge of God is fragmentary, and his reflections on Isa. 7:9 drove him to highlight that weakness in faith is our root problem. In that Augustinian spirit then, I feel I have to preface this thesis with the words of a modern Lutheran scholar, himself a great admirer of Augustine:

> We must guard against the error that the history of theology is one of continuous growth in truth. In almost equal measure it is a history of forgetting the truth. Theology is undertaken by sinners and thus needs forgiveness as sinners themselves do. Even at best our work is in vain. Thought, including theological thought, is part of this work. Like all our work, it can go forward only as a justified work.[1]

1. Helmut Thielicke, *The Evangelical Faith*, vol. 1 (Edinburgh: T&T Clark, 1974), 124.

All translations are my own. I have aimed for a literal translation approach; the more colloquial translations of Augustine's *Sermones* by Edmund Hill have been consulted.

Abbreviations

b. vita.	De beata vita	*On the Happy Life*
c. Acad.	Contra academicos	*Against the Skeptics*
c. adu. leg.	Contra adversarium legis et prophetarum	*Against the Adversaries of the Law and the Prophets*
c. Faust.	Contra Faustum Manicheum	*Against Faustus the Manichee*
civ. Dei.	De civitate Dei	*The City of God*
conf.	Confessiones	*Confessions*
cons. Ev.	De consensu Evangelistarum	*On Agreement among the Evangelists*
cont.	De continentia	*On Continence*
De trin.	De Trinitate	*The Trinity*
div. qu.	De diversis quaestionibus octoginta tribus	*On Eighty-Three Various Questions*
doctr. Chr.	De doctrina Christiana	*On Christian Teaching*
en. Ps.	Enarrationes in Psalmos	*Expositions of the Psalms*
Ep.	Epistulae	*Letters*
Gn. adv. Man.	De Genesi adversus Manicheos	*On Genesis, Against the Manichees*

Gn. litt.	De Genesi ad litteram	*On the Literal Interpretation of Genesis*
Gn. litt. imp.	De Genesi ad litteram imperfectus liber	*On the Literal Interpretation of Genesis: An Unfinished Book*
gramm.	De grammatica	*On Grammar*
imm. an.	De immortalitate animae	*On the Immortality of the Soul*
Inst.	Institutio Christianae religionis	*Institutes of the Christian Religion*
Jo. eu. tr.	In Johannis evangelium tractatus	*Tractates on the Gospel of John*
lib. arb.	De libero arbitrio	*On Free Will*
mag.	De magistro	*On the Teacher*
mend.	De mendacio	*On Lying*
mor.	De moribus ecclesiae catholicae et de moribus Manichaeorum	*On the Catholic and the Manichean Ways of Life*
mus.	De musica	*On Music*
ord.	De ordine	*On Order*
pecc. mer.	De peccatorum meritis et remissione et de baptismo parvulorum	*On the Merits and Forgiveness of Sins and on Infant Baptism*
quant.	De animae quantitate	*On the Greatness of the Soul*
Retr.	Retractationes	*Reconsiderations*

s.	Sermones	*Sermons*
simpl.	Ad Simplicianum	*To Simplicianus*
sol.	Soliloquia	*The Soliloquies*
uera rel.	De uera religione	*On True Religion*

CRITICAL EDITIONS

AB	*Analecta Bollandiana*, Brussels, 1883ff.
CCL	*Corpus Christianorum Series Latina,*: Edited by Xenium natalicium, J. Leemans, L. Jocqué, Belgium, 1953-2003.
CSEL	*Corpus Scriptorum Ecclesiasticorum Latinorum*. Vienna, 1866ff.
DOLBEAU	*Augustin d'Hippone, Vingt-six Sermons au Peuple d'Afrique*. Paris: Institut d'Études Augustiniennes, 1996.
Helen	*Encomio de Elena: Testo Critico, Introduzione e note a Cura*, ed. Francesco Donadi. Roma: Università di Padova, 1982.
Homo Sp.	*Homo spiritalis*. Festgabe für L. Verheijen, Ed. C. Mayer, K. H. Chelius, Würzburg, 1987.
MA	*Miscellanea Agostiniana*. Roma: Typis Polyglottis Vaticanis, 1930.
OCT	*Scriptorum Classicorum Bibliotheca Oxoniensis*, Oxford: Oxford University Press, 1989ff.
PL	*Patrologiae Cursus Completus*, Series Latina, 221 vols., ed. J. Migne. Paris, 1857–66.
PLS	*Patrologiae Cursus Completus*: Supplementum, Vol. 2. Paris: Éditions Garnier Frères, 1960.
RB	*Revue Bénédictine*. Belgium: Abbaye de Maredsous, 1884ff.

ReAug   *Revue des Études Augustiniennes.* Paris: Institut d'Études Augustiniennes, 1955ff.

SC   *Sources Chretiennes.* Paris, 1942ff.

SIM   *Manlio Simonetti, L'Instruzione Christiana.* Augustine's De Doctrina in Italian and Latin, Roma: Fondazione Lorenzo Valla, 1994.

SPM   *Sermones post Maurinos*, Roma: Typis Polyglottis Vaticanis, 1930.

Summary

We aim to articulate the undergirding theological convictions which shaped and informed Augustine's preaching. By doing this, we hope to provide a meaningful hermeneutic of Augustine's preaching, which may be used to interpret his *Sermones ad Populum*. The thesis involves a close reading of the *Sermones ad Populum*, which pays careful attention to the role of Scripture, and utilizes the concepts of "interiority" and "temporality" as hermeneutical keys to Augustine's preaching.

Chapter 1 offers a historical survey of the context within which Augustine preached. This is followed by Chapter Two, which analyzes the issues raised by pagan oratory. Chapter 3 explores Augustine's assumptions about the task of preaching, as expressed in *De Doctrina Christiana*.

All of the above lays the foundation for Chapter 4, which explores our hermeneutical keys: interiority and temporality. These are then used in Chapters 5 to 7 to explicate key themes of Augustine's preaching. In this way, we seek to show that interiority and temporality are valid terms with which to understand Augustine's approach to preaching. Our conclusion sums up our findings before highlighting the contemporary value of our study and further avenues of research. Augustine's preaching has been neglected in current scholarship. This thesis makes a contribution by offering a guide to the *Sermones ad Populum* and suggesting that our understanding of Augustine is distorted if his preaching is overlooked—as it has too often been.

Preface

The aim of our study is to suggest a meaningful hermeneutical key for interpreting Augustine's *Sermones ad Populum*. It is hoped that suggesting such a guide through the *Sermones* will illuminate the undergirding theological convictions which shaped Augustine's approach to the task of preaching.

There is a vast amount of scholarly literature about Augustine. However, his *Sermones* and his preaching generally, are not adequately represented in publications. The actual distribution of academic writing is disproportionate. Augustine's corpus comprises over five million Latin words, yet 15 percent of modern publications on Augustine focus on only two of his writings: *Confessiones* and *De Civitate Dei*.[1]

When the *Sermones ad Populum* are mentioned in academic studies, it is often in a surprisingly dismissive manner. The *Cambridge Companion* series is a benchmark publication, generally accepted across many fields as representative of the current state of scholarship. Yet the *Cambridge Companion to Augustine* describes the *Sermones* as having a "short and scrappy focus on issues of pastoral urgency."[2] An academic lecture complains that "much of what Augustine says in his preaching is unexceptional, even banal."[3]

When Augustine's preaching is overlooked, an imbalanced portrait of Augustine is given. Arguably, this is present wherever people imagine him as merely a philosophical theologian, associate him solely with the refutation of heresies, or link him only with controversial doctrines like original sin. Augustine distinguished himself from other bishops by devoting himself to the ministry of preaching. Many others made only a cursory effort at the task, or held back altogether for fear of Donatist reprisals. We may assume that preaching to the congregation at Hippo demanded of Augustine less knowledge and ability than writing the treatises for which he is famous. However, he himself thought that preaching would require of him an intimidating depth of Scriptural knowledge.[4]

---

1. Hubertus R. Drobner, "Studying Augustine, an Overview of Recent Research," in *Augustine and His Critics*, ed. Robert Dodaro and George Lawless (London: Routlege, 2000), 23.

2. James O' Donnell, "Augustine: His Time and Lives," in *The Cambridge Companion to Augustine*, ed. Eleonore Stump and Norman Kretzmann (Cambridge: Cambridge University Press, 2001), 11.

3. David G. Hunter, "Sex, Sin and Salvation: What Augustine Really Said" (Washington Theological Union, 2002).

When academics marginalise the *Sermones*, the real Augustine is not represented accurately. It may appear at first glance that these deal mainly with matters of pastoral urgency but at the same time, for example, they provide an essential resource for understanding how Augustine articulated his doctrine of the trinity[5] or the resurrection.[6] One of many reasons that Augustine was so influential arose from the shift he made from secular life to Christian ministry. Understanding precisely how he developed from a pagan orator into a Christian preacher is essential for the sake of historical fidelity.

Studying Augustine's preaching will not only yield us a truer understanding of his life and concerns, but may also help us explore areas which today are of considerable importance. We need to articulate methods of persuasion which do not succumb to manipulation and abuse of power. This is a concern in many areas of human endeavour. In the church, there is also the added pressure that many assume preaching is a hopelessly outmoded ministry which ought to be replaced by more visual or interactive experiences. The church needs to reflect on how to communicate the message of God's salvation in Christ to a secular society which assumes God is at best an irrelevance, and at worst, a dangerous idea. Those who engage in Christian ministry often wonder how, or to what extent, they may benefit from utilizing secular learning and means of communication. In addressing all these issues, a study of Augustine's preaching may be valuable.

Classical scholars and historians have begun to notice the immense historical and cultural significance of the Christian sermon. *The Edinburgh Companion to Ancient Greece and Rome* argues that the sermon was Christianity's foremost contribution to ancient culture, representing "nothing less than a revolution in the politics of literary production, a democratisation theorised, in fact, by Augustine himself."[7]

Preaching was a distinctive form of communication which had long term ramifications for secular society. It also was the main way in which the church interacted with Scripture: "Dans la tradition chrétienne, tout au long de la période patristique, c'est l'homélie liturgique actualisante qui constitue la part de loin la plus importante de la littérature exégétique."[8] There is significant value

---

4. *Ep.* 21.3–4 (CSEL 34,1).

5. *s.* 52 (RB 74, 15).

6. *s.* 361 (PL 39, 1599); 362. (PL 39, 1611).

7. Clifford Ando, "Christian Literature," in *The Edinburgh Companion to Ancient Greece and Rome*, ed., Edward Bispham, Thomas Harrison, and Brian A. Sparkes (Edinburgh: Edinburgh University Press, 2006), 405.

to be gained from exploring more carefully what Augustine believed he was doing when he preached.

As stated above, Augustine's preaching has not received the attention it merits. Our book seeks to make an original contribution in a number of ways. We aim to suggest two hermeneutical keys in our discussion, and test them for their explanatory power in three areas of Augustine's preaching. The case studies which form these test cases are extensive engagements with the Latin texts of Augustine's *Sermones*. Since the corpus is so vast, these chapters offer a reader the opportunity to read through large amounts of the material, with our hermeneutical terms providing a guide. The majority of what work has been published on the *Sermones* focuses on textual and reception matters. Very little is concerned with what we are studying—the theological convictions which shaped Augustine's preaching.

There are a small number of doctorates which speak on aspects of the issue, which will be discussed in our book. Robert Dowler's thesis is related to the subject matter of ours, though it is on the *Ennarationes*.[9] Gowans' (published) thesis[10] on the *Sermones* is discussed in Chapter Four. An (unpublished) dissertation from Boyd-MacMillan[11] is considered in our conclusion. None of these pieces of work aim to offer hermeneutical guides such as we attempt—ones which are general enough to help make sense of the entire preaching project of Augustine, but distinctive enough to genuinely highlight that which is so characteristic of his contribution. The small number of other writings in our subject area remind us that our project can neither claim to offer an exhaustive reading of Augustine's *Sermones*, nor provide the only valid interpretation of his preaching. Nevertheless, it is hoped that the project is found to be a coherent, meaningful and valid reading which helps make sense of the act of preaching Augustine valued so highly.

Our book accepts Augustine's judgement that his *Sermones* formed a distinct body of literature, which had he lived longer, he intended to edit.[12]

---

8. "In Christian tradition, throughout the patristic period the liturgical homily constituted by far the most important form of exegetical literature." François Dreyfus, "Du Texte À La Vie," *Revue Biblique* (1979), 23.

9. Robert Dowler, "Songs of Love: A Pastoral Reading of St Augustine of Hippo's Enarrationes in Psalmos", PhD diss., Durham University, 2006.

10. Coleen Hoffman Gowans, *The Identity of the True Believer in the Sermons of Augustine of Hippo, a Dimension of His Christian Anthropology* (New York: Edwin Mellen Press, 1998).

11. Ronald Boyd-MacMillan, "The Transforming Sermon: A Study of the Preaching of St. Augustine, with Special Reference to the Sermones Ad Populum, and the Transformation Theory of James Loder", PhD. diss., University of Aberdeen, 2009.

Our research is not a historical or text-critical study; rather, it is an exercise in theological interpretation, aiming to elucidate the doctrinal convictions which guided Augustine in his development from pagan orator to Christian preacher.

We recognise that doctrine is formed in historical settings, and so we will give some treatment of contextual influences in Chapter One. Chapter Two also contains some background context, but its real focus is on the beliefs and concerns which animated the pagan orators who influenced Augustine. From that point on, we read the *Sermones* as they have been read for the majority of history—a delineated section of the Augustinian corpus.

Our hermeneutical keys, which will shape our study, are interiority and temporality. These are explicated in Chapter Four, though they develop out of our preceeding study of *De Doctrina Christiana* in Chapter Three. We aim to "give increased attention to the existential attitudes underlying the dogmatic edifices we encounter."[13] In this way, our two hermeneutical keys help expose the undergirding beliefs and attitudes Augustine held to concerning preaching. Scripture was central to Augustine's preaching; our reading of *De Doctrina Christiana* orientates us to his self-conscious, overarching approach to Scripture. The hermeneutical keys give coherence to our selections and interpretations in subsequent case studies.

The *Sermones ad Populum* contains all the preserved *Sermones* from Augustine which were not gathered and edited into a continuous commentary on Scripture. They total about 590 sermons, ranging in length from a paragraph to a short treatise. Though our two hermeneutical terms are introduced before the inductive case study chapters, they arose from extensive reading through the source material.

The two hermeneutical keys are then tested in Chapters 5, 6, and 7. There we provide case studies on three areas which feature prominently in Augustine's preaching – Riches, Death and Relationships. These sections offer an opportunity to test the validity of our terms as interpretive keys, and at the same time serve to illumine further their potential significance. Throughout, the paramount importance of Scripture is highlighted.

Thus there is a logical development through our book. The first three chapters give various contexts to Augustine's preaching, such as their historical setting, pagan rhetoric and his own views as expressed in *De Doctrina Christiana*. Out of this, we develop our hermeneutical keys in Chapter Four. These are then utilized in the three subsequent case study chapters. Our conclusion will

---

12. *Retr.* 2.67 (CCL 57, 142).

13. Pierre Hadot, *Philosophy as a Way of Life* (Oxford: Blackwell, 1995), 104.

explore whether the keys of interiority and temporality are valid and useful; consideration will be given to their possible refinement and implications for matters of contemporary importance.

It is hoped that readers who follow this process through will find themselves exposed to Augustine's preaching in a way which is sufficiently structured to overcome some of the challenges posed by such a large corpus of writings. It is our aspiration that readers will desire to read the *Sermones* for themselves, and integrate the insights they glean from them into their appreciation of Augustine. If our thesis has the desired impact on scholarship, it will encourage others to include increased consideration of Augustine's preaching in presentations of Augustine's significance and doctrinal legacy.

Introduction

Preachers often ponder the state of preaching. The influence, methods and reception of mentors are weighed. When this is done, there is frequently fearfulness about the future of preaching. So Tim Keller spoke at the American memorial to John Stott, saying, "John Stott reinvented expository preaching. I'm still worried that younger evangelical leaders are increasingly thinking that they need to get beyond expository preaching."[1]

Since preaching has been central to the Church from its inception, it is surprising that what revival of the expository ministry there has been in the modern church has been nurtured with a notable lack of historical awareness. Hughes Oliphant Old commented on this: "Some of these contemporary preachers may have been aware that Augustine or Origen or Calvin [practiced expository preaching], as indeed they did, but they did not argue for it for that reason. It was mostly because it seemed to be a good way of preaching. It seemed appropriate."[2] A form of preaching embraced on the basis of pragmatism will, of course, be neglected when it is 'out of season' (2 Tim 4:2). The same goes for a model of ministry followed due to the influence of a charismatic leader. Even the claim that one's approach to preaching is biblical will, in time, be eroded by the apparently equal weight of claims made by other methods upon that title.

Learning through and from preachers in church history develops a deeper self-awareness about the practice and possibilities of preaching. Getting beyond a superficial imitation of past preachers to the timeless convictions and debates bequeaths tools and confidence for the task today. In that spirit, we consider the possibilities Augustine's preaching opens for the contemporary preacher. Augustine's ministry resources contemporary preachers as they reflect upon at least five important areas of homiletics.

---

1. http://www.youtube.com/watch?v=n3WkR0LPCxM (Accessed 19.12.13)

2. Hughes Oliphant Old, *The Reading and Preaching of the Scriptures in the Worship of the Christian Church: The Patristic Age*, vol. 7 (Grand Rapids; Cambridge: Eerdmans, 2010), 172.

The Role of Secular Insights to Communication

Augustine was the first figure in church history to write a guide on preaching. Since he had been a tutor of pagan rhetoric, he was able to reflect in a self-aware manner upon both the value and danger of secular insights. Augustine's book *De Doctrina Christiana* was "really the first Manual for Preachers that was written in the Christian Church. As such it deserves careful reading."[3]

Cicero had, in Augustine's view, much to teach Christian preachers. The idea of fitting one's manner of speech to the setting was one of several areas in which Augustine's advice was dependent upon the ancient world's most famous pagan orator. Augustine gave considerable time to encouraging preachers in the task of learning how language functions—the study of what we would today know as hermeneutics. Secular knowledge about science, mathematics and history all aid the faithful interpreter of Scripture.[4]

However, in seeking to assess Augustine's views on the value of secular studies for preaching, we must take care not to accept—and then impose upon Augustine—the assumptions of contemporary secularity. While most would today assume that a subject such as mathematics is a secular discipline, it was not straightforwardly so for Augustine. The church father recognized that mathematics stood at some remove from strictly biblical disciplines; nevertheless, he did not perceive as neat a division between pagan and divine endeavors as many today do. Augustine wrote, "It must be clear to the dullest of wits that the discipline of arithmetic has not been instituted by human beings, but rather discovered and explored."[5] Regardless of what the pagan scholars themselves believed, the useful insights of secular culture were in the final analysis not established apart from God:

> Their teachings contain liberal disciplines which are more suited to the service of the truth, as well as a number of most useful ethical principles, and some true things are to be found among them about worshiping only the one God. All this is like their gold and silver, and not something they instituted themselves, but something which they mined, so to say, from the ore of divine providence, veins of which are everywhere to be found. As they for their part make perverse and unjust misuse of it in the service of demons, so Christians ought, when they separate themselves in spirit from their

3. John Ker, *History of Preaching* (London: Hodder & Stoughton, 1887), 105.

4. *doctr. Chr.* 2.27.41.

5. *doctr. Chr.* 2.38.56.

hapless company, to take these things away from them for the proper use of preaching the gospel.[6]

Such nuanced reflections on the relationship between God and secular knowledge enabled Augustine to both commend the value of secular studies for preaching, and to warn against thinking pagan knowledge could lead to happiness or divine wisdom. A preacher with the time, skill and option to do so, could benefit from studying the writings of pagan orators such as Cicero. However of greater importance was prayer:

> If Queen Esther prayed, when she was going to speak in the king's presence for the temporal salvation of her people, that God might put suitable words into her mouth, how much more should you pray to receive such a favor, when you are toiling in word and teaching for the people's eternal salvation?[7]

The Role of Doctrine

How doctrine relates to preaching is a contested area. For some, doctrine is seen as a threat to the integrity of preaching. For others, doctrinal explication provides the normal form of the sermon. How can a preacher embody a faithful handling of the Scriptural text (with its narrative, poetry and redemptive historical form) alongside doctrinal fidelity and comprehensiveness? Is there such a thing as a doctrine of preaching? Engaging with such questions is essential for any who wish to transcend pragmatic or shallow preaching.

Augustine provides rich resources in his teaching and example for those who seek to explore the role of doctrine in preaching. In his observation that Scripture's aim is to cultivate love of God and neighbor,[8] Augustine made a doctrinal claim which was shaped by the contours of redemption history and the words of Jesus. Holding forth love as the goal of Scripture gave Augustine a doctrinal standard by which to measure the faithfulness of his preaching. If a sermon did not in some way help listeners love God and each other, the preaching must in some way be sub-biblical.

As he preached through books of the Bible, Augustine gave attention to the particularities of whatever passage was before him—its position in salvation history, its imagery, and its tone. Having an overarching doctrinal aim for his preaching helped give some self-critical control. The question of what

6. *doctr. Chr.* 2.40.60.

7. *doctr. Chr.* 4.30.63.

8. *doctr. Chr.* 1.35.39.

hermeneutical controls ought to inform all our preaching of Scripture still exercises preachers and those who train them. Augustine's focus on the cultivation of love is a doctrinal claim about the Bible which commends itself on substantial exegetical, pastoral and theological grounds. Doctrinal insights about the Bible had a leading role in shaping Augustine's expositions.

While Augustine usually preached through books of the Bible consecutively—afterwards writing up his sermons as commentaries—on occasion, he preached a straightforwardly doctrinal sermon. These were often prompted by a saint's day, festival, a false teaching or pedagogical concern. In the latter category, his two sermons on the resurrection are striking. *Sermones* 361 and 362 are by far the longest sermons from Augustine we have records of. They are a doctrinal study on the nature of the resurrection, aiming to reassure and educate believers who have doubts. They are evidence that Augustine could, for pastoral reasons, deviate from his normal routine of preaching through a Bible book in its entirety. As he taught doctrine to his congregation, Augustine was aware that some listeners were tempted to align themselves with heretical sects; others were not yet believers. His pastoral heart is on display through his awareness of different perceptions of the doctrine and various stumbling blocks to orthodoxy, and the importance of doctrinal preaching for educating a church.

The relationship doctrine ought to have to preaching through the Bible is a matter which should concern all preachers. One needs a doctrine of Scripture and preaching in order to critically assess the act of preaching. One also needs to form a view on the role of preaching which sets aside the more expository method for a doctrinal approach. There are pastoral needs and spiritual dangers on all sides of these debates. Augustine was one of the first people to write about the relationship between doctrine and preaching. He did so as a practitioner and theologian whose works still repay study today.

Freedom and Order

One of the reasons that Augustine is thought by many to be a highpoint is patristic preaching is that he embodied a compelling vision of both freedom and order. His style of preaching was to meditate on a passage in advance, and then to speak without notes on the issues he felt were important or potentially confusing to his congregation. Augustine was happy to keep speaking till he felt listeners understood what was being said. Questions and demurrals from the gathered congregation helped him judge the response. These are recorded for us in his *Sermones* since the transcribers preserved them.

Presumably, Augustine would have edited these out as he did for his sermon series on the Psalms when he turned preaching into a commentary. He intended to edit his *Sermones* after his *Epistulae*, but died after completing the task for only his correspondence. From the perspective of the modern reader, the lack of editing makes the *Sermones* all the more engaging and valuable. If Augustine felt his congregation was tiring due to length of time standing, or the heat, he was willing to pause his exposition abruptly. He would after all resume where he left off when he next sat in the teacher's chair.

The passage of Scripture then provided Augustine with an ordered control for preaching. He was determined to explain the text's meaning, set it in the context of salvation history and use it to promote orthodox doctrine. However the way he went about this gave considerable room for the passage to be refracted through his own personality, experiences and reflections. The actual presentation of the sermon, without notes or script, gave space for interaction with the listeners and a deeply relational engagement with preacher. The high value Augustine placed on prayer surrounding preaching meant that he was open spiritually in the moment of delivery to God's prompting and sovereign leading.

Subsequent generations of African preachers became more rigid and formulaic in their preaching, limiting their length of time speaking and letting themselves be bound more firmly to a lectionary. Augustine's *Sermones* maintain a vivid sense of exploration and personal exploration. The listeners join in the preacher's search for God's message. Augustine's life was one of self-critical theological reflection. He dove deep into the waters of scripture, and when he emerged for breath he had treasure to share with all who listened. As one scholar observed:

> Since theological reflection has great potential for formation, Augustine envisioned communities of people, not simply church leaders, engaged in reflection. His style of preaching, for example, encouraged listeners to develop a theologically reflective approach to life. Just imagine, with Augustine, entire communities of believers engaged in theologically reflective living. Imagine a God who has already given us the biblical words with which to do our reflection. Imagine believers, soaking in the marinade of those words, attentively, inquisitively, prayerfully spurring each other on to testimonies of praise. Just imagine.[9]

9. David Rylaarsdam, "Theological Reflection and Augustine's Confessions," in *For God So Loved the World*, ed. Arie Leder (Belleville: Essence, 2006), 99–100.

Augustine's approach to preaching, with its remarkable combination of freedom and order, modeled for people a way of viewing not only the Bible, but God's world. To look at life through the Scriptures, and feel one's heart warmed by God's love there revealed: these were theologically-reflective arts modeled by Augustine when he preached.

RELATIONSHIP TO PASTORAL MINISTRY

One of the most beautiful aspects of preaching is that it is a message conveyed through a preacher who knows his flock. Augustine felt keenly the weight of responsibility towards the people in his church. He was in huge demand as a counselor, confessor, and arbiter of disputes. He frequently complained about the incessant burden of administration, but doubtless it served as a means of drawing him closer into the minutiae of people's daily lives.

In the modern information-technology age, it is tempting to focus on the aspect of preaching which involves communicating information. Without a doubt, preaching does involve that, but Augustine's painstaking care over the personal lives of his listeners reminds us that real teaching necessarily involves personal relationship and encounter. The attitude of the preacher to his people, and to his own progress in the faith, both shape the ability of listeners to learn. And so, Augustine counseled:

> Let us not be too proud to learn what has to be learned with the help
> of other people, and let those of us from whom others are taught
> hand on what we have been given without pride or envy.[10]

The ability to teach others well requires the humility to learn. People must get to know the preacher well enough to be reassured that the one teaching them is himself humble enough to learn. The virtues essential for communication are practiced and observed in relationship. There is no better forum for them to be encountered than the pastoral ministry of a church.

One of the reasons the *Sermones* of Augustine have been relatively neglected in scholarship is that they appear to be less academic and significant than his more philosophical texts. This is surely a view of Augustine—and learning itself—that is overly influenced by an Enlightenment favoring of rationality over relationality. Augustine's life of preaching, in a context where he offered sacrificial pastoral care, challenges not only those modern preachers who wish to teach while avoiding engagement with people; it calls into

10. *doctr. Chr.* prooem. 5.

question the validity of the academic outlook which prizes detached rational inquiry apart from personal relational encounter. If we really are people with restless hearts, created to dwell together in God's eternal city, it may be that Augustine's preaching in the context of pastoral ministry provides deeper insights about how we learn and flourish than his more famous academic writings.

Training Preachers

The issue of how to grow and train preachers was one Augustine gave much thought and prayer to. His manual for training preachers, *De Doctrina*, is significant not least for being the first such book. It is also instructive in the way Augustine held off writing the concluding chapter till he had nearly completed his lifetime of preaching. Augustine seemed to feel keenly the need to be a practitioner if he was to train others. His mind was quick and his memory prodigious, but that did not in and of itself qualify him to train preachers. There is something gained through time, experience, and relationships which enables one to speak in a way that is heard, understood, and loved. Embodying both the humility and honor of preaching is no easy task for a sinful human. It takes time to embrace the existential conflicts that arise from being a sinful human, bringing a message from God's word to other sinners.

Many of the other areas where Augustine's preaching resource contemporary practice contribute to his vision for training. For example, if Augustine's views on the value of secular learning are accepted, that impacts how one trains preachers. The same goes for his teaching on freedom, order and so forth. Today there is a renewed interest in Britain, America and worldwide, in how we can best train preachers. In Britain, the 'Cornhill Training Course' has done much to equip people for the task of preaching.[11] Founded in 1991 by Rev. David Jackman and Preb. R. C. Lucas, the Cornhill Training Course has trained several hundreds of students in the art of preaching. This training course was able to devote exclusive time and attention to the training of preachers in a way that seminaries were unable to. Focused on constructive feedback for practical preaching exercises which are done in relational community, many of the strengths of the training given there stand in traditions which Augustine would have been happy to be a part of.

Much of the best preaching and training for preaching in the contemporary church has been developed without any explicit engagement

---

11. http://www.proctrust.org.uk/cornhill. A similar training work is done in America by the Simeon Trust http://www.simeontrust.org.

with Augustine. Where we have best practices, we have often stumbled into them by following gifted leaders or intuition. My own experience has been that engagement with the preaching of Augustine over a number of years has deepened my core convictions about God speaking to his people through Scripture being preached. It has also alerted me to areas of reflection and practice where I have been weak. We all have much to learn; the humility to admit as much was, for Augustine, the first step towards becoming a competent teacher.

1

The Historical Context of Augustine's Preaching

It is not too much to say that Augustine revived the church in North Africa by reviving preaching.[1]

For Augustine his Bible is primarily the Bible of a preacher.[2]

The concerns of this book are primarily doctrinal, in that our intent is to expose the undergirding philosophical-theological assumptions which informed Augustine's preaching. Nevertheless, doctrine is neither formulated nor promulgated in an historical vacuum. In order to give due recognition to the relevance of historical setting for doctrinal expression, this chapter offers a historical context for Augustine's preaching.

We shall proceed from a broad overview towards a narrower focus. Thus North African culture in general will be outlined first, followed by a consideration of the Church in that area. We will then study, with representative examples, North African preaching. All of this will lead to some concluding observations on Augustine's preaching style.

This contextual material cannot exhaustively represent the state of historical knowledge about fourth-century North African ecclesiastical matters. Neither can it prematurely demonstrate the doctrinal claims made in subsequent chapters. However, it is hoped that a modest link may be perceived between the historical context and our philosophical-theological interpretation of Augustine's preaching. That connection flows from a thread which runs through each of our sections of historical context – the interplay between order and passion.

1. Edmund Hill, "St. Augustine's Theory and Practice of Preaching," *Clergy Review* 45 (1960), 590.

2. Anne-Marie la Bonnardière, "Augustine: Minister of the Word of God,", *Augustine and the Bible*, ed. Pamela Bright (Indiana: Notre Dame Press, 1999), 245.

As doctrine cannot be formulated apart from historical context, so historical context cannot be recounted without interpretation. Our interpretive suggestion is that a tension or interplay between order and passion was a leading feature of the situation from which Augustine preached. This insight informs our presentation of material in this chapter, and lays a foundation for the doctrinal explorations taken further in following chapters.

NORTH AFRICAN CULTURE

Invasion and subjugation were repeated features of classical North African history. The Phoenicians ruled by means of their naval might until about the second century B.C.E. The Romans inaugurated the imperial age which endured until the Vandals captured Carthage in C.E. 439. At the end of C.E. 533, Emperor Justinian's forces conquered Carthage. As civil war and instability weakened the Byzantine rule of North Africa, Islamic forces spread with remarkable speed from Mecca. Egypt was conquered by the Muslims in C.E. 641, Cyrenaica in C.E. 642, and Tripoli and Eastern Fezzan in C.E. 643. Byzantine resistance paused the Islamic conquests. The city of Kairouan was founded as a permanent outpost of Islam in C.E. 669; by C.E. 700, North Africa was fully subdued by the Muslims.[3]

North Africa was an immensely prosperous region, and therefore attractive to invaders. However, the wealth of North Africa was not a straightforward result of it possessing plentiful resources. Capitalisation of resources was inextricably intertwined with the infrastructure imposed by conquering nations. The prosperity of North Africa was, to a great degree, the result of its flourishing under order imposed from without.

The period of history within which Augustine flourished is that of late Roman rule in North Africa. He lived in an age that inherited the legacy of Roman order and infrastructure. By the mid-third century, Roman soldiers had laid twelve thousand miles of roads. A vast network with miles demarcated by the famous Roman milestone facilitated military movement, tax collection and domestic travel. Once soldiers had conquered a region, they worked as unpaid engineers to survey land and build the desired infrastructure. Today, their fifty

3. Victor Davis Hanson, "Holding the Line: Frontier Defense and the Later Roman Empire," in *Makers of Ancient Strategy: From the Persian Wars to the Fall of Rome* (Princeton: Princeton University Press, 2010); "*Roman Africa*", in Graham Shipley et al., ed., *The Cambridge Dictionary of Classical Civilisation* (Cambridge: Cambridge University Press, 2006); Roger le Tourneau, "North Africa to the Sixteenth Century," in P.M. Holt, Ann K.S. Lambton, Bernard Lewis, ed. *The Cambridge History of Islam: The Indian Sub-Continent, South-East Asia, Africa and the Muslim West* (Cambridge: Cambridge University Press, 1970); David Bentley Hart, *The Story of Christianity* (London: Quercus, 2010), 108–13.

mile aqueduct still stands over the River Miliana. Usable maps were drawn up, showing the connections between towns. So effective was the marriage of Roman rule and African resources that by the middle of the second century, North West Africa produced two-thirds of the wheat needed by Rome.

City life was embraced by North Africans.[4] By the third century there were close to six hundred cities; two hundred of these were surrounded by fertile farming land. Often they were no more than eight miles apart. Most had populations between five thousand and fifteen thousand. Carthage was probably the only city with a six figure population and included some impressive Christian buildings.[5] The aqueduct for Caesarea could provide water for forty thousand people. Excavations have revealed that Hippo, a "typical provincial town"[6] had a forum, baths, theatre, residential quarter and ecclesiastical area. Augustine's preaching against the games[7] strongly suggests an (undiscovered) amphitheatre. Augustine was aware of disparity in wealth between town and country.[8]

Historians have observed the enthusiasm with which Africans took to the building program and wealth creation which Rome's infrastructure harnessed:

> The inhabitants of Roman Africa eagerly followed their new masters' example: their towns were built of stone, and embellished with handsome and often grandiose temples, forums, market places and public baths.[9]

The Romans created new ways of building not only cities, but also careers. Many talented Africans developed a taste for Latin as a language of law, poetry and politics. Rich educations in Carthage appealed to those who felt the allure of Rome itself. One of the most famous examples of such men was Apuleius—lawyer, poet, student of Platonic philosophy, mystery religions and

4. Claude Lepelley, "The Survival and Fall of the Classical City in Late Roman Africa," in ed., John Rich, , *The City in Late Antiquity,* (London: Routledge, 1992).

5. Simon Hornblower and Antony Spawforth, ed., *The Oxford Companion to Classical Civilization* (Oxford: Oxford University Press, 1998), 143; Naomi Norman, "Carthage," in *Augustine through the Ages*, ed., Allan Fitzgerald (Grand Rapids: Eerdmans, 1999), 132–3; "Cities", "Town Planning", in *The Cambridge Dictionary of Classical Civilisation*, in ed., Shipley, et al.

6. F. Van Der Meer, *Augustine the Bishop: The Life and Work of a Father of the Church*, (London: Sheed and Ward, 1961), 16.

7. *s.* 51.1–2. (RB 91, 23)

8. W.H.C. Frend, "Town and Countryside in Early Christianity," in *The Church in Town and Countryside, Studies in Church History*, ed. Derek Baker (Oxford: Blackwell, 1979), 42.

9. Susan Raven, *Rome in Africa* (London: Routledge, 1993), 103.

orator. In many respects, the path Augustine later trod through life bears striking resemblances to him. Africans who sought to make their fortunes in the Roman world were assured of their legitimacy in the Imperial world. After all, the African Septimus Severus had ascended to the supreme position of Roman emperor in C.E. 193.

Augustine, living from C.E. 354–430, experienced the latter days of this Roman North Africa. His life reveals him to be typical of the African debutant aspiring to cosmopolitan success. The love of Latin, dabbling in religious groups, Platonism and collegial friendships were typical of the passionate Africans who were, in their studious affectations, more Roman than the Romans. One study of early bishops presents the highly educated, secular, scholar-convert, as a well recognised category.[10] Such Latinised African leaders were passionate and driven—by their culture, aspiations and semi-acceptance within the upper stratas of Roman society. Augustine's *Confessiones* attempted to impose order on the rich passions of an inner life, much as Roman roads navigated the fertile lands of Africa. After the production of his most famous work, the outstanding question was whether a similar order could be imposed on the passions of the turbulent African Church.

THE CHURCH IN NORTH AFRICA

Africa had a long tradition of embracing martyrdom as an expression of faithfulness to God. One of Tertullian's earliest writings, *Ad Martyras*, was a spirited encouragement to believers awaiting execution. When Augustine was received into the North African Church, he entered into a Church which remained proud of its famous martyrs; of these, none ranked higher than Cyprian (martyred in C.E. 258) and Perpetua (martyred in C.E. 203). The former represented ecclesiastical leadership and scholarly theology, sealed in blood. The latter was a reminder that women, children and anonymous African Christians made up the majority of martyrs. Remembered in liturgy, sermons and festivals, the African Church's collective memory was dominated by martyrdom.[11]

The order of Roman rule may have led to financial prosperity for North Africa, but it also meant persecution. The Diocletian Persecution was enforced with particular ferocity in Africa, with laity as well leaders being charged and

10. Claudia Rapp, *Holy Bishops in Late Antiquity: The Nature of Leadership in an Age of Transition* (Berkley: University of California Press, 2005), 186.

11. Anna Leone, "Christianity and Paganism in North Africa," in *The Cambridge History of Christianity: Constantine to c. 600*, ed. Augustine Casiday and Frederick W. Norris (Cambridge: Cambridge University Press, 2007). See also François Decret, *Early Christianity in North Africa* (Eugene: Cascade Books, 2009).

executed. By contrast, the rulers of Gaul and Spain did not apply such strict enforcement.[12] Interstingly, one of Dioceltian's other historical achievements, alongside presiding over famously fierce persecution, was a phemonal expansion in government workers. Under Caracella (c.e. 211–217) there were about three hundred career civil servants. This became thirty thousand to thirty-five thousand.[13]

The fortitude of the African church under persecution and the Church's honouring of martyrs speaks much of their passion for faithfulness. That same temperament, admirable in so many ways, manifested itself in Donatism—the single most influential feature of the North African Church in explaining Augustine's context.[14]

By c.e. 300, the burden of taxation upon North Africans was so punitive as to cause social unrest.[15] Against a backdrop of such discontent and persecution, Donatism divided the Church into those who accepted repentant leaders who had denied the faith under persecution and those who would not. The Donatists were in the majority and often had the support of the poorer people.

Nevertheless, the influence of sociological factors ought not obscure the fact that substantive theological issues were at stake. Alexander gives a balanced appraisal: "schism cannot be explained in too narrowly religious terms. Nevertheless, it seems likely that the persistence of Donatism owes much to theology."[16] These had a direct impact upon Augustine: "The African Church had been unable to celebrate the unity of the baptised for more than seventy years when Augustine returned to his homeland after the joy of his own baptism."[17] Whenever Augustine mentions African Christianity specifically in preaching, the feature he most often highlights is Donatism and the resulting disunity.[18] Disunity was a prevalent and serious feature of the Donatist

---

12. W.H.C. Frend, *Martyrdom and Persecution in the Early Church: A Study of a Conflict from the Maccabees to Donatus* (Oxford: Blackwell, 1965), 477–535; Paul Keresztes, *Imperial Rome and the Christians: From the Severi to Constantine the Great*, vol. 2 (Lanham: University Press of America, 1989), 95–113.

13. Ramsay MacMullen, *Christianity and Paganism in the Fourth to Eighth Centuries* (New Haven: Yale University Press, 1997), 83. For further details of the ways Christianity impacted government workers, see Michele Renee Salzman, *The Making of a Christian Aristocracy: Social and Religious Change in the Western Roman Empire* (Cambridge: Harvard University Press, 2002), 107–37.

14. A.H.M. Jones, *The Later Roman Empire* (2 vols.; Oxford: Blackwell, 1973), 2:1034.

15. W.H.C. Frend, *The Donatist Church* (Oxford: Clarendon Press, 1952), 63.

16. James Alexander, "Donatism," in *The Early Christian World*, ed. Philip F. Esler (London: Routledge, 2000), 961.

17. Pamela Bright, "North African Church," in *Augustine through the Ages*, ed. Fitzgerald, 185.

18. *s.* 162A.10. (MA 1, 98)

controversy, which provided a crucial context for Augustine's ministry. The disunity meant that an authority had to be sought other than mere popularity and numbers. Until Augustine Donatism had attracted the "abler and more learned leadership."[19] By many measures, the Donatists had good grounds to present themselves as the legitimate church. Augustine supported various strategies, at different times, for dealing with it. These included writing theological treatises, preaching sermons, supporting state repression,[20] calling an ecclesiastical conference and affirming repentant Donatists. In all of these endeavours, Augustine sought to impose order on a disunited Church. The order was intended to be theological, universal, ecclesial and charitable.

It may be suggested that the context of Donatism informed much of Augustine's preaching. His authority as a bishop was exercised from a "clerical monastery."[21] One study highlights the way he increased the authority of Rome by appealing there for disciplinary and ecclesiastical guidance.[22] That said, his main power came from theological teaching. He could support and turn to the state, but even then, his main role was to provide a theological rationale for such action. Donatism encouraged Augustine to emphasise the worldwide catholicity of the Christian Church, the love and acceptance Christians should offer to repentant brethren, the validity of rightly administered sacraments, and the impossibility of removing sin from the Church in this age. That these are recognisable as distinctly Augustinian theological themes serves to underline how deeply Donatism shaped his teaching. If the passion of the North African Church was a constituent element of the popularity of Donatism, then an important goal of Augustine's preaching ministry became imposing a catholic theological order upon it.

PREACHING IN NORTH AFRICA

Though we intend to focus on a few North African preachers, our intention in so doing is to amplify the historical context for Augustine's preaching. That being the case, we shall begin by briefly mentioning Ambrose (c.e. 337–397).

19. Frend, *The Donatist Church*, 227.

20. For summary of development of Augustine's views on state repression, see Maijastina Kahlos, *Forbearance and Compulsion: The Rhetoric of Religious Tolerance and Intolerance in Late Antiquity* (London: Duckworth, 2009), 111–17, and Michael Gaddis, *There Is No Crime for Those Who Have Christ: Religious Violence in the Christian Roman Empire* (London: University of California Press, 2005), 137–50.

21. Andrea Sterk, *Renouncing the World yet Leading the Church: The Monk-Bishop in Late Antiquity* (London: Harvard University Press, 2004), 76.

22. J.E. Merdinger, *Rome and the African Church in the Time of Augustine* (London: Yale University Press, 1997).

Though he preached in Milan, his singular impact on Augustine obliges us to reflect on his significance. The travels Augustine made outside Africa remind us that he was an educated Latin North African; his context was the imperial world, not just his homeland.

AMBROSE (C. C.E. 337–397)

The distinctive feature of Ambrose's preaching was its saturation in Scripture.[23] Form and content were together intensely scriptural. At first, Augustine was unimpressed with Scripture. He thought Cicero more elegant and he was unable to penetrate Scripture's interior: "Indeed my pride recoiled from its metre, and my wit could not penetrate its interior."[24] Even before conversion, Augustine recognised that Christianity was centred on the Scriptures. As he looked back, he interpreted his failure to appreciate Scripture's interior mystery as a failure in his own interiority. Scripture demanded to be approached humbly: "But I disdained to be a little one and swollen with pride saw myself as lofty."[25] These reflections show how Augustine saw Scripture as central to his eventual conversion. Interiority is a key hermeneutical category which arose from this engagement with Scripture.

Intrigued by his life and preaching, Augustine remarked upon Ambrose's unusual habit of reading to himself silently.[26] Ambrose's preaching so presented Scripture that Augustine's view of it changed. He began to rejoice in what had previously seemed childish.[27] In Ambrose's preaching we see the importance of Scripture in Augustine's conversion. Scripture famously takes centre stage in the garden scene where the words of Romans 13:13 resonated with Augustine's

23. Frances Young, Lewis Ayres, and Andrew Louth, ed., *The Cambridge History of Early Christian Literature* (Cambridge: Cambridge University Press, 2004), 309–12; Neil B. McLynn, *Ambrose of Milan: Church and Court in a Christian Capital* (Berkeley: University of California Press, 1994); D.H. Williams, *Ambrose of Milan and the End of the Arian-Nicene Conflicts*, Oxford Early Christian Studies (Oxford: Clarendon Press, 1995); Craig A. Satterlee, *Ambrose of Milan's Method of Mystagogical Preaching* (Collegeville: Liturgical Press, 2002); Steven M. Oberhelman, *Rhetoric and Homiletics in Fourth-Century Christian Literature: Prose Rhythm, Oratical Style, and Preaching in the Works of Ambrose, Jerome and Augustine*, in *American Philological Association American Classical Studies*, ed. Matthew s. Santirocco (Atlanta: Scolars Press, 1991); Miriam Annunciata Adams, *The Latinity of the Letters of Saint Ambrose* (Whitefish: Kessinger Publishing, 2007); Boniface O.P. Ramsey, "Ambrose," in *The First Christian Theologians*, ed. G.R. Evans (Oxford: Blackwell, 2004).

24. "Tumor enim meus refugiebat modum eius et acies mea non penetrabat interiora eius." *conf.*3.9. (CCL 27, 31).

25. "Sed ego dedignabar esse paruulus et turgidus fastu mihi grandis uidebar." *conf.*3.9. (CCL 27, 31).

26. *conf.*6.3. (CCL 27, 75).

27. *conf.*6.6. (CCL 27, 77).

life experiences.[28] He reminds the reader of Ambrose by mentioning that in the garden he read the words of Paul "*silentio*"; as Ambrose had read in sermon preparation, so Augustine read in conversion.[29] In this way, Augustine links his stylised conversion experience not just with Scripture but also with Ambrose's reading and preaching of Scripture. Scripture was the crucial medium through which Augustine experienced God call him into the Christian life.

When Scripture so impacted Augustine, he consciously explored the nature of that impact with his hermeneutic of interiority and temporality. Thus in place of the earlier inability to appreciate scripture, the text impacted his heart: "Suddenly at the end of this sentence, as if by a light, peace poured into my heart and all of doubt's darkness dispersed."[30] An interior change of heart had been set up as essential due to the earlier presentation of his interior pride and inability to appreciate the mystery of Scripture. Augustine has previously described himself as, "I was not yet loving and was loving to love."[31] Through Ambrose's preaching, Scripture so impacted his interiority that his heart could believe and love anew.

Scholars have generally agreed with our assessment that Ambrose practised a particularly scriptural form of preaching, weaving the text of scripture around his observations on the text. Thus, for example:

> The bishop's constant recourse to Biblical quotation and paraphrase suggests what was truly distinctive about his pastoral style. For Ambrose reproduced in his sermons the texture and rhythm of the Bible itself: his preaching was nothing less than an exercise in scriptural mimesis.[32]

While this interpretation is reasonable, it should be remembered that Ambrose was also able to make substantive use of secular illustrations. Perhaps his most striking recorded example being from his treatment of Luke 4. Here Ambrose offers an extended contrast between the temptations of Christ and Ulysses. Gabriel Tissot suggests this may have been added by a later editor – but it would have been well within the knowledge base of Ambrose, and reads as not inappropriate to its context.[33]

---

28. *conf.*8.29. (CCL 27, 131).

29. The same word "silentio" appears in *conf.*6.3 (CCL 27, 75) and 8.29 (CCL 27, 131).

30. "Statim quippe cum fine huiusce sententiae quasi luce securitatis infusa cordi meo omnes dubitationis tenebrae diffugerunt." *conf.*8.29. (CCL 27, 131).

31. "Nondum amabam et amare amabam." *conf.*3.1. (CCL 27, 27).

32. McLynn, *Ambrose of Milan: Church and Court in a Christian Capital*, 238.

Ambrose bequeathed to Augustine a relentless focus upon Scripture, and an enthusiasm to open its inner meaning to listeners who were deaf to its message. Augustine would develop his own style – more conversational[34] and on occasion more willing to prosecute the text in search of an answer to a question. Nevertheless, his indebtedness to Ambrose remains noticeable.

TERTULLIAN (C.E. 160–220)

Famous for his rigour, passion and rejection of secular philosophy, Tertullian was a highly-honored African church leader.[35] One would expect his opposition to paganism to drive him towards a simplicity of style in prose. Surprisingly, "Tertullian is notoriously the most difficult of all Latin prose writers".[36] Others scholars concur, singling Tertullian out for his complexity:

> Latin literature had a tendency to admire complicated, sometimes even contrived, diction . . . With the exception of a few early Christian writers, such as Tertullian, the Latin Fathers struggled against the current.[37]

Tertullian's striving to state every matter fully in secular Latin diction may have been a secular counterpart of the high standards he held in Christian ethics.[38] It fits with the assumption that he had a legal training, and the fact that most of the material he wrote, which may be considered sermonic, is actually topical. Addresses given to deal with occasional problems of ethics or persecution may permit a level of obscurity which regular congregational preaching would expunge.

Augustine adopted in preaching a more fluid, conversational style than Tertullian. If Ambrose's style was saturated with Scripture, Tertullian's topical

33. Gabriel Tissot, ed. *Ambrose of Milan: Traité Sur L'évangile De S. Luc*, vol. 45 & 52 (Paris: Les Éditions du Cerf, 1956, 1958).

34. McLynn, *Ambrose of Milan: Church and Court in a Christian Capital*, 239.

35. Geoffrey D. Dunn, *Tertullian, The Early Church Fathers* (London: Routledge, 2004); Eric Osborn, *Tertullian: First Theologian of the West* (Cambridge: Cambridge University Press, 1997); Eric Osborn, "Tertullian," in *The First Christian Theologians*, ed. Young, Ayres, and Louth (Oxford: Blackwell, 2004), 133–9.

36. Tertullian, *Treatises on Penance: On Penitence and on Purity*, vol. 28 (London: Longmans, Green and Co, 1959), 6.

37. Hughes Oliphant Old, *The Reading and Preaching of the Scriptures in the Worship of the Christian Church: The Patristic Age*, vol. 2 (Grand Rapids: Eerdmans, 1998), 366.

38. Gerald Bray, *Holiness and the Will of God: Perspectives on the Theology of Tertullian* (London: Marshall, Morgan & Scott, 1979).

addresses stand at the opposite extreme. Augustine integrated the two approaches; his conversational preaching probed and explored passages of Scripture in a way that both enlivened scripture and permitted a degree of topical doctrinal speaking.

CYPRIAN (C.E. 208–258)

Augustine called Cyprian[39] the most beautiful of teachers.[40] After analysing every Scriptural citation in Cyprian's corpus, Fahey concludes:

> Cyprian was not a profound or creative theologian gifted with rich and original insights, yet this may prove to be more of an advantage than disadvantage, since Cyprian records a prevalent attitude in his contemporary Church toward Scripture rather than his own highly personalised view.[41]

This observation is generally true; however, some difference can be seen between Tertullian and Cyprian. For example, while the former blended Scriptural citation into the body of his own words, the latter rarely cited scripture without some kind of introductory formula. This may indicate the development of a more self-conscious submission to Scripture's authority.

The treatises written by Cyprian between C.E. 247 and his martyrdom appear originally to have been sermons or parenetic exhortations.[42] Cyprian's style is quite distinctive; warm, assured and concise. Thus, Fahey somewhat overstates his case, saying that "Cyprian totally disregarded the miracles of Jesus and narrative passages in scripture which held no importance for him."[43] Cyprian may not have cited them so frequently because narrative does not lend itself to citation as readily as doctrine. He could nevertheless mention them without citation. So, for example, Cyprian warmly commends Hannah's praying for a son.[44] The stories of Cain, Esau and Saul are all referred to as examples of jealousy.[45] Such piling up of Scriptural images has a homiletic feel,

---

39. J. Patout Burns, *Cyprian the Bishop* (London: Routledge, 2002); G. *s.* Murdoch Walker, *The Churchmanship of St. Cyprian* (Cambridge: James Clarke, 2003); *The Cambridge History of Early Christian Literature*, ed. Young, Ayres, and Louth, 152–160.

40. *doctr. Chr.* 2.61. (SIM 162).

41. Michael Andrew Fahey, *Cyprian and the Bible: A Study in Third-Century Exegesis* (Tübingen: J. C. B. Mohr, 1971), 624.

42. Ibid., 18.

43. Ibid., 625.

44. *De Dominica Oratione*, 5. (CCL 3A, 92)

45. *De Zelo et Liuore*, 5. (CCL 3A, 77)

and suggests that there was a close relationship between Cyprian's preaching and his preserved treatises.

The moralistic tone of Tertullian continues in Cyprian. Not only is he very concerned with ethical issues, but when he speaks of them, he stresses the importance of obedience.[46] Acting Christianly takes priority over Christian contemplation. Some of this is due to the difficulties created by persecution, but part of the issue is that Cyprian's preserved writings are topical rather than expository. Sermons which move through the lectionary tend to introduce more emphasis upon the contemplative, with the demands of the text blunting the urgency of external circumstances.

Augustine managed to combine the ethical and expository in a more integrated way than his predecessors. He did indeed preach through books of Scripture – turning the sermons into commentaries when complete. As he preached he engaged with the text and the ethical concerns of listeners, exploring both and relating each to the other.

PETER CHRYSOLOGUS (C.E. 406–450)

In stark contrast to his predecessor Augustine, Peter Chrysologus ministered in an age when the Roman empire no longer held preeminence.[47] We do not know when Peter was given the honorific title "Chrysologus"; evidently somebody thought the Western Church ought to have its own Chrysostom, and Peter was given the position. We have 179 sermons from Chrysologus.[48] Unlike Cyprian, he frequently preached from the Gospels. His style has very pastoral, focused upon the needs of his congregation. A determination to uphold expository sequential treatment of books is evidenced in his method of preaching.[49] For example, consecutive sermons on Romans moved through the epistle section by section. After a break for other topical sermons, Romans was resumed at the precise point at which it had been left.

---

46. *De Habitu Virginum*, 2 (CSEL 3.1, 185–205).

47. William B. Palardy, "Peter Chrysologus' Interpretation of the Raising of Lazarus," in, *Studia Patristica*, ed., Elizabeth A. Livingstone (Leuven: Peeters, 1991).

48. Peter Chrysologus, *Sermons and Homilies*, vol. 1, *The Fathers of the Church* (Washington D.C.: The Catholic University of America, 1953); Peter Chrysologus, *Sermons and Homilies*, vol. 2, *The Fathers of the Church* (Washington D.C.: The Catholic University of America, 2004); Peter Chrysologus, *Sermons and Homilies*, vol. 3, *The Fathers of the Church* (Washington D.C.: The Catholic University of America, 2005). Some, such as Palardy accept 183 sermons as authentic.

49. *s.* 114 (CCL 24A, 694–8).

It is often suggested that Augustine's sermons were a "revolution"[50] or represented the high watermark of classical preaching.[51] The sermons of preachers before and after Augustine support what at first glance appears to be a hagiographical assessment. Chrysologus was reliable in his interpretation of scripture and pastoral care. However, there is a marked decline from Augustine's warm, extemporary engagement with text and listeners. At a very basic level, this is seen in the consistent brevity of Chrysologus' preaching. Each sermon could not have taken more than ten or fifteen minutes to preach. Chrysologus was so committed to brevity that he frequently broke up Scriptural passages into separate short addresses. For example, the "Parable of the Prodigal Son" received five distinct brief sermons.[52] Old seems to find it difficult to accept a preacher could speak for such a short length of time, and suggests that medieval scribes truncated the material due to decreased "literary facility."[53] But there is no evidence for this assertion.

It seems more likely that the texts have been accurately preserved, and that Chrysologus did indeed preach very short sermons. Two observations from the sermons bear this out. First, Chrysologus expressed a desire to break off his sermon out of deference to the customs and expectations of his church.[54] Second, it seems that the custom to which he referred was the practice of preaching three sermons in each church service, an approach which naturally demanded brevity. So Chrysologus mentions a threefold preaching from the Psalms, Gospels and Paul.[55] Evidence of this custom is seen in *s*.6, which is on a psalm and opens with reference to the previous sermon on a Gospel.[56] It appears that both sermons took place within the same service.

The brevity of Chrysologus may be due to the liturgical customs within which he operated, but whether or not this is the cause, his sermons lack Augustine's fluidity and vitality. Augustine interacted with text and listener in such a manner that he felt free to cease preaching only when he knew the congregation had either tired or else accepted his message. Augustine tried various approaches to communicate the insight he felt was his message from God. There was, in Augustine, a flexibility in presentation. Chrysologus appears

50. Ando, "Christian Literature," 405.

51. Old, *Reading and Preaching: The Patristic Age*, 344; George Kennedy, *The Art of Rhetoric in the Roman World 300 B.C.– A.D. 300* (Princeton: Princeton University Press, 1972), 612–13.

52. *s*. 1–5 (CCL 24, 15–42).

53. Old, *Reading and Preaching: The Patristic Age*, 418.

54. *s*. 2 (CCL 24, 25).

55. *s*. 115 (CCL 24A, 699).

56. *s*. 6 (CCL 24, 43).

more bound by his preparation, technique and customs than Augustine, who preferred to imbibe the Scriptural text and preach it as the occasion demanded. By the time of Chrysologus, liturgical custom had largely normalised sequential sermons on Scripture, but the resultant order necessitated a decline from Augustine's vital interplay between Scripture, preacher and listeners.

Augustine's Preaching Method

By Augustine's time, only bishops were permitted to preach. Edmund Hill sees this as evidence that the North African church had "sunk into a dejected and fossilised formalism."[57] The situation was even worse than ecclesiastical order inhibiting the ministry of preaching. Many bishops were too busy to preach, or frightened of the Donatists. Bishop Valerius was himself a product of this situation, a Greek speaker unable to preach in the Latin tongue of his congregation. It is difficult to know whether Augustine's ordination as priest and assistant to Valerius was the result of the bishop's talent spotting, or his congregation's frustration. Whichever was the case, Bishop Aurelius of Carthage appreciated the potential Augustine possessed. Aurelius broke with ecclesiastical tradition and ordered the young priest to preach. After he was ordained bishop, Augustine was frenetically active, but never too busy to preach.

ARCHITECTURE AND ATTENDANCE

The historical development of preaching was intertwined with architecture. During persecutions, such as that under Decius, Christians had to meet secretly, in small groups. Preaching could not take the form of public discourse in such a restricted setting. After Constantine gave his backing to the Christian church, funds and freedom permitted the architecture within which preaching as public discourse could flourish.[58] When Augustine preached, he interacted with listeners in the assured manner of a trained orator. The unedited records of these interjections give his *Sermones* a sense of warm immediacy. The intimacy is all the more remarkable when it is remembered that Augustine spoke from the *cathedra*—an imposing seat modelled on Roman marble *cathedra* for passing judicial rulings. The irony of a Christian preacher speaking from the same kind

---

57. Hill, "St. Augustine's Theory and Practice of Preaching," 590.

58. Gordon Campbell, ed. *The Grove Encyclopedia of Classical Art and Architecture* (Oxford: Oxford University Press, 2007), 155; Johannes Roldanus, *The Church in the Age of Constantine: The Theological Challenges* (London: Routledge, 2006), 41.

of seat as that from which Pilate condemned Christ would not have been lost on listeners.[59]

While Augustine sat in the raised position of authority, his congregation stood around him.[60] It is possible that the building Augustine preached in had Donatist origins – they were after all the majority church. It is probable that Augustine's church has been excavated. The site is difficult to visit now. In 2001, Prof. James O'Donnell[61] visited and photographed the site with Serge Lancel.[62] Examination of O'Donnell's photograph and report suggests the building could have held a maximum standing congregation of three hundred.[63] It is difficult to reconcile the architecture with Van der Meer's occasional attendance figure of two thousand.[64] Perhaps such numbers could gather around the buildings on festival days, for they could not have fitted inside the main church. People would have crowded around the buildings for the Easter Vigil and baptismal processions from baptistry into church. The stenographical recording of the *Sermones* is evidence that Augustine's preaching garnered a wide interest. There was demand for copies of the *Sermones*, and in all likelihood a certain amount of excitable retelling of the preached content.

It has been common to assume that Augustine's listeners were drawn from all sections of society: rich and poor, educated and barbarian. Van der Meer portrays the setting thus,[65] as does Doyle.[66] This is certainly the impression one gets from reading the *Sermones*, as they refer to slaves and the poor being present. Readers naturally assume that Paul's assessment of Corinth held true for Hippo.[67]

In an important article, Ramsay MacMullen challenged this view of a mixed congregation.[68] He argued that the belief in a mixed congregation comprising diverse social strata was little more than romanticism. The limited

59. Matt 27:19.

60. *s.* 355.2. (SPM 1, 124)

61. Copyright is held by Prof. J. O'Donnell. He has given permission for reproduction.

62. Serge Lancel, *St Augustine* (London: SCM Press, 2002).

63. I am grateful to Prof. O'Donnell for his correspondence on the matter, and generosity in letting me reproduce his photograph as part of my PhD.

64. Van Der Meer, *Augustine the Bishop*, 23.

65. Ibid., 389; G. Wright Doyle, "Augustine's Sermonic Method," *Westminster Theological Journal* 39 (1977), 221.

66. Doyle, "Augustine's Sermonic Method," 221.

67. "There were not many wise according to the flesh, not many mighty, not many noble." 1 Cor 1:26. New American Standard Bible.

68. Ramsay MacMullen, "The Preacher's Audience (AD 350–400)," *Journal of Theological Studies* 40 (1989), 503–11.

size of church buildings suggested to him that only the wealthy could attend. With specific reference to Augustine, MacMullen contended that the appearances of a mixed congregation were illusory. He suggests that the poor would not have been beggars but rather middle class landowners; poor only in a relative sense compared to the upper class.[69] Augustine's acceptance that almost all households have slaves suggests a genteel outlook unfamiliar to those who could not afford slaves.[70]

MacMullen's thesis is a helpful corrective to an idealisation of Augustine's audience. However, his view ought not be taken too far. Maxwell does not accept his conclusions with regard to one of the other preachers MacMullen considers: Chrysostom. She points out that while laborers and artisans may not be actual beggars, they would have felt themselves to be poor in comparison to others, and in absolute terms, compared to equivalent workers today, they were indeed poor.[71] Pickpockets were certainly present at Chrysostom's services, though it is difficult to know whether that was to steal or listen.[72] In a similar manner, we can discern definite social distinctions among Augustine's congregation: children, slaves, church leaders, farmers and the poor.

It is difficult to be precise about exactly what financial means each group enjoyed. MacMullen assumes that a small building would lead to attendance being restricted to rich people who would not associate with the poor. But it could just as easily be the case that rich people would be attracted to a meeting where they can show off in front of the poor. That would fit with the sort of rebukes Augustine gave the wealthy in his preaching.[73] In addition it should be remembered that Augustine was involved in regular legal cases and public matters to do with property ownership, wages and slave manumission.[74] This aspect of his ministry would have brought him into frequent contact with the poor, some of whom may have subsequently attended his preaching. In summary, MacMullen offers a helpful corrective to imagining Augustine's congregation as thousands of people united in a utopia which transcended all social barriers. The reality was more modest; however, it was still a genuine inclusion of several diverse representatives of society.

---

69. Ibid., 509.

70. Ibid., 505.

71. Jaclyn L. Maxwell, *Christianization and Communication in Late Antiquity: John Chrysostom and His Congregation in Antioch* (Cambridge: Cambridge University, 2006), 74.

72. Ibid., 75.

73. E.g., *s.* 178.2–7 (PL 38, 961).

74. Joseph B. Bernardin, "St. Augustine as Pastor," in *A Companion to the Study of St. Augustine*, ed. Roy W. Battenhouse (New York: Oxford University Press, 1955), 74.

THE LITURGICAL SERVICE

As physical architecture imposed a certain order on Augustine's preaching, so the liturgical service also shaped the *Sermones*. Augustine's listeners had expectations that their preacher would follow accepted liturgical readings. On the occasions that Augustine departed from the normal reading, they could be upset.[75] The liturgical calendar impressed Scripture deeply upon listeners:

> The Bible, solemnly read or sung each year, was recalled incessantly on numerous occasion. . . . Augustine and his congregation knew the liturgical lessons and their related Psalms by heart.[76]

The order of liturgical readings was not overly restrictive to Augustine, as he could select a reading from the service to preach upon, or could use a reading to treat a topic of pastoral importance. It appears that there were two programs of readings throughout the liturgical year – one fitting with the seasons, the other with saints. *Sermones* from both of these categories are considered in our case study chapters. In addition to these, a number of the *Sermones* do not appear to fit either set of readings. These would include occasions where Augustine was travelling and addressed another congregation on some local matter, or considered a pastoral issue such as a freed slave or the forgiveness of a repentant Donatist.

It appears that though there were the aforementioned cycles of readings, and expectations were present, a liturgical calendar for readings was not fixed rigidly. Willis confirms that in Augustine's time, liturgical calendars for reading had been developed, but were not yet obeyed rigidly. He suggests that the focus on relevant passages during the liturgical seasons such as Easter and Lent was a catalyst towards fuller embracing of liturgical order.[77] Augustine's *Sermones* are consistent with this observation. Thus, there was both freedom and order in the readings. In a service of Eucharist, there were three readings, from the Old Testament, Epistles and Gospels. Additionally, there would have been a Psalm sung.

The usual days for preaching were Sunday and Saturday; however, Augustine could preach at more than one service or church on a given day. In addition to the normal Sunday pattern, several points in the liturgical calendar increased preaching responsibilities. Lent required a sermon every day; Easter demanded more than one sermon a day, in addition to baptismal preparation.

---

75. *s.* 232.1. (SC 116, 260)

76. Bonnardière, "Augustine: Minister of the Word of God," 250.

77. G.C. Willis, *St. Augustine's Lectionary* (London: Alcuin Club Collections, 1962), 6.

Augustine did not preach only at his own church. According to Verbraken's analysis,[78] 146 of the *Sermones* were preached at Hippo and 109 in Carthage. Twelve others can be traced to smaller cities, but the rest cannot be placed with any certainty.

The significance of the liturgical service and calendar will be considered further in our case studies, particularly with reference to Easter, Christmas and martyrs. At this point in our book, we merely draw attention to the important role liturgy had in ordering Augustine's preaching. The order was not rigid or restrictive; pedagogically, the liturgy helped listeners learn the Scriptures. This was not simply through repetition, but by inviting them to step into the rhythm of a year which melded with the sweep of Scriptural narrative. Augustine was conscious of the manner in which liturgical celebrations could make the passion of Christ in the past, appear in a spiritual manner in the present.[79] The congregation was empowered to feel an appropriate sense of being possessed by Scripture, and possessing Scripture. It was their Scripture, for they loved and knew it. As the Scripture was memorized by repetition, the Scriptural images and stories encroached upon the daily rhythms and seasons of life. Clearly there was a danger that familiarity and memorization could engender pride, complacency or boredom. Thus, a great part of the preacher's responsibility was to preach so as to avoid those possibilities created by the liturgical ordering.

AUGUSTINE'S STYLE OF PREACHING

Augustine's style of preaching appears on a first reading to be pedestrian and casual. His manner is more temperate than Tertullian or Cyprian, less stylised that Chrysologus and less elegant than Ambrose. Major philosophical and doctrinal themes associated with his other writings, such as predestination, are mentioned very infrequently.[80] Though one of these instances suggests a full blown doctrine of double predestination,[81] this is not developed or defended as it is elsewhere in Augustine's corpus. Sermonic application of predestination

78. Pierre-Patrick Verbraken, *Etudes Critiques Sur Les Sermons Authentiques De Saint Augustin*, vol. 12, *Instrumenta Patristica* (Steenbrugis: 1976).

79. *Ep.* 98.9. (CSEL 34, 2:530)

80. *s.* 111 (RB 57, 112), 138.5 (PL 38, 765), 158 (PL 38, 862) and 260D.1 (MA 1, 499) contain the only mentions of predestination in the *Sermones.* 229S mentions predestination in a manner uncharacteristic of Augustine before the Pelagian controversy, suggesting it may be inauthentic. See J. Patout Burns, "From Persuasion to Predestination: Augustine on Freedom in Rational Creatures," in *In Dominico Elquio, in Lordly Eloquence: Essays on Patristic Exegesis in Honour of Robert Louis Wilken*, ed. Paul M. Blowers, et al (Cambridge: Eerdmans, 2002).

81. *s.* 260D.1 (MA 1, 499).

is focused more on urging the predestined to prove their election by offering hospitality.[82] As mentioned in our preface, such features as these have led to a marginalisation of Augustine's *Sermones*. Not only do they appear less impressive than other ancient preachers' efforts, they do not fit with the image people have built up of Augustine himself, on the basis of his three or four best known writings.

A small number of academics have realised that the informal style of Augustine's preaching is pregnant with theological significance. The pastoral context of congregational preaching shaped Augustine's manner of speaking:

> It was Augustine's pastoral concern that so deeply engaged him with his congregation. It is the pastoral concern which saves him from making his preaching a personal display, and individualistic performance or a work of oratorical art or self expression.[83]

It is difficult to prove Old's intriguing suggestion that the Jewish synagogue's style of teaching supplanted secular rhetoric as the dominant influence on Augustine's manner of preaching.[84] Nevertheless, something must be offered as an explanation of Augustine's approach to preaching. Augustine's description of his earlier attitudes to rhetoric show what a substantive change his beliefs had undergone. One way to measure the immensity of the revolution is to compare *De Dialectica*[85] with *De Doctrina* and the *Sermones*. The greatest influence was most likely—as we shall argue when we consider *De Doctrina*—his immersion in the Scriptures themselves.

An earlier writer who offered insightful comment on Augustine's style was Fredrick van der Meer:

82. *s.* 111.4. (RB 57, 116)

83. Old, *Reading and Preaching: The Patristic Age*, 365.

84. Ibid., 349.

85. There is a debate about the authenticity of *De Dialectica*. A strong case for Augustinian authorship is given in B.D. Jackson, *Augustine's De Dialectica* (Dordrecht: D. Reidel Publishing Company, 1975). Jackson's reconstruction of the context of the treatise, and its relationship to the Augustinian corpus is compelling. I accept his conclusion: "Complete certainty eludes us, of course, but we can say that it is more probable that it is Augustine's than that it is not his. " (p. 30) As he admits, doubts arise due to the medieval manuscript traditions. We will not make further use of *De Dialectica* in our work, as the historical work has already been done ably by other scholars. The most significant thing about *De Dialectica* is that it is an unremarkable, efficient summary of some principles of ancient rhetoric. Even if Augustine was not the author, it is a good example of the kind of thing he would have used to teach his students rhetoric.

> The average sermon of Augustine makes such a disorderly impression that his unpretentious manner seems almost to suggest downright carelessness... He made his sermons deliberately artless, and at the same time showed positive genius in his strict observance of all artistic rules.[86]

There appear to have been two aspects of Augustine's style which merit comment: the rhetorical and the theological. On the rhetorical side, his casual manner was the mark of a man skilled and gifted enough in his profession to wear his learning lightly. He did not need to labor or draw attention to his ability in rhetoric; neither was his use of rhetorical devices formulaic.

However, that would only be a partial explanation of Augustine's style; a theological component is necessary to build a convincing case. His studied ambivalence about rhetoric and embracing of a homely, personal manner of discourse was profoundly theological. It flowed from his conviction that God loved and cared for his listeners, regardless of their status or learning. It arose from his belief that the same God who spoke to a learned preacher through the Scriptures, addressed the listener who stood to hear a sermon from a book he could never afford to purchase. Convictions such as these led Augustine to prefer keeping the Scriptural translation his listeners were familiar with, even if that necessitated not making use of scholarly advances.[87] The warm colloquial style of Augustine also flowed from his doctrinal convictions about the centrality of the desirous heart. Warm words from God intended to inculcate love naturally demand a preacher to speak with heartfelt warmth.

Thus, rhetoric and theology together shaped Augustine's preaching style. The result was an extemporaraneous manner of preaching which satisfied rhetorical and theological agendas. Deferrari studied Augustine's preaching on John in depth, and concluded that we have:

> The practically unrevised and unaltered longhand transcripts of shorthand verbatim reports made at the time when the sermons were delivered, the sermons themselves were spoken off-hand without much preparation.[88]

---

86. Van Der Meer, *Augustine the Bishop*, 418–19.

87. Ep. 28.2 (CSEL 34, 1:105); 71.3–6 (CSEL 34, 2:250); 82:34–5 (CSEL 34, 2:385); *civ. Dei* 18.43 (CCL 48, 638).

88. Roy Joseph Deferrari, "Verbatim Reports of Augustine's Unwritten Sermons," *American Philological Association* 46 (1915), 35.

In a subsequent paper, Deferrari extended his research to cover other *Sermones*, and focused on the method of preparation Augustine utilized.[89] A compelling case is made that Augustine's habit was to meditate upon the passages of scripture which would be read in a service,[90] and then speak extemporaneously upon the passage. He would not use notes or memorization, and felt free to adapt and change his approach to fit the listeners' reactions and interjections. Since Augustine did not live long enough to edit his *Sermones*,[91] the marks of improvisation and interaction are more than evident.

Quintilian had expressed dissatisfaction with speakers who relied overly upon scripts or memorisation of speeches.[92] Augustine's preference for extemporaneous preaching meant that he utilized the methods recommended by the best secular orators. His style had rhetorical purpose:

> Augustine knew that if a man truly mastered a subject, he had only
> to say what was in his mind with honesty and conviction; then he
> would have no difficulty in remaining in the popular vein and being
> at all times understood.[93]

However, the theological concerns were even more important than the rhetorical agenda. Theologically, Augustine's preference for extemporary preaching which flowed from prior contemplation upon Scripture generated a concern for relationality between God, preacher and listeners. The preacher's prayers for listeners, and requests that God would enlighten his understanding, drew all parties into a spiritual union and shared journey. Augustine's method of preaching required far more than mere information transfer; it necessitated the opening of a preacher's heart to God and a subsequent outpouring of the heart's love to listeners. Van der Meer makes the connection between extemporary style and relationality when he observes that Augustine "spoke from the fullness of his heart" and was "in living contact with his audience."[94]

Thus we can see that Augustine's style of preaching set him apart from other ancient preachers, and flowed from not only his rhetorical training but also his theological beliefs. If the *Sermones* have been neglected, then it is

89. Roy Joseph Deferrari, "St. Augustine's Method of Composing and Delivering Sermons," *The American Journal of Philology* 43, no. 2 (1922).

90. *s.* 225.3 (PL 38, 1097), 352.1. (PL 39, 1550).

91. *Retr.* 2.67. (CCL 57, 142)

92. Quintilian, *The Orator's Education*, 2.10.3.

93. Van Der Meer, *Augustine the Bishop*, 432.

94. Ibid., 419.

reasonable to suggest that an important aspect of Augustine's legacy has been undervalued. A style which at first appears to be casual and pedestrian is actually the fruit of profound theological convictions.

CONCLUSION

We have considered aspects of the context within which Augustine preached, the North African culture and the North African Church. We have shown some of the commonalities and distinctives of Augustine's preaching compared to other relevant preachers. All of this has highlighted the interplay, in various ways, between order and passion. Order and passion manifested themselves in North African culture generally. These two terms have been helpful in organizing our historical study. However, our subsequent chapters will prefer to utilize the hermeneutical keys of interiority and temporality, as these terms for investigation are more nuanced theologically than passion and order. They may be viewed as developments which build upon order and passion, but make for more constructive delineation of Augustine's undergirding assumptions and convictions.

In Augustine's preaching we highlighted the ordering roles of architecture, liturgy, rhetoric and theological convictions. Passion is evident in his devotion to extemporary preaching, which allowed room for his love of God and listeners to be expressed in prayerful meditation and spontaneous interaction. A central aim of the subsequent chapters is to elucidate the supremely important role Scripture took in ordering and shaping the preaching of Augustine. Scripture enlarged the passions of Augustine for God and people. It shaped and ordered his convictions and gave him the means to urge others to experience what he enjoyed. It is well known that the *Confessiones* represented a new kind of literature which flowed from the pen of an author saturated in Scripture. Our goal is to expose some of the ways Scripture shaped and informed his preaching. In the next chapter, we shall consider another vital part of the context which informed Augustine's preaching: the heritage of pagan oratory.

2

Pagan Oratory

Augustine holds a foundational place in the development of the Christian sermon. This is partly due to the fact that he began life as a professional teacher of rhetoric. His conversion led to him being changed from a professor of rhetoric into a Christian preacher. His unique experiences put him in the position of being able to offer self-conscious reflection upon the nature of preaching and its relationship to oration. The fruit of this is seen in *De Doctrina Christiana*, which will be considered in a subsequent chapter.

Augustine knew well that there was debate about the relationship between pagan oratory and Christian thought; he mentioned Julius' edict forbidding the teaching of rhetoric to Christians.[1] When he heard the Manichee, Faustus, Augustine was initially impressed with his oratory, only to be disillusioned by the lack of underlying knowledge.[2] As Augustine reviewed his secular career as an orator, he was hesitant about the profession's value, writing "I was selling the skill of speaking, if it is possible to excel through being taught."[3] Augustine attempted to distinguish between good and bad uses of rhetoric: " And without deceit I was teaching deceits, not that they might use these against the head of the innocent, but in due course on behalf of the head of the guilty."[4]

The goal of this chapter is to help us understand how Augustine's experiences of oratory prepared him to formulate the views on preaching which he developed. We shall first consider the contributions of five orators who in various ways impacted Augustine. We shall then attempt to extrapolate what secular oratory bequeathed to Augustine as a preacher.

---

1. *conf.* 8.10 (CCL 27, 119).

2. *conf.* 5.11–12 (CCL 27, 62).

3. "Ego uendebam dicendi facultatem, si qua docendo praestari potest.", *conf.* 8.13 (CCL 27, 121).

4. "Et eos sine dolo docebam dolos, non quibus contra caput innocentis agerent, sed aliquando pro capite nocentis," *conf.* 4.2 (CCL 27, 40).

How did pagan oratory seek to change people?

To persuade and change people was the goal of oratory. Considerable effort was devoted by rhetoricians to considering the methods and morality of oratory. Augustine wrote harshly of his time as a professional orator in *Confessiones* and gave a more nuanced opinion in *De Doctrina Christiana*. That he reached the level of teaching rhetoric for a living suggests the extent of his immersion in the art. It may be that the disdain he expresses for oratory in *Confessiones* has led to its significance being passed over by modern interpreters. Peter Brown helpfully reminds us that Augustine's educational background had deep consequences for his outlook; it focused his life upon words and eloquence.[5]

As we explore the debates had by pagan orators about how listeners may be changed, we hope to capture something of Augustine's outlook as a pagan orator; his Christian preaching cannot be seen for what it was without due reference to pagan rhetoric. From the wide selection of sources which could be profitably studied, we have selected five who, in various ways, had substantive connections to Augustine, via quotation, influence, admiration or proximity.

The most famous figure who influenced Augustine's rhetoric was Cicero. However, we need to appreciate that Cicero himself embodied earlier orators' insights. Augustine's thought looked back "chronologically and intellectually to the pre-Christian world of Cicero, Augustine's principal model, but Cicero himself enshrined a generic retrospection."[6] For this reason, not only Cicero but also earlier orators whom he engaged with contributed to Augustine's views of rhetoric. Cicero's retrospective embodiment of other orators' insights means that we must, in due course, consider some of his most important interlocutors: Gorgias and Plato.

Gorgias (483–375 b.c.e.)

Gorgias may be presented as merely glorying in the brute power of words to overcome opposition;[7] he did indeed write "Speech is a powerful ruler."[8] However, *The Encomium of Helen* suggests that Gorgias did not merely present

5. Peter Brown, *Augustine of Hippo* (London: Faber & Faber, 2000), 36–7.

6. Catherine Conybeare, "The Duty of a Teacher: Liminality and Disciplina in Augustine's De Ordine," in *Augustine and the Disciplines, from Cassiciacum to Confessions*, ed. K. Pollmann and Mark Vessey (Oxford: Oxford University Press, 2005), 50.

7. Colin Higgins, "Gorgias," in *The Sophists: An Introduction*, ed. Patricia O' Grady (London: Duckworth, 2008); Soteroula Constantinidou, *Logos into Mythos: The Case of Gorgias' Encomium of Helen* (Athens: Institut Du Livre, 2008).

8. Helen, 8. Helen Encomio de Elena: Testo Critico, Introduzione e note a Cura, ed. Francesco Donadi (Roma: Università di Padova, 1982).

a straightforwardly authoritarian view of rhetoric. It is significant that Gorgias' *Helen* is ostensibly about a woman famed for her beauty and wickedness: Helen of Troy. For when Gorgias talks of the power of words to deceive, the imagery is of seduction and desire.

Bons argues that this was a conscious association.[9] The wider context of seduction and desire means that when we consider Gorgias' claim that rhetoric has power, we should remember that it is power of a particular sort, analogous to seduction and erotic desire. At the end of *Helen*, the listener is to find herself seduced by the whole experience. As one scholar described it:

> When we ourselves are made to pity Helen and execrate Paris, are persuaded (perhaps) that persuasion is manipulation, enjoy the deception with which Gorgias amuses us even as we discern it, we feel in our own souls the seduction of rhetoric.[10]

This context of seduction which arises from the intention of *Helen* to acquit the most beautiful of women helps explain Gorgias' view of rhetoric. Gross argues that the internal dynamic of rhetoric found a natural home in the world of amorous persuasion. Coming to terms with this is of more value than to "merely catalogue a list of rhetorical figures and proofs."[11] Gorgias explicitly endorsed the important role love played in persuasion. He suggested four possible powers that could overwhelm Helen and therefore excuse her actions: the gods, force, speech or love.[12] The final suggestion is not developed as a separate point till *Helen* 19, where it serves as an illustration of the power of speech to seduce. This suggests that Gorgias intended to present the power of speech as a power analogous to that of erotic seduction. Therefore, while it is correct to say that he makes a case for the power of rhetoric to overwhelm, it would not do Gorgias justice to present his case for power as simply that of naked authoritarianism or deception:

> Gorgias's *technê* for moving audiences to action is aesthetic, using the emotional response of an audience to the immediate rhetorical context. To demonstrate reason and truth in the relative context a

9. Jeroen A.E. Bons, "Gorgias the Sophist and Early Rhetoric," in, *A Companion to Greek Rhetoric*, ed. Ian Worthington (Oxford: Blackwell Publishing, 2007), 44.

10. Robert Wardy, *The Birth of Rhetoric: Gorgias, Plato and Their Successors* (London: Routledge, 1996), 51.

11. Nicolas P. Gross, *Amatory Persuasion in Antiquity* (London: Associated University Presses, 1985), 20.

12. *Helen*, 6.

particular situation is important; yet it is also important for rhetorical uses of language to elicit a certain emotional response in the audience.[13]

Thus the "powerful ruler"[14] of speech is amorous because rhetoric is aesthetic. Gorgias' rhetoric requires a partner, permits ambiguity and ultimately invites collusion on the part of those who are seduced. He may argue that rhetoric overpowers, but his is a "rhetoric of seduction."[15] This is a less authoritarian portrait of his rhetoric than is usually presented, but one that is shown to be accurate by the final sentence of *Helen*:

> I have taken away by speech the shame of a woman, I have kept the plan which we established at the start of the speech, I have attempted to end the injustice of blame and the ignorance of reputation, I intended to write a speech which would be a praise of Helen, but for me a game.[16]

The final word of *Helen*, "game", invites the listener to collude with the embrace of Gorgias's rhetoric. He suggests that his speech is really a game, a joke. One can laugh at his joke. He has only in jest attempted to acquit the universally acknowledged villainess of the ancient world; or has he? Were all his arguments really nothing more than "a magic spell"[17] or "drug"[18] that overcame the audience? Did not his arguments earth themselves in well accepted truisms concerning the ability of coercion to mitigate blame? Was not Helen known for beauty as well as evil, and could the former explain why one's laughter is slightly nervous? To the original hearers, Gorgias's rhetorical joke would evoke hesitant laughter because listeners could not entirely escape the feeling that they had colluded and acquiesced in allowing his rhetoric to seduce.

Thus the contribution of Gorgias to the development of rhetoric is underestimated when reduced to one of unquestioning exaltation of rhetoric's authoritarian power. His real significance lies more in his presentation of rhetoric as an erotic power which seduces and invites collusion.

---

13. Bruce McComiskey, *Gorgias and the New Sophistic Rhetoric* (Carbondale and Edwardsville: Southern Illinois University Press, 2002), 28.

14. *Helen*, 8.

15. Gross, *Amatory Persuasion in Antiquity*. 32.

16. *Helen*, 21.

17. Ibid., 10.

18. Ibid., 14.

PLATO (424–348 B.C.E.)

The quarrel between Plato[19] and the orators remains one of the longest standing and most bitter of philosophical debates: "If Plato protests that Gorgias is not a true philosopher, perhaps he protests too much, since he addresses Gorgias' ideas explicitly or implicitly in a dozen dialogues."[20] Plato's contribution to the pagan discourse on oratory raises two important issues which formed part of Augustine's conceptualisation of rhetoric. We shall first consider the role of philosophy in persuasion, then the apparent failure of philosophical persuasion.

19. Julia Annas, *Plato: A Very Short Introduction* (Oxford: Oxford University Press, 2003); Richard Kraut, ed., *The Cambridge Companion to Plato*, Cambridge Companions (Cambridge: Cambridge University Press, 1992); Catherine Pickstock, "Justice and Prudence: Principles of Order in the Platonic City," *The Heythrop Journal* 42, no. 3 (2001): 269-282; G.L. Dickinson, *Plato and His Dialogues* (London: Unwin Brothers Ltd., 1931); C.J. Rowe, *Plato* (London: Bristol Classical Press, 2003); Charles H. Kahn, *Plato and the Socratic Dialogue: The Philosophical Use of a Literary Form* (Cambridge: Cambridge University Press, 1996); Ramona A. Naddaff, *Exiling the Poets: The Production of Censorship in Plato's Republic* (Chicago: University of Chicago Press, 2002); Richard Marback, *Plato's Dream of Sophistry* (Columbia: University of South Carolina, 1999); Seth Benardete, *The Rhetoric of Morality and Philosophy: Plato's Gorgias and Phaedrus* (London: University of Chicago Press, 1991); Devin Stauffer, *The Unity of Plato's Gorgias: Rhetoric, Justice and the Philosophic Life* (New York: Cambridge University Press, 2006); Michael Gagarin, "Probability and Persuasion: Plato and Early Greek Rhetoric," in *ersuasion: Greek Rhetoric in Action*, ed. Ian Worthington (London: Routledge, 1994); Fred D. Miller, "Plato on the Parts of the Soul," in *Plato and Platonism*, ed., Johannes M. Ophuijsen (Washington D.C.: The Catholic University of America Press, 1999); Otis M. Walter, "Plato's Idea of Rhetoric for Contemporary Students: Theory and Composition Assignments," *College Composition and Communication* 35, no. 1 (1984): 20–30; Edward Schiappa, *The Beginnings of Rhetorical Theory in Classical Greece* (New Haven: Yale University Press, 1999); Harvey Yunis, "Plato's Rhetoric," in *A Companion to Greek Rhetoric*, ed., Ian Worthington (Oxford: Blackwell Publishing, 2007); Alastair Blanshard, "Rhetoric," in *The Edinburgh Companion to Ancient Greece and Rome*, ed., Edward Bispham, Thomas Harrison, and Brian A. Sparkes (Edinburgh: Edinburgh University Press, 2006); James L. Kastely, "In Defence of Plato's Gorgias," *PMLA* 106, no. 1 (1991): 96–109; George Klosko, "The Insufficiency of Reason in Plato's Gorgias," *The Western Political Quarterly* 36, no. 4 (1983): 579–95; George Klosko, "The Refutation of Callicles in Plato's "Gorgias'," *Greece & Rome* 31, no. 2 (1984): 126–39; William H. Race, "Shame in Plato's Gorgias," *The Classical Journal* 74, no. 3 (1979): 197–202; Devin Stauffer, "Socrates and Callicles: A Reading of Plato's Gorgias," *The Review of Politics* 64, no. 4 (2002): 627–57; Patrick Quinn, *Aquinas, Platonism and the Knowledge of God* (Aldershot: Avebury, 1996); Mark Julian Edwards, *Origen against Plato* (Aldershot: Ashgate, 2002); Lloyd P. Gerson, *Knowing Persons: A Study in Plato* (Oxford: Oxford University Press, 2003); John Beversluis, *Cross-Examining Socrates: A Defense of the Interlocutors in Plato's Early Dialogues* (Cambridge: Cambridge University Press, 2000).

20. Scott Porter Consigny, *Gorgias, Sophist and Artist* (Columbia: University of South Carolina Press, 2001), 37.

THE ROLE OF PHILOSOPHY IN PERSUASION

Gorgias admitted that rhetoric lost some of its power when listeners had full knowledge of the issue being spoken of.[21] The possibility of deception being used to persuade was repugnant to Plato. He thought that philosophy, not rhetoric, should be relied upon to persuade people. He agreed with the orators that people had to be persuaded; it was whether or not philosophy should be the key to persuasion that divided the groups:

> To understand Socrates' mission, then, one must realise that he pursued a political end, the reform of his fellow citizens, but without recourse to political means. He lived and died in the conviction that logical arguments alone were enough to sway people to the pursuit of virtue.[22]

The goal of Plato's persuasion was the living of a good life and the soul's purification. The worst thing that could happen to somebody would be to have a corrupt soul.[23] Plato thought that orators did not speak with a view to what was best for listeners.[24] Since philosophy was the means to understanding the true nature of reality, the soul and people, any attempt to persuade people in such a way as to benefit them had to be philosophical. As a physician must know the nature of a body to heal it, so an orator must know the nature of the soul to persuade a person.[25] Since rhetoric apart from philosophy is only a technique and cannot give philosophical knowledge of the soul and world, true rhetoric must be philosophical: "Unless he philosophises competently, he will never be sufficient to speak about anything… Is not rhetoric as a whole an art which leads the soul by words?"[26]

The decisive position in persuasion, given to philosophy by Plato, ensured that all future discussion of rhetoric would have to grapple with the role of virtue, truth, cosmology and epistemology. By connecting all these issues, Plato did not end debate about the nature of persuasion. However he provided the framework of related concerns which a defence of persuasion would have to account for.

21. *Helen*, 11.
22. Klosko, "The Insufficiency of Reason in Plato's Gorgias," 584.
23. *Platonis Opera* (OCT 3), 511a.
24. *Platonis Opera* (OCT 3), 502e.
25. *Platonis Opera*, (OCT 2), 270b.
26. *Platonis Opera* (OCT 2), 261a.

THE APPARENT FAILURE OF PHILOSOPHICAL PERSUASION

In light of the seminal influence of Plato upon the future of philosophical thought, it is surprising how often his philosophical persuasion is portrayed as apparently failing when his works are read. The struggle to persuade is the issue with which Plato's *Republic* opens. Socrates is accosted en route to Athens. His interlocutors demand that he remain with them to discuss what they want to speak about. They remind Socrates that they are stronger than he is, and Socrates asks if it would be possible for him to persuade them to release him. They answer with a question: "And would you be able to persuade us," he said, "If we are not listening?"[27]

Frequently, Socrates is left alone, having failed to persuade opponents of the truth he was championing. The traditional explanation for this is twofold. First, the genre of dialogue aims to provoke and stimulate thought in readers. Second, acceptance of philosophical truth requires an inner engagement or disposition which is open to dialogue. This standard explanation has been challenged by John Beversluis, who argues that Plato presented in Socrates a figure who utilised such poor arguments and so misrepresented his opponents that he never really intended to persuade others. Socrates' actual intent "was not to improve anyone, but simply to win arguments."[28]

The reason Beversluis's thesis has not won widespread acceptance is that it necessitates positing a Plato who created a fictional character, but one with such lack of ability that almost any reader could spot the flaws in his efforts. However his argument serves to underline the point which even traditional scholars accept: Socrates often fails to persuade those he dialogues with. In addition to the explanations mentioned above, the genre of dialogue and the need to be inwardly open to dialogue, a number of factors are mentioned which impact the conditions of possible persuasion. Thus those who are older in age may be more willing to debate and be persuaded.[29] Sometimes Plato resorts to myth and traditional gods to champion some aspect of his argument.[30] It is also important to note that some are described by Plato as changing their views as a result of dialogue with Socrates.

CONCLUSION

It is easy to get drawn into taking sides in the debate about the value of rhetoric or philosophy in which Plato engaged. However, the real value of Plato as

27. *Platonis Republicam* (OCT), 327c.
28. Beversluis, *Cross-Examining Socrates*, 36.
29. *Platonis Opera* (OCT 5), 634d.
30. *Platonis Opera* (OCT 2), 246a–257b.

regards the topic under discussion is not that he offers a watertight argument against the practice of rhetoric, but rather that he underlines for us the tentative nature of truth claims. Plato makes arguments for the need of philosophical truth in persuasion; some external authority or reality must be appealed to by the orator. Yet, as he represents Socrates so often failing to persuade, Plato reminds us that there is a certain fragility and tentativeness to truth claims. As soon as arguments are made to persuade others, there is a need for appropriate disposition and external circumstances conducive to persuasion. The act of persuasion occurs not in a logical vacuum, but within an interconnected web of relationships, dispositions and assumptions.

Thus Plato brought to the attention of orators both the necessity and fragility of philosophical truth in persuasion. Augustine's preaching, if it was to satisfy the aspirations secular oratory bequeathed him, had to find a way of giving meaningful external sources of persuasion alongside genuine internal resources for moulding interior disposition.

CICERO (106–43 B.C.E.)

Quoted 176 times in the extant works of Augustine, Cicero had immense influence upon Augustine's views of oratory. His dialogue *De Oratore* was quoted by Augustine eight times.[31] The importance and influence of Cicero on Augustine's views was considerable: Augustine modelled his ideal ecclesiastical orator after the pattern of Cicero's ideal classical orator.[32] Traditionally there have been three main scholarly approaches to assessing the nature of Cicero's rhetorical persuasiveness. These were outlined by C. J. Classen as: First, studying each speech in its particular historical context. Second, comparing Cicero's practice with his advice on oratory. Third, observing repeated tactics utilised in speeches.[33] Each of these is helpful in forming a view of Cicero's oratory. Since we are particularly concerned with the reception of Cicero in Augustine, we will keep an awareness of these approaches as controls to our study, but pay more attention to the way Cicero was perceived by others to persuade. We wish to summarize what sort of legacy Cicero left for others. This was formed by the broad contours of his teaching on rhetoric and its impact. The popular reception of Cicero's oratory is an aspect of research that has been developed more recently and is discussed, for example, by Morstein-Marx.[34]

---

31. Five times in *doctr. Chr.*; once in each of *uera rel.*; *Jo. eu. tr.* and *gramm.*

32. James Burnette Eskridge, *The Influence of Cicero Upon Augustine in the Development of His Oratorical Theory for the Training of the Ecclesiastical Orator* (Menasha: George Banta Publishing, 1912), 55.

33. C.J. Classen, "Ciceros Kunst Der Überredung," in *Rhétorique et Éloquence Chez Cicéron* , ed., W. Ludwig (Genève: Fondation Hardt, 1982), 149–84; 149–50.

Cicero viewed oratory as a self-evidently good thing and thought himself an excellent practitioner of it. This self-assessment has been the near universal opinion of those who have evaluated his contribution. Views of those who regarded rhetoric as dangerous or immoral were not accepted by Cicero, since he rejected the divorce between philosophy and rhetoric. A good orator would know philosophy and not devalue it. However Cicero's attempt to avoid the philosophers' charges contained a certain evasiveness, for when he stated that the orator should know philosophy, he was commending a general knowledge which included many topics and would serve to increase persuasiveness: "The philosophy of his orator consists in knowing about philosophy, and philosophy is only one of the things he must know about."[35]

This is a considerably less exalted place for philosophy than that which Plato intended. The manoeuvre on Cicero's part reveals a central aspect of his persuasion: a pragmatic settling of issues flowing from a focus on the general. In *De Oratore*, Cicero instructed students to shift the grounds of a debate from the species to the genus, as the latter could be argued for more powerfully. Once talking about an issue in general terms, an orator could fortify himself on territory about which he had prior knowledge and would be more able to frame a speech which forced a dilemma upon listeners.[36]

In terms of answering the actual debate between Plato, Gorgias, and the orators, Cicero's rhetorical success carried the day but did not resolve the issues. He spoke as if he had solved tensions between philosophers and orators, but in actuality "Cicero offers no concrete suggestions for resolving the division between philosophy and rhetoric."[37] There is little doubt that Cicero's ability to persuade was both very real and magnified by himself as a rhetorical technique. The large corpus of his works and their influence on following generations has confirmed his near mythical status. The assumption that he must have been brilliant because he had nothing else to rely upon than his words is compelling.

Nevertheless, one modern scholar has noted a weakness in Cicero's oratory:

34. Robert Morstein-Marx, *Mass Oratory and Political Power in the Late Roman Republic* (Cambridge: Cambridge University Press, 2004).

35. M.L. Clarke, *Rhetoric at Rome: A Historical Survey*, 3rd. ed. (London: Routledge, 1996), 56.

36. Christopher P. Craig, *Form as Argument in Cicero's Speeches: A Study of Dilemma*, American Classical Studies (Atlanta: Scholar's Press, 1993).

37. Anthony Corbeill, "Rhetorical Education in Cicero's Youth," in *Brill's Companion to Cicero: Oratory and Rhetoric*, ed., James M. May (Leiden: Brill, 2002), 37.

> It is startling to realise that in some respects Cicero is a slave to his skill. One might want to argue that he relied too heavily on oratory to take risks with it, and that, as a result, there were strict limits on the issues he discusses... I would suggest that Cicero's reliance on oratory actually restricts what he can say; his brilliance is not accompanied by freedom.[38]

The danger which Steel has discerned is one arising from too much weight being placed upon oratory. The debate with the philosophers was whether rhetoric was a neutral, good or manipulative tool. Steel's observation is that in his actual life Cicero's entire existence depended upon rhetoric's success. It was a load which could not be borne indefinitely. This aspect of Cicero's persuasiveness, his willingness to make it carry all his fortunes and security, contrasts with the moderations Augustine made to his oratory after he became disillusioned with a life centred only on rhetoric.

The contributions Cicero made to the development of oratory were manifold, and at first may suggest that it is not possible to give one straightforward answer to the question of how he sought to persuade people. Persuasion, for him, resided in appropriating the best of Greek educational principles into Roman thought.[39] It also involved his infamous use of wit[40] and humor[41] to demolish an opponent. His insights as to how one could sway the popular masses were important,[42] as was promoting an appeal to character.[43] Unashamed swaying of emotions and grandiose identification of himself with the listeners' concerns were essential parts of his persuasiveness.[44] A compelling form of structured argument was important.[45]

The sheer diversity of these aspects of persuasion may dissuade us from discovering a foundational principle of persuasion in Cicero. However, the breadth of insights is crucial to understanding his oratory. For in the end,

---

38. C.E.W. Steel, *Cicero, Rhetoric, and Empire, Oxford Classical Monographs* (Oxford: Oxford University Press, 2001), 189, 227.

39. Corbeill, "Rhetorical Education in Cicero's Youth," 29.

40. Elaine Fantham, *The Roman World of Cicero's De Oratore* (Oxford: Oxford University Press, 2004), 186–208.

41. Clarke, *Rhetoric at Rome: A Historical Survey*, 79.

42. Morstein-Marx, *Mass Oratory and Political Power in the Late Roman Republic*.

43. James M. May, *Trials of Character: The Eloquence of Ciceronian Ethos* (London: University of North Carolina Press, 1988).

44. James M. May, "Ciceronian Oratory in Context," in *Brill's Companion to Cicero: Oratory and Rhetoric*, ed., James M. May (Leiden: Brill, 2002), 67.

45. Craig, *Form as Argument in Cicero's Speeches: A Study of Dilemma*.

Cicero attempted to persuade not by any one of these techniques, but rather by encouraging the formation of a certain type of person: an orator who had a grasp of, and was gripped by, the multifarious aspects of oratory. The orator himself, embodying the liberal educated ideal, was the essence of Cicero's conception of persuasiveness:

> He spoke as a "connoisseur" and not as a "schoolmaster"; his aim was not to furnish precepts, but to show what sort of orator and to what style he gives his own personal approval.[46]

Cicero recorded objections that his vision of the orator was beyond the reach of any person. This was not a concern to Cicero, who recognised that he was setting before people an ideal: "For always, whatever art or faculty is inquired into, it is common practice that according to the complete and perfect it be inquired into."[47] Thus, while Cicero had opinions about techniques, practice, learning and training, he thought they had been overly relied upon. Instead, he put the main emphasis upon the orator himself. The cardinal need was to possess a certain quality and breadth of ability, which though related to training and techniques, transcended them. The ideal orator, who was to be aspired to, enjoyed mastery over emotions, skills and the political circumstances which surrounded a speech.

When Augustine, as a young student, aspired to become an orator, it would have been Cicero's image which was set before him. The ambition to embody the unachievable, the ideal orator, could only temporarily motivate and reward. As we noted above, Cicero put so much value upon it that it actually restricted his freedom. Augustine gave up on this Ciceronian ideal; he found it promised much but could not deliver happiness.[48] However, as we shall see, Augustine moderated but never fully turned his back on Cicero's ideal orator. Augustine's ecclesiastical orator bore more than a passing family resemblance.

QUINTILIAN (C.E. 35–98)

The important contribution Quintilian made to the development in oratory was his focus on teaching rhetoric.[49] Of all Roman orators, he was the one quintessentially concerned with the methods of educating and forming a young

---

46. Emanuele Narducci, "Orator and the Definition of the Ideal Orator," in *Brill's Companion to Cicero: Oratory and Rhetoric*, ed. James M. May (Leiden: Brill, 2002), 430.

47. "Semper enim, quacumque de arte aut facultate quaeritur, de absoluta et perfecta quaeri solet." *De Oratore* (OCT 3), 22.84.

48. *conf.* 6.9–10 (CCL 27, 79).

boy into a mature orator.[50] Quintilian adopts a fairly conservative approach to rhetoric, following the established categories and methods. He worries that lack of originality will make his work unappealing: "[The Institutio] which mostly contains things not invented by me, but passed on by others."[51] In the end, it was not originality that Quintilian would come to be known for, but rather his drawing together and systematising of traditional principles of rhetoric. This was done with the intent of educating and training young boys so that they would grow into orators. The first book of his *Institutio* considers principles for educating boys; the final book portrays an idealized vision to which the orator aspired. Taking *Institutio* as a coherent work, we find that Quintilian sought to change listeners through educating and inspiring young boys to become the best orators that they could be. We shall consider and evaluate these two aspects of his project in turn.

EDUCATING ORATORS

Quintilian is best known for his contribution to education. Perhaps he developed an interest in how to pass on the skills of rhetoric because he had himself learned them from his father.[52] After twenty years' experience of educating others, Quintilian set down his principles and methods in writing.[53] The process of educating a young boy in rhetoric was intended to inculcate dramatic changes. Quintilian reflected carefully on the capacity and nature of those he wished to educate. Therefore he considered their family environment, insisting that a father ought to hold high expectations of his son's capacity to learn.[54] This advice was reasonable, in Quintilian's view, as it reflected the natural aptitude of humanity. If a child grew up to be unaccomplished

49. F. Edward Cranz, "Quintilian as Ancient Thinker," *Rhetorica* XIII, no. 3 (1995): 219–39; Robert G. Hall, "Ancient Historical Method and the Training of an Orator," in *The Rhetorical Analysis of Scripture: Essays from the 1995 London Conference*, ed., Stanley E. Porter and Thomas H. Olbricht (London: Continuum International Publishing Group, 1997); James J. Murphy, *Quintilian on the Teaching of Speaking and Writing* (Carbondale: Southern Illinois University Press, 2003); George Kennedy, *Quintilian* (New York: Twayne Publishers, 1969); Fernández López, "The Concept of Authority in the Institutio Oratoria Book One," in *Quintilian and the Law: The Art of Persuasion in Law and Politics*, ed., Olga Eveline Tellegen-Couperus (Leuvan: Leuvan University Press, 2003).

50. Maud W. Gleason, *Making Men: Sophists and Self-Presentation in Ancient Rome* (Princeton: Princeton University Press, 1995), 114.

51. "Quod pleraque non inuenta per me sed ab aliis tradita continebat." *Institutio Oratoria* (OCT 1, 3.1.5.), 130.

52. Ibid. (OCT 2), 9.3.73. 528.

53. Ibid. (OCT 2, 1), pr.1. 3.

54. Ibid. (OCT 1) 1.1.1. 7.

"obviously it is not the fault of nature but nurture."[55] In all these observations Quintilian presents his views as observations which will become self-evidently clear to any other sensible person who examines the nature and progress of students learning.

His discussion continues to explore whether education is best carried out at home or school. Quintilian agrees that schools may encourage immorality, but the determining factor will be the actual nature of the individual student. Thus if a student lacks virtue then he will be immoral in private as much as public.[56] Two points where Quintilian argues against the popular views of his day, are in the areas of physical beating[57] and memorization.[58] He challenges over-reliance on these methods, with observations about the natures of students and what will best suit their capacities.

Quintilian's *Institutio* is a student-focused educative programme, not that he advocated indulging or spoiling a child. As he warned: "What will he not desire as an adult, if he crawls in purple [garments]?"[59] While disdaining indulgence and refusing to spoil a student, Quintilian repeatedly bases his advice for education upon his observations about the actual nature of the learner. In this sense, Quintilian was student-focused. This led to his hope that a teacher would care for the individual and note their needs. Even in a crowded school, a good teacher would so speak that "we will never be in a crowd."[60] Therefore educating and changing people, according to Quintilian, required a sensitive appraisal of human nature and listeners' capacities. The setting was always relevant and the individual always central.

INSPIRING ORATORS

Quintilian frequently complained in his work that the task he had embarked upon was lengthy and arduous. However, the fact that he managed to complete an ordered account of the various techniques and approaches to oratory was itself an inspiration to younger students in their learning. There is an aesthetic appeal in completeness and order. Quintilian's invitation was an apprenticeship to a body of thought that had been collated by an older expert. He himself meditates upon the retirement of an elderly orator, suggesting the appropriate moment to retire: "So before he becomes ensnared in the traps of age, he should

55. "manifestum est non naturam defecisse sed curam." Ibid., 1.1.2. 8.

56. Ibid. (OCT 1) 1.2.4. 15.

57. Ibid., (OCT 1) 1.3.14–18. 21.

58. Ibid., (OCT 1), 2.7. 92–3.

59. "Quid non adultus concupiscet qui in purpuris repit?" Ibid., (OCT 1), 1.2.6. 15.

60. "Ita numquam erimus in turba." Ibid., (OCT 1), 1.2.15. 17.

announce a retreat and he will arrive in the harbour with an intact ship."[61] When retired, the goal should be to keep passing on the knowledge and skills learned in the service of oratory. The future hope of educating the young is held up as an inspiration and motivation to both the older and younger orator. Retirement is something to relish as it affords more time to teach others, and if taken early enough, one is strong enough in body and mind to make a meaningful contribution to this task. Quintilian's *Institutio* was itself clearly a work of maturity, something he had longed to produce when younger and now relished setting down. Consequently the *Institutio* aims to inspire orators by taking in the full sweep of not only the art of rhetoric, but of life itself. This joining of lived experience with precise instruction was essential to Quintilian's approach: "A reward worthy of the work comes when precepts and experiences come together with each other."[62] A young boy who embarked on learning rhetoric could feel the inspiration of being tutored into a school of lived experience and technique which had a grand tradition and high aspirations.

Quintilian's desire to inspire young orators is also seen in the way he echoes Cicero by writing of an ideal orator. He concludes *Institutio* with a portrayal of the perfect orator, setting before his readers an image of perfection to pursue. He is less clear than Cicero about the attainability of his image of perfection. Cicero had been clear that the ideal orator was just that: an unattainable ideal with pedagogical value. Quintilian seems to oscillate between attainability and idealisation. He states that Cicero was the perfect orator,[63] yet as even Cicero thirsted after the perfect orator, he must still be sought.[64] The standards Quintilian set were high; the perfect orator would not only master all the methods of rhetoric, but would utilise them with ease.[65] He pondered, "Shall I not dare to say that something, in this remaining eternity, may be found more perfect than that which has happened previously?"[66]

Quintilian's lack of precision about the possibility of becoming a perfect orator can be understood as arising from lack of clarity about the interior conditions for virtue. Thus Quintilian states that he wishes to go beyond

61. "Quare antequam in has aetatis veniat insidias, receptui canet et in portum integra nave perveniet." Ibid., (OCT 2), 12.11.4., 741.

62. "Tum dignum operae pretium venit cum inter se congruunt praecepta et experimenta." Ibid. (OCT 2), 12.6.7. 714.

63. Ibid. (OCT 2), 12.1.19. 695.

64. Ibid. (OCT 2), 12.1.20. 695–6.

65. Ibid. (OCT 2), 12.10.77. 739.

66. "Ego non audeam dicere aliquid in hac quae superest aeternitate inveniri posse eo quod fuerit perfectius?" Ibid., OCT 2, 12.1.21. 696.

Cicero's treatments of style and consider morals.[67] He insists that virtue is essential in the good orator: "Now I am not only saying this, that he who is an orator must be a good man, but that it will not even be possible to be an orator unless he is a good man."[68] This insistence alone, in such unqualified terms, would create difficulties. However, he goes further, stating that it is impossible for virtue and vice to dwell in the same person.[69]

Whatever words are spoken by an orator flow from his interior and reveal him as either good or bad. The bad man may speak well, but his feelings are out of step with his words: "Now the bad man necessarily speaks differently than he feels."[70] Thus Quintilian links his consideration of the perfect orator with virtue. He is clear about this from the outset: "We are educating the perfect orator, who cannot exist unless he is a good man. And so much so that we require not only an extraordinary faculty of speaking in him but also all the virtues of character."[71] His conception of virtue is not nuanced enough to enable him to clarify what kind and amount of virtue may actually be attained. The gifted student will use his talent for just reasons rather than in jest.[72] Virtue is crucial to Quintilian's conception of the good orator. However, it is so discussed by him that the uncertainties surrounding the expectations of progress and perfection in rhetoric may be traced to this lack of precision concerning virtue. He perhaps senses that his argument has brought him to fasten hopes of progress in rhetoric, upon an increase in virtue.

What is clear from Quintilian's comments on virtue and the ideal orator is that he wishes to inspire readers towards effort and progress: "So let the young, or more properly every age (for it is never too late for a good resolution), strive for this with all our minds, taking pains in this: perhaps it might be possible to reach perfection."[73] The goal of inspiring orators to increase their ability, virtue and the ease with which they discharge their profession, explains much of the structure of *Instituio* and comes to the foreground in the final book. The linking of perfection with virtue and the unexamined or imprecise nature of that virtue

67. Ibid. (OCT 2), 12.pr.4. 691–2.

68. "Neque enim tantum id dico, eum qui sit orator virum bonum esse oportere, sed ne futurum quidem oratorem nisi virum bonum." Ibid. (OCT 2), 12.1.3. 692.

69. Ibid. (OCT 2), 12.1.4. 692–3.

70. "Vir autem malus aliud dicat necesse est quam sentit." Ibid. (OCT 2), 12.1.30. 698.

71. "Oratorem autem instituimus illum perfectum, qui esse nisi vir bonus non potest, ideoque non dicendi modo eximiam in eo facultatem sed omnis animi virtutes exigimus." Ibid. (OCT 1), 1.pr.9. 4.

72. Ibid. (OCT 1), 1.3.2. 19.

73. "Quare iuventus, immo omnis aetas (neque enim rectae voluntati serum est tempus ullum), totis mentibus huc tendamus, in haec elaboremus: forsan et consummare contingat." Ibid. (OCT 2), 12.1.31. 698.

introduces a certain ambivalence and ambiguity to the sort of expectations of success Quintilian entertained. The lack of precision in analyzing virtue, which marks Quintilian's presentation, was a heritage of Stoic ethics. For the Stoics, "virtue was an absolute term: it was a state such that its possessor would always do what was right."[74] Recent research has emphasised the idealistic and absolutist ethics of Stoicism. While Paul's epistles distinguished love between Christians from honorable behaviour among the pagans, Stoics expected ethical commitments to be free of such graduation and differentiation.[75]

CONCLUSION

Quintilian testifies that though talents and physical capacity are essential,[76] there is real value in training people how to become orators. Training and teaching people requires experience, maturity and attention to the individual. Cultivation of the skills Quintilian values is a matter of more than simply passing on the techniques; students must be inspired to become virtuous. Lack of clarity about how sufficient virtue could be achieved in light of high standards suggests that *Institutio Oratoria*, while containing much which Augustine would affirm, leaves room for an approach to rhetoric that interacts with a more nuanced approach to interior virtue.

APULEIUS (C.E. 123–180)

In view of the large number and length of quotations in Augustine's work,[77] "no post-classical Latin author has such a place in Augustine's writings as Apuleius."[78] The two orators shared a common rhetorical style[79] and much more besides. As Augustine noted, the two men were not only fellow Africans but had both been born in Numidea and studied in Carthage.[80] Commonalities in career have been followed by scholarly observations on similarities in output.

---

74. F.H. Sandbach, *The Stoics* (London: Chatto & Windus, 1975), 28.

75. Runar M. Thorsteinsson, *Roman Christianity & Roman Stoicism: A Comparative Study of Ancient Morality* (Oxford: Oxford University Press, 2010), 194.

76. *Institutio Oratoria* (OCT 1), 1.pr.26. 7.

77. Apuleius, *Rhetorical Works*, (Oxford: Oxford University Press, 2001); S.J. Harrison, *Apuleius: A Latin Sophist* (Oxford: Oxford University Press, 2000); Julia Haig Gaisser, *The Fortunes of Apuleius and the Golden Ass* (Princeton: Princeton University Press, 2008).

78. Harold Hagendahl, *Augustine and the Latin Classics*, vol. 2, *Studia Graeca et Latina* (Göteborg: Acta Universitatis Gothoburgensis, 1967), 680.

79. Ibid., 686.

80. *Ep.* 138.19 (CSEL 44, 147).

For example, Augustine's attribution of his pre-conversion errors to "*curiositas*" may have been modelled upon Apuleius's self-assessment.[81]

Augustine's main concern when quoting Apuleius is to engage with the implications of the belief that he was a magician, and to challenge his explanations of demons.[82] For our purposes, the most significant thing about Apuleius is his reputation and image as an orator. While all orators cultivated their public image, Apuleius is of particular interest since his background was known to Augustine and he represented the life from which Augustine had turned away.

When on trial for being a magician Apuleius was accused of carrying a pocket mirror.[83] The insinuation was that the mirror fostered vanity and was used for occult purposes. Apuleius' response was to express his pleasure at seeing himself in a mirror: "Do you not know that there is nothing a natural-born (normal) man would rather look at than his own form?"[84] He went on to argue that while he personally enjoyed the vividness and movement visible in a mirror's portrait, he thought statues were necessary monuments to men such as himself since they lasted longer. This incident serves as a vivid illustration of the self-promotion endemic in ancient orators. While hyperbole must always be assumed to be present in their own recounting of achievements, it was still the case that Apuleius was well known as an orator, Platonic philosopher and society figure. His career was very close to that which Augustine had for so long sought. A hint of jealousy is detectable in Augustine:

> For Apuleius, since I can speak particularly about him, who as an African is better known to us African*s*. With all his magical arts he was not able to secure any judicial office never mind a kingdom; despite being born into a place of honour in his own country, being educated liberally and endowed with great eloquence.[85]

---

81. Pierre Courcelle, *Les Confessions De Saint Augustin Dans La Tradition Littéraire: Antécédents et Postérité* (Paris: Études Augustiniennes, 1950), 107.

82. *civ. Dei.* 8.14–19 (CCL 47, 230).

83. *Apologia*, Bibliotheca Scriptorum Graecorum et Romanorum (1963), 13.5.

84. "An tu ignoras nihil esse aspectabilius homini nato quam formam suam?" *Apologia*, Bibliotheca Scriptorum Graecorum et Romanorum (1963), 14.2.

85. "Apuleius enim, ut de illo potissimum loquamur, qui nobis Afris Afer est notior, non dico ad regnum sed ne ad aliquam quidem iudiciariam rei publicae potestatem cum omnibus suis magicis artibus potuit peruenire honesto patriae suae loco natus et liberaliter educatus magnaque praeditus eloquentia." *Ep.* 138,19 (CSEL 44, 147).

Apuleius enjoyed the career and success which Augustine rejected. He typified the spirit of not just orators in general, but the particular North African, Latinised ideal which had captivated Augustine's pre-conversion heart. "Apuleius was a quintessential product of his time, for both were bicultural, prosperous, nostalgic for the classical past, and enamoured of display."[86] Since this aspiration so closely resembled that which shaped so much of Augustine's rhetorical training, Apuleius reminded Augustine, as well as us, that the Christian preacher had been, and to some significant degree remained, an orator.

Thus Apuleius is an apposite bridge between considering pagan orators' methods of persuasion and the attitudes they bequeathed Augustine the Christian preacher. As Augustine could not refrain from engaging with secular orators, neither could he erase their influence upon his approach to preaching.

WHAT DID PAGAN ORATORY BEQUEATH AUGUSTINE THE CHRISTIAN PREACHER?

In our subsequent chapter, we will consider the arguments Augustine made in *De Doctrina Christiana* concerning the appropriation of secular rhetoric in preaching. At this point, we are interested in establishing the philosophical-theological connections and assumptions, through which the above description of secular oratory prepared the way for Augustine's convictions about preaching. Pagan oratory both provided categories and posed problems for Augustine's approach to preaching. The resolutions which he embodied in his preaching are illumined when we see how they were forged from interactions with Scripture, read through the hermeneutical concepts of interiority and temporality. We will focus on two important concerns: authority and transformation. These are better understood when we appreciate Augustine's creative use of interiority and temporality in his preaching of Scripture.

AUTHORITY

Plato's insistence upon the need for philosophical truth in oratory pointed towards the need for an external authority in persuasion. However, the apparent failure of philosophical persuasion in many of Plato's writings reveals the need for something more than the sort of philosophical truth which he utilized. The approach which Augustine took to authority can be seen as a resolution of the tensions which we outlined in regard to Plato's concerns. In order to demonstrate this, we need to explore how Augustine moved beyond the

86. Gaisser, *The Fortunes of Apuleius and the Golden Ass*, 2.

framework bequeathed to him by Plato and in his use of interiority and temporality, submitted to the external authority of Scripture.

To preach without any submission to an external authority would be too much a replication of Cicero's exaltation of rhetoric. Persuasion was the goal of Augustine's preaching, but it could not be a goal that subsumed all other concerns, and neither could it be the ultimate test of faithfulness. There had to be some form of authority which could take the role of Plato's philosophical truth. That authority had to be configured in a way which ensured it was more successful than the philosophical truth which so often failed Plato. What Augustine submitted to in preaching was Scripture. The interaction and philosophical-theological relationships which he engendered between interiority and temporality ensured that this authority was invested with power to effect that which he prayed God would do through preaching.

That Scripture was the authority to which Augustine submitted in preaching may be seen from several vantage points. The liturgical setting of a church service meant that every time Augustine preached he did so after a number of Scripture passages had been read, or in the case of the Psalm, sung. An Old Testament reading, Epistle, Gospel and a chanted Psalm comprised the normal Scriptural content of a Eucharist service.

Occasionally Augustine commented on the fact that there had been several readings: "We have heard the apostle, we have heard the Psalm, we have heard the Gospel; all the divine readings agree, that we should place hope not in ourselves, but in the Lord."[87] There were two annual cycles of liturgical readings, one associated with the special liturgical seasons and the other with memorials of the saints.[88] Both are represented in the extant *Sermones* of Augustine. The liturgical seasons emphasised by these cycles, including Christmas, Easter, Ascension and Lent were aimed at impressing a Christian temporality upon pagan interpretations of life.

In Augustine's day the celebrant still had freedom to select his own choice of readings on ordinary days.[89] It was Augustine's normal practice, in this area where he had discretion, to work his way systematically through books of scripture. This shows that he operated with a view of scripture's authority which respected the temporal flow of the scripture text. He understood that the

---

87. "Apostolum audiuimus, Psalmum audiuimus, euangelium audiuimus; consonant omnes diuinae lectiones, ut spem non in nobis, sed in domino collocemus." *s.* 165.1 (PL 38, 902).

88. Anne-Marie la Bonnardière, "La Bible 'Liturgique' De Saint Augustin," in *Jean Chrysostome et Augustin* (Paris: Actes du colloque de Chantilly, 1975), 154.

89. Willis, *St. Augustine's Lectionary*, 6.

authority was mediated through books which demanded to be understood as just that; books with introductions, narrative flow and conclusions.

In words echoing *De Doctrina Christiana*[90] Augustine expounded how his preaching submitted to Scripture's authority:

> In the consideration and interpretation of holy scriptures, dearest brethren, the most manifest authority of those same scriptures ought to guide our thinking. This is in order that those scriptures which are spoken openly might be faithfully examined for our edification, and those which are spoken more obscurely, for our training.[91]

Scripture suffused Augustine's preaching, whether he was working through a book in an orderly manner or speaking in memory of a saint. He sought to open up truths from Scripture, drawing on his meditations upon the readings and other passages where he found them relevant. Scripture was the authority to which Augustine appealed in his preaching. The unfolding of meaning from the text was central to his endeavours: "Now having admired this paragraph, let us search a little bit more carefully for the meaning of the text."[92] The extent to which his sermons were commentaries on scripture may be seen not only from the unedited *Sermones ad Populum* but also from the ease with which Augustine could make a few editorial alterations and turn his sermon series on the Psalms into an actual commentary.

The importance of Scripture, as it performed this role of authority, may appear so pedestrian as to be overlooked. Our earlier study of the debates concerning the role of philosophical truth in oratory, particularly associated with Plato, serves to highlight the monumental significance of Augustine's submission to Scripture's authority. Every time Augustine sought to explain not his thoughts, but those of Paul or Moses, he embodied a fresh answer to the apparent failure of philosophical truth which had plagued earlier secular orators. They spent hours preparing for a speech by rehearsing the techniques and methods of Cicero; Augustine's preparation for preaching was meditation upon Scripture.

---

90. *doctr. Chr.* 2.8 (SIM 82).

91. " Sensum nostrum, fratres carissimi, in scripturis sanctis considerandis atque tractandis regere debet earumdem scripturarum manifestissima auctoritas; ut ex eis quae aperte dicta sunt ad nutriendos nos, ea quae obscurius dicta sunt ad exercendos nos, fideliter disserantur." *s.* 363.1 (PL 39, 1634).

92. "Uerumtamen post articulum admiratum litteraturae huius significationem paulo adtentius requiramus." *s.* 110A.1 (DOLBEAU 141, 23–4).

The change from orator to preacher was nothing less than Copernican. No longer did the authority and success of persuasion reside merely within the orator and his skills. An external authority could be appealed to; the speaker demonstrated not flamboyance but faithfulness. This was seen in the preacher becoming a servant of the text, forging a new, appropriately humble, form of speech. The "*sermo humilis*"[93] was born from Augustine's popularisation of scripture as his authority in preaching.

This revolutionary role of Scripture was far from the totality of Augustine's contribution to a solution of the challenges bequeathed him by pagan oratory. The true nature of his approach to preaching is seen more fully when we examine how he forged philosophical-theological doctrines which enabled his use of Scripture to interact with both interiority and temporality. It was these creative connections which ensured that Scripture's authority in preaching did not repeat the apparent failures of Plato's use of philosophical truth. Augustine did not simply use Scripture as Plato used philosophical truth; he set Scripture within a network of doctrines which enabled its authority to stand where others had fallen.

The network of doctrinal connections Augustine made to preserve the authority of scripture in preaching revolved around interiority and temporality. As the scripture is brought to the exterior of a person, through preaching which brings words to the ears, so there is an Inner Teacher who awakens the person to respond appropriately: "For we have an Inner Teacher–Christ."[94] The same Christ who speaks through scripture is the Inner Teacher, who self-evidently teaches interiorly. In preaching, Augustine made explicit the contrast between his speaking and Christ the Inner Teacher: "Therefore return to the heart: and if you are believers, you will find Christ there; he himself is speaking to you there. For I am shouting: but truly he in silence teaches more."[95]

Augustine's development of a theology of the "*cor*" as the desirous centre of human identity was an essential part of this actualizing of Scripture in preaching. The heart's desires are the interior realities to which a preacher must minister: "Indeed the intention of the human heart; what it is directed towards and what it desires, it is this that needs observing."[96] If the center of human identity was rationality, then clarity of explanation would suffice to empower

---

93. Ando, "Christian Literature," 405.

94. "Habemus enim intus magistrum Christum." *Jo. eu. tr.* 20.3 (CCL 36, 204).

95. "Redite ergo ad cor: et si fideles estis, inuenietis ibi Christum; ipse uobis loquitur ibi. ego enim clamo: ille uero in silentio plus docet." *s.* 102.2 (PL 38, 611).

96. "Intentio quippe cordis humani quo dirigatur et quid exspectet, intuendum est." *s.* 54.3. AB 100, (1982) 263–9.

external authority. If the *cor* is at the centre, then internal desires and longings need to be re-ordered and healed, so that they can be fixed upon something more attractive than what was previously sought. Gowans correctly notes that in the *Sermones* the *cor* is the interior which is addressed: "the heart must be the focal point around which his preaching necessarily revolves . . . the term *cor* stands for the person in the deepest centre of being."[97]

This anthropology was forged by Augustine over time. His views developed from the Cassiciacum days when he frequently mentioned the *mens* and *animus*, through a period when he used *cor* to describe the moral quality of a person,[98] to a mature position where *cor* signified the essence of a person as a loving being above and before all else. The main factor fueling this development was Augustine's immersion in scripture—evidenced by increasing use of Bible texts in writing *Confessiones*—and also his engagement with the inadequate anthropologies of Pelagianism and Stoicism.

Christ as the Inner Teacher, the *cor* as the interior listener: these two doctrines of interiority enabled Augustine to bring the authority of Scripture to bear upon listeners in a way that surpassed secular rhetoric. Since Christ was teaching, the actual final act of persuasion did not depend upon human efforts. However, the preacher knew that the *cor* was where his words had to be aimed. His common human sympathy and pathos couched terms and appeals in such a way that the *cor* could be swayed and moved. It is the contention of our book that the temporal nature of Scripture itself aided Augustine's efforts to preach in such a way that the interior listener experienced God's authority. Scripture, which is temporal in form and has narrative flow, is well suited to this task. As a temporal narrative, the Scripture appeals to imagination and seductively invites listeners to position themselves within its temporal framework. As listeners hear of the temporal dealings between God and Israel and are enticed by the images and allegories Augustine expounded, he appeals to their imaginations. Auerbach suggested that this temporal appeal to imagination was one of the prime explanations for the spread of Christianity in the Ancient World. Its "integral, firmly teleological view of history and the providential order of the world gave it the power to capture the imagination and innermost feeling of the convert nations."[99] Thus Augustine could warn listeners of the danger of spiritually experiencing the curses Egypt suffered: "Therefore I think that all

97. Gowans, *The Identity of the True Believer*, 47.

98. E.g. *uera rel.* 24 (CCL 32, 202).

99. Erich Auerbach, "Figura," in *Scenes from the Drama of European Literature: Six Essays* (Gloucester: Meridian Books, 1973), 56.

who scorn and do not observe the Ten Commandments, suffer spiritually that which the Egyptians suffered physically."[100]

When Augustine so preached, he was inviting his congregation to imagine themselves in the temporal narrative of Scripture. As people were drawn into this grand narrative, they could be forgetful of their prior self-interpretations. In their interiors, they could experience the Inner Teacher renewing and reordering loves. In this way Augustine's preaching brought an authority to bear upon listeners with an inner power which surpassed that available to secular rhetoric. The sermonic form and nature of this authority arose from the explicitly temporal nature of the scripture which was itself the authority. Few scholars put so much emphasis upon Augustine's valuing of interiority as Phillip Cary. Yet even he can say of Augustine "the most important shift in his thought has to do not with our need for inner grace but our humiliating need for external authority."[101] Cary's interpretation of Augustine posits an ever more developed sense of the interior. That he highlights the need for external authority supports our view that scripture shapes and authorises Augustine's focus on interiority.

Virtuous Transformation and the Cultivation of Virtue

Secular oratory was obviously aiming to persuade and thus in some way transform listeners. Our earlier investigation of secular speakers revealed that this transformation, in various ways, was hindered or advanced by the speakers' understandings of virtue and the nature of transformation. This impacted both listeners and speakers. For example, Gorgias has been understood as so exalting the power of speech as to overwhelm both listeners and ethical considerations. The ability to persuade was its own ethic and needed no virtue beyond the fact that it could transform. Cicero and Quintilian agreed that a persuasive orator ought to be a virtuous person. Cicero highlighted the pragmatic benefit of having an audience who admired and trusted the speaker. Quintilian was more absolute than Cicero in insisting on the necessity of virtue in a speaker. Plato aimed to create virtue in those with whom he spoke; his efforts appeared often to be frustrated.

This background of pagan oratory bequeathed to Augustine an agenda to pursue in preaching; how can a preacher virtuously transform listeners to cultivate virtue in listeners? Augustine's approach required that he address both

---

100. "Arbitror ergo omnes qui decem legis praecepta contemnunt et non obseruant spiritaliter pati ea quae Aegyptii corporaliter passi sunt." *s.* 8.2 (CCL 41, 80).

101. Phillip Cary, *Inner Grace: Augustine in the Traditions of Plato and Paul* (Oxford: Oxford University Press, 2008), 5.

preacher and listener. We will explore his advice to the preacher in our chapter on *De Doctrina Christiana*. For now our focus will be upon Augustine's attempt to transform listeners.

These efforts to transform listeners involved preaching Scripture within the constellation of doctrines which he developed around the loci of interiority and temporality. This enabled him to expect transformation superior to that which was possible under the paradigms of secular rhetoric. Scripture told Augustine of a reason to seek people's transformation. Christ had died with the intent of changing people: "Christ died for the wicked: but by no means that they might remain wicked."[102] This salvation event, narrated in Scripture, demanded to transform the wicked. The question—central to our study—is how the preacher was to bring this salvation event, as recorded in Scripture to listeners in such a way that it had a transformative impact? Our suggestion is that it was by preaching the Scriptures with a particular attention to issues of interiority and temporality.

Crucial to Augustine's expectation of transformation was his understanding of virtue. We noted above that Quintilian's view of virtue was influenced by Stoic philosophy and as such had an absoluteness to it. Augustine, by situating virtue within a network of doctrinal loci, worked with a more graduated and nuanced understanding. In Augustine's preaching virtue was urged with reference to interiority and temporality. As regards interiority, virtue was presented as an inner love, desire for and delight in God. Cultivating such virtue involves reconfiguring loves: "Since a concise and true definition of virtue is the ordering of love."[103] When people desire earthly things, there are consequences for both the interior and exterior. People are left with: "Nothing outside, nothing inside: an empty wallet, an emptier conscience."[104] What needs to be aroused is an interior desire for God. Augustine uses the temporal narrative of Scripture to stir up this inner desire:

> Now, if it pleases you, let the Ark of the Covenant enter into your heart, and may it overthrow Dagon. So now listen, and learn to desire God, learn to prepare to see that same God. Blessed, he says, are the poor in heart, for they will see God. Why are you preparing the eyes of the body? What can be seen in this way? Whatever can be seen will occupy a place. He who is everywhere at once does not occupy a place. Clean that from which he may be seen.[105]

102. "Christus pro impiis mortuus est: non utique ut impii permanerent." *s.* 375A.2 (MA 1,2).
103. "Quod definitio breuis et uera uirtutis ordo est amoris." *civ. Dei.* 15.22 (CCL 48, 487).
104. "Foris nihil, intus nihil: inanis arca, inanior conscientia." *s.* 105.13 (PL 38, 624).

In this quotation, we see Augustine utilize the narrative of 1 Samuel 5 and Jesus's teaching from Matthew 5. Listeners are drawn into the temporal narrative of Scripture as they are reminded of the story of Dagon falling in front of the Ark of the Covenant. This temporal narrative is internalized as Augustine applies it to listeners' hearts. The imagery of eyes and sight is used in doctrinal works, such as *De Doctrina Christiana* 1.11. However, it is in his preaching that Augustine makes particularly evocative use of Scripture's temporal narrative to create an interior impact.

Virtue, conceived of as an interior desire for God, has a graduation and subtlety to it which naturally lends itself to a process of temporal development: "For desire is in someone who wants to attain to what he does not have."[106] Thus, desire draws one into a journey of seeking to possess that which is longed for. With virtue conceived as desire for God, Augustine could not present a view of the Christian life which focused primarily upon a single turning point; cultivating virtue was not simply a one off turning towards God. Listeners had to be encouraged to turn away regularly from earthly loves to God; to turn more deeply, more lastingly. In contrast to the God who revealed himself in Christ,

Augustine complained, "How great and how vain is the happiness of people."[107] In his preaching, Augustine aimed to use Scripture in order to help listeners discover this repeatedly—again and again seeing afresh the supreme desirability of God. The temporal narrative of Scripture had to be preached in such a way that listeners felt themselves drawn into the narrative. We shall see more examples of this in our case studies of Augustine's preaching. He drew people into the temporality of the narrative both by use of allegory and encouraging listeners to look back or forward to God's works. Their own temporal journey could thus be refigured as one in which desire for God is ever more deeply cultivated in their interior.

Conclusion: The Appropriateness of Scripture

We have seen that secular oratory bequeathed Augustine a framework for seeking to transform and change listeners. Augustine's Christian preaching both utilized and transcended this secular background. In the two key areas, of

---

105. "Iam in cor tuum, si placet, intret arca testamenti, et ruat Dagon. Audi ergo nunc, et disce deum desiderare, disce eundem deum uidere praeparare. Beati, inquit, mundicordes, quoniam ipsi deum uidebunt. Quid praeparas oculos corporis? Si sic uidebitur, quid uidebitur? In loco erit quod uidebitur. Non est in loco qui ubique totus est. Munda unde uideatur." *s.* 53.7 (RB 104, 24).

106. "Desiderium est enim homini, qui uult peruenire ad quod non habet." *s.* 177.6 (SPM 1, 68).

107. "Quanta hominum, et quam uana laetitia." *s.* 142.7 (MA 1, 700).

authority and virtuous transformation, Augustine forged his Christian doctrine of preaching by utilizing a number of Christian teachings which he developed around the *loci* of interiority and temporality. We have suggested several ways in which Scripture motivated, shaped and facilitated Augustine's use of interiority and temporality. Highlighting the appropriateness of Scripture for this task is one of the aims of our study. We have attempted to do this by exposing the philosophical-theological connections Augustine worked with in his preaching. This is necessarily an inductive investigation. However, did Augustine himself, in his preaching, state that scripture is a singularly appropriate tool for shaping people's interiority and temporality?

The suitability of means to effecting an outcome was certainly something to which Augustine had given thought. At one point he had suggested that the thing which distinguishes the elect from the non-elect is that the former are called in a manner suitable to them: "For the elect are those who have been appropriately called."[108] In this passage Augustine is making the point that God is able to call people to himself in a manner suitable to ensure that they respond as he intends. The issue may be raised with regards to Augustine's preaching whether he explicitly stated that scripture is "*congruenter*" to reordering people's loves and drawing them into relationship with God?

The suggestion of an answer may be seen when we consider the connections he makes in his preaching between the Holy Spirit, love and the Scriptures. Augustine insists that "the various riches of divine scriptures, the most extensive teaching, my brothers, is grasped without any error, and kept without any effort, by him whose heart is full of love."[109] We have seen how central love was to the desired transformation his preaching aimed at inculcating. Romans 5:5 is quoted thirty-five times in the *Sermones*. Taken together, the impact of these verses, as utilised by Augustine, is to emphasise that it is God's work, through his Holy Spirit, to create love within listeners. Augustine does not simply preach about God's love or love for God; he expects and prays that God will create love within people. Such a work will overcome the limits one imagines the human heart may have; God's Spirit can create space for his love to be shed abroad.[110] The love that Augustine wants listeners to experience is radically God-centred; it can involve nothing less than being caught up into God's own love.[111]

---

108. "Illi enim electi qui congruenter uocati." *simpl.* 1.2.13 (CCL 44, 37).

109. "Diuinarum scripturarum multiplicem abundantiam, latissimamque doctrinam, fratres mei, sine ullo errore comprehendit, et sine ullo labore custodit, cuius cor plenum est caritate." *s.* 350.1 (PL 39, 1533).

110. *s.* 23.7 (CCL 41, 313); 163.1 (PL 38, 889); 169.15 (PL 38, 923).

With reference to Romans 5:5, we are urged, "may we love God with God."[112] Even more radically, "So in order that you may love God, may God live in you, and may he love himself through you. That is, may he move you, enflame you, illumine you and awaken you, to his love."[113] Thus, in his use of Romans 5:5 Augustine makes clear that it must be God who transforms listeners and creates within them his own love. However, in one reference to this verse, he states explicitly that the Scripture's authority is the means God uses to form this love: "By believing the scriptures God has given love to you."[114] Thus it may be seen that as Augustine sought through his preaching to utilise and transcend the principles which secular oratory had bequeathed him, he did so self-consciously using the means of scripture. Byassee overstates his case, but he is surely correct to highlight the importance of scripture: "For Augustine, theology is nothing more (or less!) than a reading of Scripture."[115] As a Christian preacher he had come to the conviction that the Scriptures were peculiarly suitable to being used by God to shape the interiority and temporality of listeners.

111. Donald Fairbairn, *Life in the Trinity* (Downer's Grove: Intervarsity Press, 2009) introduces this motif in the Church Fathers.

112. "Amemus deum de deo." *s.* 34.3 (CCL 41, 424).

113. "Ut ergo ames deum, habitet in te deus, et amet se de te; id est, ad amorem suum moueat te, accendat te, illuminet te, excitet te." *s.* 128.4 (PL 38, 715).

114. "Credendo de scripturis deus tibi dedit caritatem." *s.* 145.4 (PL 38, 793).

115. Jason Byassee, *Praise Seeking Understanding: Reading the Psalms with Augustine* (Grand Rapids: Eerdmans, 2007), 56. As evidence that Byassee overstates the point, I would refer to Augustine's measured evaluation of the role secular studies play in Scriptural interpretation, *doctr. Chr.* 2.38–57.

3

Training Preachers: *De Doctrina Christiana*

Let him learn without pride, and as one through whom another is taught, without pride or envy may he hand on what he has received.[1]

This chapter is a study of *De Doctrina*. Our attempt to expose the undergirding doctrinal assumptions of Augustine's preaching would be incomplete without a consideration of this extremely rich book. *De Doctrina* was the first (and remains one of the most stimulating) Christian writings on the task of preaching. Having explored some of the background and context to Augustine's preaching, we now consider his own explanations of the task of understanding and preaching Scripture.

Though short, *De Doctrina* is a dense work. We cannot aim to do more than outline how our terms of investigation feature here, and suggest how they may be helpful in appreciating Augustine's doctrine of preaching. Along the way, we will attempt to show that our reading does more to explain Augustine's practice than simply assessing the extent to which he was indebted to pagan rhetoric. It is hoped that this chapter is a compelling reading of *De Doctrina* which coheres with our study and lays foundations for our hermeneutical keys of interiority and temporality. Though it cannot claim to be an exhaustive treatment of *De Doctrina*, out of this study will come our more precise configuration of interiority and temporality in Chapter Four.

---

1. "Sine superbia discat et, per quem docetur alius, sine superbia et sine inuidia tradat quod accepit." *doctr. Chr.* prooem. 5 (SIM 10, 59).

The Significance of *De Doctrina*

De Doctrina is one of the most studied texts in the Augustinian corpus.[2] Kannengiesser regards it as the theoretical foundation of Augustine's approach to doctrine,[3] influencing medieval[4] and later[5] hermeneutics. The first authentic writing of Augustine to be printed on a printing press was *De Doctrina IV* in 1465 by John Mentelinus in Strasbourg.[6]

Augustine began writing *De Doctrina* as soon as he was ordained bishop.[7] One of the most striking features of the work is the thirty-year hiatus Augustine left between writing Books 1–3 (c.e. 396) and Book 4 (c.e. 426). He lived a frenetic life and often paused his writing to attend to another matter. However, the normal pressures of his ministry do not account adequately for such a long pause in writing. Augustine revealed in correspondence that around the time he began *De Doctrina*, he thought that he understood enough Scripture for himself, but not enough to teach others.[8] That being the case, it is reasonable to conclude that a sense of his own inexperience in preaching led Augustine to pen the three books on understanding Scripture, but to refrain from composing the fourth book on preaching what was understood. If this is a reasonable deduction, then two observations may be made: first, it would seem likely that a major reason Augustine wrote *De Doctrina* was to aid the training of preachers; second, he thought that his knowledge of secular rhetoric was insufficient to prepare him for that task. Thirty years of preaching the Scriptures would be a greater qualification.

This interpretation of *De Doctrina* as primarily aimed at training preachers has been suggested by several scholars such as O'Donnell, who observes that it

2. Drobner, Hubertus R. "Studying Augustine: An Overview of Recent Research," in *Augustine and His Critics: Essays in Honour of Gerald Bonner*, ed. by Robert Dodaro and George Lawless (London and New York: Routledge, 2002),, ch. 3, p. 18–34. and Frederick Van Fleteren, "Comments on a Recent Edition of De Doctrina Christiana," *Augustinian Studies* 34, no. 1 (2003), 126–37.

3. Charles Kannengiesser, *Handbook of Patristic Exegesis: The Bible in Ancient Christianity*, vol. 2 (Leiden: Brill, 2004), 1149.

4. E.D. English, ed., *Reading and Wisdom: The De Doctrina Christiana of Augustine in the Middle Ages* (Notre Dame: Notre Dame Press, 1995).

5. Duane W.H. Arnold and Pamela Bright, ed., *De Doctrina Christiana: A Classic of Western Culture* (Notre Dame: University of Notre Dame Press, 1995).

6. Thérèse Sullivan, "S. Aureli Augustini Hipponiensis Episcopi De Doctrina Christiana Liber Quartus: A Commentary, with a Revised Text, Introduction and Translation" (PhD, The Catholic University of America, 1930), 1.

7. Carol Harrison, "De Doctrina Christiana," *New Blackfriars* 87, no. 1008 (2006), 121.

8. *Ep.* 21. (CSEL 34, 1)

"has been a silent authority for much of the best of Christian preaching from Augustine's time to the present."[9] A similar assessment was made by Kennedy, who thought Christian rhetoric achieved "its full theoretical expression in the second part of Augustine's *De Doctrina*."[10] Meer contends that "it is a book definitely intended for preachers and its assumption is that whoever ascends the pulpit must have a thorough knowledge of Holy Scripture."[11]

Others have instead focused upon the treatise as a program for education,[12] or an outline of the relationship between Christianity and secular culture.[13] Clearly the short work *De Doctrina* is polyphonic. Perhaps Press is overly dogmatic in rejecting some readings when he says that "one can construct a cultural or educational program out of the book, but that is just not what the book sets out to do."[14] For our purposes, we merely claim that a key but not necessarily exclusive, aim of the text was that it train Christian preachers. This training involved considering hermeneutics, education and secular culture. In line with our book, it may be seen that Augustine's approach to preaching Scripture did not engage with these issues randomly but by means of interiority and temporality. We shall consider the ways Augustine utilized interiority and temporality, first in understanding Scripture and second, in preaching Scripture.

INTERIORITY AND TEMPORALITY IN UNDERSTANDING SCRIPTURE

The opening three books of *De Doctrina* focus upon understanding Scripture.[15] It is tempting to dismiss the first book as merely an introduction; however, it may be argued that while the second book outlines the fitting mindset for approaching secular learning, the first aims to develop in readers the mindset appropriate for understanding Scripture.[16] Augustine was aware that some

9. J. O' Donnell, "De Doctrina," in Fitzgerald, ed., *Augustine through the Ages* (Grand Rapids: Eerdmans, 1999), 280.

10. Kennedy, George, *The Art of Rhetoric in the Roman World 300 B.C.–A.D. 300* (Princeton: Princeton University Press, 1972),, 612–13.

11. Van Der Meer, F., *Augustine the Bishop: The Life and Work of a Father of the Church* (London: Sheed and Ward, 1961),, 404.

12. Catherine M. Chin, "The Grammarian's Spoils: *De Doctrina Christiana* and the Contexts of Literary Education," in *Augustine and the Disciplines, from Cassiciacum to Confessions*, ed. K. Pollmann and Mark Vessey (Oxford: Oxford University Press, 2005).

13. R.J. Forman, *Augustine and the Making of a Christian Literature: Classical Tradition and Augustinian Aesthetics*, vol. 65, *Text and Studies in Religion* (New York: Edwin Mellen Press, 1995).

14. G.A. Press, "The Content and Argument of Augustine's *De Doctrina Christiana*," *Augustiniana* 31 (1981), 181.

15. *Retr.* 2.4.

would "*reprehensuri*"[17] his book. He saw the root of potential unjust censure as being found in "*tentationes superbissimas.*"[18] Such pride led people to imagine they could understand Scripture without teachers or principles. The opening book of *De Doctrina* follows on logically from the prologue, restraining pride by engendering a humble mindset conducive to understanding Scripture. Such a humble mindset is appropriate since Scripture contains much that is obscure and needs to be opened up to readers.

Our study recognizes that Scripture took a central role in Augustine's theological project. Stock observes that, "From the spring of 386, when his interest in Christianity was renewed, he attempted to situate his inquiries into transfers of meaning within a programme of scriptural studies."[19] This meant that Augustine's search for a higher understanding was conducted "in the presence of a sufficiently authoritative text (such as the Bible)."[20] Our analysis of the use Augustine made of interiority and temporality is made with specific reference to his use of Scripture in preaching. In this sense, Scripture is necessarily central to our investigation of Augustine's preaching. Bochet's study of Augustine's hermeneutic recognizes that Scripture played an increasing role throughout his life in shaping his methodology and self-understanding. Having given due regard to the impact of the Manichees and pagan philosophy, she argues that Augustine's movement between reflection and application reveals that Scripture is the metaphysic, or "firmament" for humanity.[21] There is an increasing realization among scholars that, not only was Scripture central to all of Augustine's theological endeavors, but its formative nature was rich and polyvalent. Implications for our hermeneutical keys of interiority and temporality will be drawn out in the subsequent chapter. But for now, we shall explore some of the relevant ways interiority and temporality manifest themselves in *De Doctrina*.

THE UNIVERSE OF SIGNS

Augustine presents his view of the universe in the following way: "So there are some things which should be enjoyed, others which should be used."[22]

---

16. Peter Sanlon, "An Augustinian Mindset," *Themelios* 33, no. 1 (2008).

17. "Censure, reject, criticise." *doctr. Chr.* prooem. 1 (SIM 6).

18. "Most proud temptations." *doctr. Chr.* prooem. 6 (SIM 12).

19. Brian Stock, *Augustine the Reader: Meditation, Self-Knowledge and the Ethics of Interpretation* (Cambridge: Harvard University Press, 1996), 1.

20. Ibid.

21. *Isabelle Bochet, 'Le Firmament de l'Écriture': L'hermeneutique augustinienne*, Collection des Études Augustiniennes, Série Antiquité, 172 (Paris: Institut d'Études Augustiniennes, 2004).

Something which is enjoyed is loved and desired for its own sake; that which is used is referred to an object of enjoyment, and ought not to be a terminus of desire in itself. The Trinity is to be enjoyed, while all created things should be used.[23] Self and other people should not be enjoyed, but rather used.[24] Augustine realized that this could appear callous and suggested people should not be offended. O' Donovan correctly notes that Augustine was in this text working out his theology of use and enjoyment for the first time:

> Augustine has not yet achieved a final disposition of these terms in the first book of *De Doctrina Christiana*; it is best to read that book as an exploratory study, in which he is still feeling his way towards a satisfactory conception of the *ordo amoris*.[25]

That said, Augustine never retracted the argument, and continued to employ it in teaching.[26] While the idea that one should use people can appear unappealing, what Augustine was attempting to do was promote a view of the universe in which every created thing is related to, and traced back to, God. No created thing should be loved apart from being referred to the God who made it. To so prematurely "terminate human desire"[27] would amount to a disordered love which constitutes idolatry. An example of Augustine applying this approach in preaching is found in *s.* 336.2.

Augustine's theology of use and enjoyment envisioned a universe of signs.[28] All created things point beyond themselves, beckoning people to enter deeper and seek the one God worth enjoying. As Rowan Williams observed, "Only when, by the grace of Christ, we know that we live entirely in a world of signs are we set free for the restlessness that is part of our destiny as rational creatures."[29] Against such a backdrop, Augustine's task of ordering and shaping interior loves makes sense. Commenting on *De Doctrina*, Brian Stock makes an observation which coheres with that of Rowan Williams, but extends his analysis to highlight the central role Scripture plays in Augustine's view of

22. "Res ergo aliae sunt quibus fruendum est, aliae quibus utendum." *doctr. Chr.* 1.3 (SIM 20, 1).

23. *doctr. Chr.* 1.5 (SIM 22).

24. *doctr. Chr.* 1.21 (SIM 40).

25. Oliver O' Donovan, "Usus and Fruitio in Augustine, De Doctrina Christiana 1," *Journal of Theological Studies* 33, no. 2 (1982), 363.

26. *s.* 177.8 (SPM 1); 50.8 (CCL 41, 629).

27. Rowan Williams, "Language, Reality and Desire in Augustine's *De Doctrina*," *Literature and Theology* 3 (1989), 145.

28. *doctr. Chr.* 2.1. (SIM 74)

29. Williams, "Language, Reality and Desire in Augustine's *De Doctrina*", 141.

reality. As Stock argues, "Scripture creates for him a readerly universe that is never fully knowable."[30] Scripture is understood as words which are signs. Some of these scriptural signs are clear; others are obscure.[31] Readers must discover themselves in the Scripture as entangled in the love of this world and by nature far from the love of God.[32] Progress in understanding the obscurities of Scripture enables one to use all created things in the way for which they were intended: as signs that direct our loves through and beyond themselves, to God. Allegory and the Inner Teacher played leading roles in helping readers understand Scripture. We will consider each in turn and note how both rely on an appreciation of interiority and temporality.

ALLEGORY

To modern readers, allegory can appear an uncontrolled hermeneutic. *De Doctrina* provides the theoretical framework within which Augustine attempted to interpret Scripture allegorically. Before outlining this, we might consider an example which suggests allegory may not be as uncontrolled as is sometimes assumed. Consider the example of Augustine's allegorizing of lentils. He preached on the story of Esau who sold his birthright to Jacob for a bowl of lentils. He allegorized the lentils to be firstly the food of Egypt and then argued that they represented all the errors of the Gentiles.[33] At first, this appears to be an uncontrolled use of allegory; however, the fact that Augustine mentions Esau's lentils in *Confessiones*[34] as an example of lust and greed alerts us to the possibility that he is not randomly focusing on a detail of the narrative, but is latching on to a detail that he sees as significant within his overarching theological schema. The transition from Esau to Egypt is an example of his allegories utilizing the knowledge of the natural world that he encouraged as a helpful tool in interpreting signs,[35] since he observed that lentils are a food of Egypt.[36] The subsequent step to treat the lentils as an allegory which represents all the errors of the Gentiles builds on the link with Egypt and meshes with his framework of redemptive history. In *De Civitate Dei* Augustine drew attention to this redemptive historical framework.[37] The lentils were an allegory that reflected

30. Stock, *Augustine the Reader: Meditation, Self-Knowledge and the Ethics of Interpretation* (Cambridge: Harvard University Press, 1996), 206.
31. *doctr. Chr.* 2.8 (SIM 82).
32. *doctr. Chr.* 2.10 (SIM 84).
33. *s.* 4.12 (CCL 41, 28).
34. *conf.* 10.46 (CCL 27, 180).
35. *doctr. Chr.* 2.23–24 (SIM 108).
36. *s.* 4.12. (CCL 41, 28).

and fitted with Augustine's framework there, which argued there are two cities throughout time. Esau represented one and Jacob the other. The lentils could thus be inwardly applied to listeners using Israel as a warning to the Gentiles; as Israel turned her heart back to Egypt, so she ate lentils.[38]

Thus, it can be seen that Augustine's allegorizing of the lentils is not as uncontrolled as one may at first assume. His use of the image in several works demonstrates that his sermon on the issue is not a unique piece of excessive interpretation, and that the overarching framework of redemptive history is a guide to his allegory. This use of allegory catches the listener up into the narrative of redemption itself. From lentils, to Egypt, to Israel, to Augustine's listeners: the details draw listeners into the story. The narrative of Scripture, portrayed in allegorical connections such as this, is carried to the interior of listeners; such a movement has been observed by Brian Stock:

> In Augustine's view, narrative thinking has its basis in a sequence of sounds or images impinging on the senses, which subsequently pass through the *sensus interior* to the mind.[39]

De Doctrina teaches the theoretical framework that gave form and control to Augustine's allegories. The most important point is that Augustine felt it was the nature of Scripture itself which drove responsible interpreters to use allegory. Specifically, it was necessary due to the Scriptures comprising an Old and New Testament: "So, although all the doings, or almost all of them, in the books of the Old Testament, are to be understood not only in their literal sense, but also figuratively [. . .]"[40] Allegory was thus an attempt to make sense of Scriptures which comprised two testaments. It was intended to be a form of reading appropriate to the text. As De Lubac has noted:

> The Christian tradition understands that Scripture has two meanings. The most general name for these two meanings is the literal meaning and the spiritual ('pneumatic') meaning, and these two meanings have the same kind of relationship to each other as do the Old and New Testaments to each other. More exactly, and in all strictness, they constitute, they are the Old and New Testaments.[41]

---

37. *civ. Dei.* 16.38 (CCL 48, 543).

38. *s.* 4.12 (CCL 41, 28).

39. Brian Stock, *Augustine's Inner Dialogue* (Cambridge: Cambridge University Press, 2010), 181.

40. "Ergo, quamquam omnia uel paene omnia, quae in ueteris testamenti libris gesta continentur, non solum proprie sed etiam figurate accipienda sint [. . .]" *doctr. Chr.* 3.32 (SIM 212).

All peoples without Christ labor under the curse of signs which are loved as ultimate goods. Israel was unique, not in that it did not live in a universe of signs, but in that she had been given signs by God specifically aimed at pointing to Christ.[42] When Israel thought the Sabbath referred merely to a weekly day of rest, or that the sacrificial system concerned only the blood of animals, she was interpreting the signs by the letter, rather than by the Spirit.[43] The Old Testament had to be read spiritually, which meant going beyond the mere letter to penetrate the hidden meaning allegorically.

Augustine went even further in his attempt to give a framework for his use of allegory. Having shown that the Scriptures themselves demanded allegorical interpretation, and that this arose primarily from the relationship between Old and New Testaments, he suggested another guideline. This principle helps explain why Augustine could also find allegories in passages of the New Testament, whereas his hermeneutic arose principally due to the need to interpret the Old Testament. The rule was that a passage in Scripture demanded allegorical reading if in its literal form it did not apply to either morals or the faith; by morals, Augustine meant the love of God or neighbor; by the faith, he meant truths about God or neighbor.[44]

The "Rules of Tychonius" are a fascinating aspect of *De Doctrina* and merit study in their own right.[45] For our purposes, it is sufficient to note that they are a fitting conclusion to the section of *De Doctrina* concerned with understanding Scripture; almost all of them are concerned with aspects of the shift from Old to New Testament. Augustine pointed out that the rules passed on were not exhaustive.[46] Rather, they were specific examples of how his general guidelines for allegorical interpretation worked out in practice.

Thus, Augustine's use of allegory saw Scripture as a text which possessed both temporality and interiority. The temporal narrative aspect of it, arising primarily from the Old and New Testament, demanded allegorical reading; such a hermeneutic permitted readers to understand the interior, spiritual reality of the Scriptures. In his work *Contra Aduersarium*, Augustine gave a clear

41. Henri de Lubac, *Medieval Exegesis: The Four Senses of Scripture*, vol. 1, *Retrieval and Renewal in Catholic Thought* (Edinburgh: T&T Clark, 1998), 225.

42. *doctr. Chr.* 3.10 (SIM 182).

43. *doctr. Chr.* 3.9 (SIM 180).

44. *doctr. Chr.* 3.14 (SIM 190).

45. Pamela Bright, *The Book of Rules of Tyconius: Its Purpose and Inner Logic* (Notre Dame: University of Notre Dame Press, 1988).

46. *doctr. Chr.* 3.42 (SIM 222).

statement of how this program of allegorical interpretation revealed Scripture's interior. Referring to the Jews' reading of the Old Testament, he wrote:

> [. . .] Because they were not understanding what they were reading, not because the books they read did not preach God and Christ. This is what it is to enter, to not be satisfied with the surface of the letter, but to enter into the interior of understanding.[47]

In this way, Augustine believed that Scripture itself possess temporality and interiority. In this respect, Scripture is a text which reflects the nature of the universe as God has created it and people experience it. A preacher needs to be acquainted with Scripture's interiority and temporality in order to understand the text correctly. When such understanding is acquired, the preacher will be able to help listeners order their loves aright and journey through the world of signs.

THE INNER TEACHER

The motif of Christ the Inner Teacher is one of the most obvious evidences that Augustine's "exegetical programme was buttressed by a number of widely held Neoplatonic doctrines."[48] Augustine's Neo-Platonic framework was inherited from Cicero, Plotinus and Porphyry. Perhaps, as Stock suggests, the most important feature of this Neo-Platonism was the concept of order or hierarchy.[49] The order of the universe portrayed the highest level of reality as absolute perfection and changelessness. Below that, in the lower levels of existence, was a world of change, decay and yearning for upward movement. The human soul occupied a mid-point between the divine and corporeal, possessing the capacity to move upwards or downwards according to desire and longing. There has been much debate about the precise role of Neo-Platonism in Augustine's conversion to Christianity. Carol Harrison helpfully warns against either underestimating or overestimating the impact of Neo-Platonism upon the early Augustine.[50] I would concur with the judgment of Matthews, who concluded that:

47. "Quia non intellegebant, quod legebant, non quia deum et Christum non praedicauerant, quos legebant. Hoc est ergo intrare, non esse contentum superficie litterae, sed ad interiora intellegentiae peruenire." *c. adu. leg.* 2.19 (CCL 49, 106).

48. Stock, *Augustine the Reader*, 10.

49. Ibid.

50. Carol Harrison, *Rethinking Augustine's Early Theology, an Argument for Continuity* (Oxford: Oxford University Press, 2006), 28.

Augustine's statement of his commitment to Christ in *Contra Academicos* marks him as a Christian at Cassiciacum. The decision probably stemmed from his conversion experience and definitely preceded his baptism. [I do] not think that this position excludes the influence of Neoplatonic philosophy in Augustine's becoming a Christian.[51]

Discerning Neoplatonic influences in Augustine's envisioning of Christ as the Inner Teacher need not cause us to assume Augustine was a Platonist in his early days. His philosophical background was just that: a background. It sensitized him to issues and framed much of his theology. As Matthews observed, "His philosophical background could be an aid or a tool; it could not be a substitute for Christian doctrine."[52]

De magistro is often associated with *De Doctrina* since both consider signs. They also both highlight Augustine's presentation of Christ as the Inner Teacher. As an early writing *De Magistro* has a lower incidence of scriptural citation than works which came after *Confessiones*. However, as Carol Harrison has argued "Augustine's early thought was not only fully Christian; it was fully Augustinian."[53] That being the case, it is unsurprising that the distinctively Augustinian emphasis on Christ as the Inner Teacher should be found in *De Magistro*[54] and *De Doctrina*; the former being an early writing, the latter composed around the time of *Confessiones*.

The important point insofar as *De Doctrina* is concerned is that Augustine believed that one could not comprehend Scripture by mere effort or unaided reason; understanding came as a gracious gift from Christ the Inner Teacher. While in *De Magistro* the focus is on the fact that it is indeed Christ who is the Inner Teacher, *De Doctrina* develops somewhat more carefully the actual means of this inner teaching. When the relevant passages are studied, it transpires that interiority and temporality are utilized to present the Inner Teacher.

Christ as the Inner Teacher is a motif which manifestly lays emphasis upon interiority. Christ, as wisdom, is present to "puro interiori oculo."[55] It

---

51. Alfred Warren Matthews, *The Development of St. Augustine from Neoplatonism to Christianity, 386–91 A.D.* (Washington: University Press of America, 1980), 32.

52. Ibid., 261.

53. Harrison, *Rethinking Augustine's Early Theology, an Argument for Continuity* (Oxford: Oxford University Press, 2006), 287.

54. It may also be observed that while Augustine had nothing negative to say about *De Magistro* when he considered it in his *Retractationes*.

55. "The pure interior eye." *doctr. Chr.* 1.11 (SIM 30).

is the inner eyes of the heart which must see Christ, God's wisdom. While, with Carol Harrison,[56] we may agree that Augustine believes and is teaching Christian doctrine, it is difficult to deny that there are strong Platonic overtones to Augustine's language at this point; talk of blind men needing inner enlightenment echoes Plato.[57] One modern scholar who has done much to emphasize the Platonic aspect of Augustine's inheritance is Phillip Cary, who comments on inner purification, writing "talk of purification by faith is as biblical as talk of justification by faith, but Augustine fills it in with specifically Platonist conceptual content."[58]

Considerable difficulties in interpretation arise if one tacitly accepts a framework for discussion which presents Augustine merely as being a virtual Platonist. His language and background may be more sympathetically grasped if he is permitted to be viewed as genuinely a Christian doctrinally, but one possessing an instinctive mindset and language indebted to Platonism. Such a mindset could accept Christian doctrine no less than a mind formed by later schools of intellectual thought such as modernity. Radical changes will be experienced by a person accepting Christian beliefs, but their underlying mindset will suggest areas for exploration and means of expression. In Augustine's case, the Platonic architecture of his mindset alerted him to issues of importance, but the doctrinal building erected was definitely Christian and Scriptural. As Stock observed of Augustine:

> Paul replaced Plotinus; progress through reading superseded the ascent of the mind on its own. Moving upwards depended less on a hierarchy of being than on a synthesis of doctrines.[59]

Thus, we may suggest that Cary's earlier cited observation should be amended; rather than explaining Augustine's emphasis on interiority as a Biblical concept filled with Platonist content, we would suggest that both concept and content are scriptural but it is a teaching highlighted, sought out and expressed by a theologian whose mindset had been formed largely by Platonism. The doctrines alluded to by Stock are discovered in Scripture, the authoritative text which shaped Augustine's Christianity and preaching. Byassee shares our view that Augustine's shift from Platonic thought was instigated by Scripture:

56. Harrison, *Rethinking Augustine's Early Theology, an Argument for Continuity* (Oxford: Oxford University Press, 2006).

57. *doctr. Chr.* 1.9 (SIM 28).

58. Cary, *Inner Grace: Augustine in the Traditions of Plato and Paul*, 13.

59.

Augustine's way of talking about salvation shifts over the course of his career—his earlier, more Platonic, other-worldly emphasis gives way to a more specifically scriptural vocabulary with which to speak of salvation as he spends a pastoral career meditating upon and preaching from Scripture.[60]

That there is more to the inner teaching role Augustine ascribes to Christ than a straightforward indebtedness to Platonism becomes apparent when we consider the relationship to temporality and Scripture.

In contrast to Platonic emphasis upon interiority, Augustine's use of it sits alongside substantive concern for temporality; Christ who enlightens the inner eyes is the wisdom who became incarnate at a particular point in time: "So she is said to have come to us not by movement though space, but by appearing to mortals in mortal flesh."[61] The crucial role of the incarnation as presented in *De Doctrina* arises from interplay between the temporal and interior: the temporal appearance of Christ enables him to be seen by people's eyes of flesh;[62] this is necessary precisely because the interior eyes have been blinded by the love of created things.[63] The ability to reorder loves so that God may be enjoyed as the ultimate good is made possible by the incarnated Christ revealing *temporally* that which was lost *inwardly*. The beautiful congruity in this healing work of Christ did not elude Augustine. He observed: "So because through pride humanity fell, she applied humility as a cure: we were deceived by the serpent's wisdom, we are released by the foolishness of God."[64]

Travelling through the created world of signs, we lose our way by clinging with excessive love to the means which ought to direct us towards God.[65] When Augustine presents the Inner Teacher as an answer to this problem, he is interpreting the incarnation with the twin hermeneutic of interiority and temporality. Both aspects of Augustine's approach need to be appreciated in order to represent him accurately.

---

60. Byassee, *Praise Seeking Understanding*, 103.

61. "Non igitur per locorum spatia ueniendo, sed in carne mortali mortalibus apparendo uenisse ad nos dicitur." *doctr. Chr.* 1.12 (SIM 32).

62. *doctr. Chr.* 1.11 (SIM 30).

63. *doctr. Chr.* 1.9 (SIM 28).

64. "Quia ergo per superbiam homo lapsus est, humilitatem adhibuit ad sanandum: serpentis sapientia decepti sumus, dei stultitia liberamur." *doctr. Chr.* 1.13 (SIM 34).

65. *doctr. Chr.* 1.4 (SIM 22).

UNDERSTANDING SCRIPTURE

We have considered three motifs used to help the preacher understand Scripture: signs, allegory, and the Inner Teacher. Having seen that interiority and temporality are part of each of these hermeneutical loci, we can attempt to summarize their cumulative significance for the understanding of Scripture. Signs, allegory and the Inner Teacher are all suggestive of what may be termed "depth."[66] That is to say Augustine perceives that Scripture and reality share a depth of being; understanding is the result of penetrating below the surface to what lies beneath. The universe will be falsely construed by the person who assumes that reality is what it initially appears to be and who lets interpretation terminate prematurely. Scripture contains a depth of allegory; creation teems with the depth of signs.

Augustine was himself a busy preacher, constantly in demand for multiple roles. He would have been all too aware of the temptation to settle for an obvious, simple interpretation of Scripture. Emphasizing the depth of Scripture and reality to his readers served to awaken within them the outlook which would not rest satisfied with the immediate or obvious, but which would search beyond the letter to engage the spirit. Augustine's hermeneutic for understanding Scripture is already suggestive of practical implications for preachers. The preacher who learns from him will need to spend time in the Scriptures; far from shying away from difficult texts he will seek them out, for they are opportunities to wade into the depths of Scripture. A personal experience of understanding is hard won, and the fruit of prayerful labor on the part of one who has embraced a mindset that perceives hidden depths and connections between Scripture and creation.

The commonality between these hermeneutical motifs suggests that Augustine wanted preachers to be sensitive to a profound connection between Scripture and creation, as the depths of Scripture illumine the depths of creation. The key to finding one's way through the depths of creation aright is to exegete a path correctly through Scripture to love. Thus Augustine recommends that a reader reflects on a passage of Scripture till he or she is led through to the kingdom of love.[67]

The task of understanding Scripture involves submission to principles of interpretation. Pride hinders some from humbling themselves to masters such as human teachers or rules of interpretation.[68] A preacher who sincerely desires

---

66. Peter Sanlon, "Depth and Weight: Augustine's Sermon Illustration," *Churchman* 122, no. 1 (2008): 61–76.

67. *doctr. Chr.* 3.23 (SIM 200).

68. *doctr. Chr.* prooem. 5 (SIM 10).

to understand Scripture must accept the inner enlightening of Christ, God's wisdom. The Inner Teacher stands as a reminder that our ability to understand has been disrupted; left to our own strength, we are blinded by disordered loves. As de Lubac argued with specific reference to Augustine's views:

> Jesus Christ brings about the unity of Scripture, because he is the endpoint and fullness of Scripture. Everything in it is related to him. In the end he is its sole object. Consequently, he is, so to speak, its whole exegesis.[69]

De Lubac is making a claim about Christ's role as interpreter of Scripture. We are in a position to expose the assumptions which led Augustine to present such a view and to extend the insight to creation.

The Inner Teacher, Christ, is able to help precisely because he stands in a unique relation to both creation and Scripture. The incarnation stands as Christ's appearance in the temporality of the Scripture narrative and, simultaneously, is the affirmation of creation's temporal narrative. The implications of this hermeneutic are vast. It suggests that creation and Scripture structure themselves around Christ, the supreme exegete. To truly penetrate the depths of either creation or Scripture requires faith in Christ. Only the Inner Teacher can so reorder inner loves that Scripture and creation are understood aright.

In conclusion, it may be suggested that Augustine's instructions as to how to understand Scripture are not appreciated in their fullness if they are treated as a collection of separate principles or pieces of advice about interpretation. Rather, we need to discern the assumptions he brings to his task of interpretation. These reveal a mindset or outlook which places Christ at the center of understanding both creation and Scripture. Acquiring this mindset is not possible apart from the gracious gift of Christ's incarnation and inner teaching.

Interiority and Temporality in Preaching Scripture

The fourth book of *De Doctrina* advises preachers on how best to communicate what has been understood from Scripture. Scholars such as Eskridge have thought of Augustine's approach as primarily a Christianization of Cicero's rhetorical strategies.[70] Others, such as Thomas Oden, have represented Augustine as being willing to use any rhetorical strategy to persuade: "Every

---

69. de Lubac, *Medieval Exegesis: The Four Senses of Scripture*, 237.

resource of rhetoric is employed to make the requirement of God as clear as possible and the eventful love of God as palpable and real."[71] While Cicero is indeed discussed, and persuasion is certainly the aim, the above explanations miss something of what makes Augustine's approach to preaching compelling and distinctive. Van Fleteran is possibly more prescient in his analysis. After accepting that Augustine does modify pagan rhetorical strategies he states that, "Augustine ended with a program of his own."[72]

Our aim is to achieve a theological understanding of what motivated this distinctively Augustinian methodology. To reach a more complete comprehension of Augustine's approach we need to expose his underlying philosophical-theological concerns. We shall proceed by considering, one after another, the preacher's view of rhetoric, Scripture and himself.

THE PREACHER'S VIEW OF RHETORIC

At first, the fourth book of *De Doctrina* may appear to voice a Ciceronian reverence for the power of rhetoric. Substantial passages from patristic writers[73] and Scripture[74] are quoted and analyzed for evidence of rhetorical principles. Cicero is alluded to reverentially[75] and his threefold manner of speaking applied to preaching, and Augustine bemoans situations where only those who teach error have the power of rhetorical persuasiveness.[76] These aspects of *De Doctrina* lead many to ponder the extent to which Augustine's view of preaching is indebted to secular rhetoric. As we have suggested, such a method of analysis, while having a degree of validity, fails to explicate the underlying assumptions that shape Augustine's views.

The originality of Augustine's doctrine of preaching arises from more than a simple modification or adaptation of secular rhetoric. While acknowledging some influence of secular rhetorical strategies, there are significant evidences of Augustine restraining the classical enthusiasm for rhetoric. He says he will not

---

70. James Burnette Eskridge, *The Influence of Cicero Upon Augustine in the Development of His Oratorical Theory for the Training of the Ecclesiastical Orator* (Menasha: George Banta Publishing, 1912).

71. Thomas C. Oden, *Life in the Spirit: Systematic Theology, Vol. III.* (San Francisco : Harper San Francisco, 1992), 79.

72. Frederick Van Fleteren, "Augustine, Neoplatonism, and the Liberal Arts: The Background to De Doctrina Christiana," in Duane W.H. Arnold/Pamela Bright (ed.), *De Doctrina Christiana: A Classic of Western Culture* (Notre Dame: University of Notre Dame Press, 1995), 14–24,, 23.

73. *doctr. Chr.* 4.46–47 (SIM 330).

74. *doctr. Chr.* 4.39–40 (SIM 312).

75. *doctr. Chr.* 4.27 (SIM 292).

76. *doctr. Chr.* 4.3 (SIM 254).

be teaching the rules of rhetoric that he learnt in the pagan schools.[77] Cyprian is rebuked for being overly rhetorical.[78] While in his younger days Augustine had been paid to teach rhetoric, he now recommends that it only be studied by the young person who has leisure for it.[79] Furthermore, he observes that people are more likely to learn eloquence from listening to good speakers than by learning the rules of rhetoric.[80] He argues that it is more important to teach the truth than to be eloquent. However, he who speaks truly ought to desire to be persuasive as well as accurate.[81]

In light of his profession and personal history, the ambivalence of Augustine towards the pagan rules of rhetoric is quite remarkable. Meer comments that it is a "minor educational revolution."[82] It cannot adequately be accounted for by simply assessing how much or how little he continued to use his rhetorical heritage. Having made various statements lowering the value placed on oratory, he goes on to make extensive use of Cicero's three styles of speaking. This seems confusing; Augustine appears to be both restraining and embracing secular rhetorical principles. While attempting to measure the scale of acceptance or rejection of pagan oratory leads to confusion, considerable progress in understanding his approach is made when we see how he relates eloquence to Scripture. This helps reveal the underlying convictions that shape his doctrine of preaching.

THE PREACHER'S VIEW OF SCRIPTURE

The fourth book of *De Doctrina* contains several long citations of Scripture, analyzed for their conformity to principles of rhetorical eloquence. These are highly significant, but not primarily because they reveal that Augustine continued to be indebted to secular rhetoric. That interpretation would fail to account for the strong element of restraint in other comments referenced above. Rather, the citations of Scripture show that Augustine believed Scripture to have its own eloquence. This point is made explicitly by Augustine: "For, where I understand them, not only does nothing seem wiser, but nothing seems more eloquent."[83] While Ciceronian eloquence helps one discern the eloquence

---

77. *doctr. Chr.* 4.2 (SIM 252).

78. *doctr. Chr.* 4.31 (SIM 298).

79. *doctr. Chr.* 4.4 (SIM 256).

80. *doctr. Chr.* 4.5 (SIM 258).

81. *doctr. Chr.* 4.8 (SIM 262).

82. Van Der Meer, *Augustine the Bishop*, 406.

83. "Nam, ubi eos intellego, non solum nihil eis sapientius, uerum etiam nihil eloquentius mihi uideri potest." *doctr. Chr.* 4.9 (SIM 264).

of Scripture, Augustine does not thereby deduce that the preacher should be taught pagan principles of rhetoric. Rather, he urges the trainee preacher to seek a closer personal experience of Scripture. The kind of personal appropriation of Scripture which Augustine desires to inculcate is described in one place as peering into the heart of Scripture: "Without doubt much more preferable than these, are they who remember the words [of scripture] less, but see their heart with the eyes of their own hearts."[84]

Here we find the fresh, distinctively Augustinian approach to training preachers. The matter of first importance for a preacher is that he see into the heart of Scripture for himself. The heart of the preacher must beat with the heart of Scripture. Focus on this inner appropriation of Scripture is not adequately represented as a Christianization of pagan rhetoric. It is a focus and mindset which flows from deeply held doctrinal convictions, embodied in the thirty or so years of preaching ministry that Augustine exercised between writing the third and fourth books of *De Doctrina*.

Augustine came to think that pagan oratory could be best learned from listening to those who are eloquent.[85] In a similar way, by the time he wrote the conclusion to *De Doctrina*, he believed that the way for listeners to learn divine truth was to be drawn into the Scriptures by a preacher who shares his own experience of that same reality. The preacher was to view himself as one who stands within the temporal narrative that is interpreted by Scripture. He needed to have an inner experience of the things of which he speaks; his contemplation of Scripture's meaning and desire to see into its heart would persuade listeners to seek the same thing. In much the same way Ambrose's preaching and silent Scripture reading had earlier entranced Augustine.[86] Inquisitiveness is often viewed as a feature of Augustine's mental approach to life. This may be so; nevertheless, in preaching his frequent meditation on a problem in Scripture was much more than a personality trait: it flowed from his doctrinal conviction that a preacher persuaded listeners to search for Scripture's meaning by welcoming them into his own search through Scripture.

It is integral to Augustine's view of preaching that some of the Scriptures are obscure. If all the Scripture was intelligible on a cursory reading, there would be no hermeneutical space left for a journey of exploration. As it is, Augustine advises that the preacher should not only deal with problems that are presented in a passage, but also address potential misunderstandings which he

---

84. "Quibus longe sine dubio praeferendi sunt qui uerba earum minus tenent et cor earum sui cordis oculis uident." *doctr. Chr.* 4.7 (SIM 260).

85. *doctr. Chr.* 4.5 (SIM 258).

86. *conf.* 6.3 (CCL 27, 75).

anticipates may arise in listeners.[87] The preacher is restless for a fresh glimpse of divine truth and his restlessness stirs up others to seek with him. The reality being sought is not immediately or easily available; a journey must be undertaken. As preacher and listeners venture forth together on this journey, they find that the eloquence of Scripture is itself an aid. It is the beauty and eloquence of Scripture that helps one persevere through confusion and uncertainty caused by obscurity.[88]

THE PREACHER'S VIEW OF HIMSELF

In light of this, it is natural that Augustine would issue instructions to preachers about how to embody the kind of person who can share what he has himself learnt from Scripture. Central to his advice is a commandment to pray. Prayer is the key to being able to draw listeners into Scripture and persuade them to embark on the same journey travelled by the preacher. If a preacher finds himself persuasive, "Let him not doubt that it is more by piety of prayer than the faculty of oratory."[89] The play on words between "*orationum*" and "*oratorum*" draws attention to the locus of Augustine's shift from pagan orator to Christian preacher. The central deciding element in the power of preaching is not skilful deployment of rhetoric, but rather humble dependence upon God. Such a mindset does not ignore secular insights any more than it condones falsity. It does more than simply moderate and restrain predilections for secular rhetoric; it sets all such matters within a profoundly Christian doctrinal framework.

The Christian preacher is trained by Augustine to regard himself as one who accesses truth in Scripture in the same way listeners do—by the graciousness of God. If, as we argue above, it is Christ the Inner Teacher who teaches the Christian, then a preacher who facilitates such an encounter must be one who experiences it himself. For Augustine, the preacher sharing his own thirst for and dependence on God is essential to the persuasiveness of Christian preaching. He must make an attempt at "mastering one's own inner dialogue."[90] The preacher who struggles to compose adequate sermons may use or borrow the words of another's sermon.[91] While original composition is optional, inner appropriation is not. The preacher's life is said by Augustine to be a sermon which must be harmonious with the message preached.[92] In all of

---

87. *doctr. Chr.* 4.39 (SIM 312).

88. *doctr. Chr.* 4.9 (SIM 264).

89. "Pietate magis orationum quam oratorum facultate non dubitet." *doctr. Chr.* 4.32 (SIM 300).

90. Hadot, *Philosophy as a Way of Life* (Oxford: Blackwell, 1995), 102.

91. *doctr. Chr.* 4.62 (SIM 358).

92. *doctr. Chr.* 4.59 (SIM 352).

this the dependence upon God enjoined by Augustine is justified, for God is in control. He could overrule any of the given norms. Thus, God may edify and convert people by sermons composed by unbelieving wicked preachers.[93] Presumably Augustine took such care writing *De Doctrina* intending that such a situation would remain a theoretical possibility with didactic value rather than the experience of his clergy.

CONCLUSION

De Doctrina is Augustine's attempt to distil the essence of his doctrine of preaching. It was written not as an arid theoretical work but as a handbook for actual preachers. This chapter has been a study of *De Doctrina*. It was necessary to include a chapter on this work because part of the goal of this study is to give readers both an insight into and experience of Augustine's preaching. *De Doctrina* makes an important contribution to our overall appreciation of Augustine's preaching since it aims to teach preachers how to understand and preach Scripture.

The central claim that has been made regarding *De Doctrina* is that the doctrine of preaching enjoined by Augustine is not adequately explained by a mere assessment of the extent to which he modifies secular rhetorical insights.[94] There is both restraint of and indebtedness to pagan rhetoric. Nevertheless, in both understanding and communication Augustine's doctrine of preaching was built upon a radical focus on interiority and temporality. These underlying concerns enabled him to explain how a preacher could understand Scripture by stepping into its temporal narrative and being taught by the Inner Teacher. Such a preacher would depend upon God in prayer and draw listeners into a similar dependent experience of being taught by God.

In all of this, the Scriptures take a leading role. They gave Augustine a vision of reality as an ever more deeply unfolding universe of signs, analogous to the very words of Scripture. Perhaps the most evocative aspect of Scripture's role in shaping his doctrine of preaching is glimpsed in considering the possible genesis of *De Doctrina*: we know that this work was begun about the same time as *Confessiones*, Augustine's most original writing that combines personal introspection with scriptural meditation to a degree previously unseen. Though it is impossible to prove the theory, it is surely very likely that the process of composing *Confessiones* pushed Augustine firmly in the direction of what may

---

93. *doctr. Chr.* 4.62 (SIM 358).

94. Such an approach is adopted in Paul R. Kolbet, *Augustine and the Cure of Souls* (Notre Dame: University of Notre Dame, 2010).

perhaps be termed contemplative obsession with Scripture. The path he trod as a result was preached in his *Sermones* for thirty years and then finally described in book four of *De Doctrina*. It takes a work of such striking originality and scriptural immersion as *Confessiones* to explain the origin of Augustine's doctrine of preaching.

4

Interiority, Temporality, and Scripture

Augustine's preaching reveals a particular concern for both interiority and temporality, and that this is due to his using Scripture to change listeners. This chapter aims to offer preliminary definitions of interiority and temporality, our two hermeneutical keys. These terms are constructive theological developments of the concepts "passion" and "order," which structured the opening chapter. Our hope is that the definitions capture the essence of the assumptions Augustine brought to his preaching, and that they can then operate as tools to help us better explicate what he believed himself to be doing as a preacher. Such a methodology was commended by Hadot when he argued that we ought to "give increased attention to the existential attitudes underlying the dogmatic edifices we encounter."[1] Our definitions were formulated through an inductive reading of the *Sermones* against the background of other major works by Augustine, especially *De Doctrina Christiana*. This chapter will include an example of how our main themes interact in one of Augustine's sermons, and will also compare our interpretation to that of three significant modern interpreters of Augustine. In this way, we approach and defend the value of our interpretation from the perspectives of Augustine's wider corpus, his *Sermones* and modern doctrinal commentators.

INTERIORITY

That Augustine was concerned with interiority needs little defense; some even attribute the very conception of interiority to his theological method.[2] Cary may be guilty of exaggerating the significance of Neo-Platonism for Augustine. If the role of Neo-Platonism in Augustine's theological method and formation

---

1. Hadot, *Philosophy as a Way of Life,* (Oxford: Blackwell, 1995),104.

2. Phillip Cary, *Augustine's Invention of the Inner Self: The Legacy of a Christian Platonist* (Oxford: Oxford University Press, 2000).

is overstated, then a number of problems ensue. The continuity of Christian convictions and doctrines between the early and late Augustine is disrupted;[3] the beauty and distinctiveness of Christianity for Augustine (as opposed to pagan philosophies such as Stoicism, Epicureanism, Manichaeism and Neo-Platonism) is minimized. This obscures the fact that:

> In the Christian assertion that God has acted in a decisive and unique way in Jesus Christ at a given point in history, Augustine sees Christianity as declaring a truth which Platonic philosophy can never understand.[4]

However, the risk of attributing an excessive role to Neo-Platonism ought not to be taken as refusing any importance whatsoever to the school of thought Augustine encountered in Plotinus and Porphyry. Augustine's study of Platonic texts sealed his rejection of Manichaeism.[5] Neo-Platonism did not give Augustine answers that he could hold to unreservedly all his life, but it did shape his mental outlook, give him insights to develop, and sensitize him to matters which remained of import within his Christian outlook. This meant that Neo-Platonism drew Augustine away from the Manichean view of evil, but in due course, Augustine could not remain satisfied with the Neo-Platonic conception of evil as a defective image of reality.[6] Neo-Platonism bequeathed Augustine a philosophical framework for ascent, progress and self-improvement. However, as this was developed theologically with Christian doctrine, "Augustine's interest in the theme of personal progress is largely replaced by a concern with the way in which men and women deal with situations in which they do not in any sense 'progress'."[7] In line with the formative role we attribute to Scripture, Stock observes that this shift of interest described in Augustine was "strenuously promoted by the Psalms, prophetic books of the Bible, and letters of St. Paul."[8]

All of this leads us to conclude that Neo-Platonism should be granted a role in developing Augustine's interest in interiority, but discerning the role of interiority in his preaching will not ultimately depend upon a detailed study of

---

3. Harrison, *Rethinking Augustine's Early Theology, an Argument for Continuity* (Oxford: Oxford University Press, 2006)

4. Daniel Williams, "The Significance of St. Augustine Today," in *A Companion to the Study of St. Augustine*, ed. Roy Battenhouse (Oxford: Oxford University Press, 1979), 3–14, 9.

5. *conf.* 8.2 (CCL 27, 113).

6. Mark Edwards, "Neo-Platonism," in *Augustine through the Ages*, ed. Allan Fitzgerald (Grand Rapids: Eerdmaans, 1999), 590.

7. Brian Stock, *Augustine's Inner Dialogue*, 12.

8. Ibid.

Neo-Platonism. In order to situate our definition of interiority, we will consider four major strands of Augustine's theological program which pertain to it. Augustine's preaching was a far more central part of his ministry and theology than is often recognized, but it did happen alongside and in the context of his other roles. Therefore, it is helpful to chart some of the contours of his thought which relate to interiority in his preaching.

SELF-REFLECTION

Augustine's reputation as a theologian of interiority arises primarily due to the self-reflective nature of his most famous work, *Confessiones*. It has been viewed as recording a transition "from the exterior to the interior self."[9] In *Confessiones*, Augustine "held a debate in the interior of the soul on the preconditions and limitations of self-knowledge."[10] Events, thoughts and memories were reflected on, with the aim of seeking not merely the self, but God. Augustine senses that his words were first spoken to him by God: "For I do not say anything right to people, which you did not hear from me first. Nor even do you hear any such thing from me, which you did not first say to me."[11] Thus, Augustine is conscious of an interior conversation between him and God which is prior to the speech heard by other people. The interior conversation is frequently revealed in *Confessiones* as he glides seamlessly from asking a question about God in the second person, via reflecting on Scripture, to converse with God in prayer.[12]

In effect, Augustine makes public his interior conversations and reflects on their significance. In earlier writings, such as *Contra Academicos* and *De Magistro*, he utilized the classical dialogue form. Such was his skill that his dialogues have been said to be the "swansong of a genre."[13] *Confessiones* is distinguished not only among the Augustinian corpus but patristic literature generally, as appearing to be a distinctly fresh genre. However, there is important continuity between *Confessiones* and earlier work, for the dialogue form is preserved, with the striking difference that the dialogue is a sharing of the dialogue between Augustine's interior and God.

9. John M. Quinn, *A Companion to the Confessions of Augustine* (New York: Peter Lang, 2002), 1.

10. Brian Stock, *After Augustine: The Meditative Reader and the Text* (Philadelphia: University of Pennsylvania Press, 2001), 11.

11. "Neque enim dico recti aliquid hominibus, quod non a me tu prius audieris, aut etiam tu aliquid tale audis a me, quod non mihi tu prius dixeris." *conf.* 10.2. (CCL 27, 155)

12. E.g. *conf.* 1.4 (CCL 27, 2).

13. G. De Plinval, *La Technique Du Dialogue Chez Saint Augustin et Saint Jerome, Actes Du Premier Congrès De La Fédération Internationales Des Associations D'études Classiques* (Paris: 1950), 311.

Augustine did more than just share his interior conversations. He presented the self-reflective inward turn as the crucial first step towards engaging God. The inward turn is described as being prompted by Scripture[14] and was first mentioned in *De libero arbitrio*.[15] While Plotinus counseled turning away from the senses, Augustine considered them and concluded that once one has looked inward, one must ascend to see the unchanging truth which is above the changeable mind. That the inward turn must be followed by an upward turn ensures that the Augustinian self-reflection is not endlessly self-referential or solipsist.[16] There is need of God's revelation, but that revelation is made at the point of inner reflection; Augustine's self-reflection created the "concept of a private inner space—the distinctively Augustinian foundation of a new and specifically Western tradition of interiority."[17]

The self-reflection outlined above reveals the importance of interiority for Augustine. The interior of a person is the space which must be examined and journeyed through in order to encounter God. It is of direct relevance to our book that *Confessiones* testify: first, that Scripture stimulates this inward turn, and second, that sharing one's interior experiences is used by God to bring others to himself.

THE INNER TEACHER

The only dialogue named in *Confessiones* is *De Magistro*.[18] In this early dialogue with his son, Augustine raises the problem that signs are used to communicate inner thoughts, but a sign cannot have meaning unless the reality designated is in some sense already known. His solution is to argue that Christ the Inner Teacher reveals true knowledge to the inner person:

> Regarding universal things however, which we understand- we consult not a speaker, who makes a sound outside of us, but that interior truth which presides over the mind. Perhaps by words we are admonished to consult it. It is Christ who is consulted and teaches, who is said to live in the interior man.[19]

---

14. *conf.* 7.10 (CCL 27, 99).

15. *lib. arb.* 2.3–2.15. (CSEL 74, 38–52)

16. Charles Taylor, *Sources of the Self: The Making of the Modern Identity* (Cambridge: Cambridge University Press, 1989), 130.

17. Phillip Cary, "Interiority," in *Augustine through the Ages*, ed. Allan Fitzgerald (Grand Rapids: Eerdmaans, 1999), 455.

18. *conf.* 9.14. (CCL 27, 141)

This passage goes beyond statements such as "in the interior man lives truth."[20] In *De Magistro*, Augustine presents interiority as the place where Christ teaches and reveals truth. The function and limitation of words is seen; they prompt one to consult the Inner Teacher, but in the final analysis, words themselves no more teach truth than human teachers.[21] When Augustine urges people to listen to the Inner Teacher, he is ruling out the possibility that humanity can know God solely on the basis of its own intelligence, virtue or effort.

The turn to contemplate the inner person is not a technique which can be performed or mastered by the self-sufficient intellectual; it is a listening to Christ who graciously reveals truth that could not be gleaned from any other source. Augustine's presentation of Christ as the Inner Teacher reminds us that Augustine believed his preaching could do little more than invite listeners to learn from Christ. Thus, the Inner Teacher enjoined upon the preacher not only a concern for the interior, but a sense of both gracious revelation from without and humility within. This concern for interiority was also demonstrated in *De Doctrina's* presentation of the Inner Teacher and concluding exhortation to prayer.

THE HEART

The *cor* became one of Augustine's central theological images for the interior as a desirous compeller. The *cor* is the innermost place of desire, longing, valuing and love. Commenting on Augustine's theology of love, one recent study emphasizes that "love has to do with human interiority."[22] The *cor* took central place in Augustine's theologizing about interior loving.

Augustine's interest in the *cor* increased with time. In the Cassiciacum writings,[23] Augustine mentions *mens* or one of its cognates sixty-nine times, but the *cor* only once: "That measure, I say, is to be kept and loved everywhere, if our return to God is in your heart."[24]

---

19. "De uniuersis autem, quae intellegimus, non loquentem, qui personat foris, sed intus ipsi menti praesidentem consulimus ueritatem, uerbis fortasse ut consulamus admoniti. Ille autem, qui consulitur, docet, qui in interiore homine habitare dictus est Christus." *mag.* 38 (CCL 29, 195).

20. "In interiore homine habitat ueritas." *uera rel.* 72 (CCL 32, 234).

21. *mag.* 45 (CCL 29, 201).

22. Werne G. Jeanrond, *A Theology of Love* (London: T&T Clark, 2010), 55.

23. These include *c. Acad.*; *b. vita.*; *ord.*, and *sol.*

24. "Modus, inquam, ille ubique seruandus est, ubique amandus, si uobis cordi est ad deum reditus noster." *b. vita.* 36 (CCL 29, 85).

In the Milan and Rome writings[25] of 387–8, Augustine refers to *cor* 32 times and *mens* 143 times. In Thagaste's compositions[26] during 388–91, *mens* continues to be the more common word, with 115 occurrences compared to 43 of *cor*. Thus in all of Augustine's treatises prior to ordination in 391 *mens* received more focus than *cor*.

It is often assumed that the seminal transition in Augustine's thought can be traced to the *Confessiones*, in which Augustine self-consciously reflected on his life and forged the image which he wished to present to the world. The power and evocativeness of this authorized narrative ensured that Augustine "succeeded in making his self-making inescapable."[27] When analyzed, the *Confessiones* do indeed reveal a change; *cor* takes central stage in Augustine's exploration of his own interiority. *Mens* there is mentioned 78 times compared to 187 uses of *cor*.

Carol Harrison has demonstrated that the early writings of Augustine display continuity with the post-396 Augustine.[28] She persuasively argues that, on the basis of Peter Brown's[29] positing of a revolution in Augustine's thought in 396, the extent of Augustine's development has been exaggerated. Our findings above support Harrison's thesis in that we see the *cor* is mentioned in one of Augustine's earliest writings; nevertheless, the stark reversal in balance of usage seen in the above statistics does demand explanation.

One method of investigation would be to check which is the earliest work in which Augustine reveals the high degree of interest in the *cor* so famously found in *Confessiones*. If *Confessiones* is not the first writing to display that focus, then it would be reasonable to doubt that the *Confessiones* themselves represent a uniquely revolutionary development in his thought. The first writing to contain more occurrences of *cor* than *mens* is *De fide et symbol*, the revised address Augustine delivered on the Nicene Creed in 393. In this, *cor* appears fourteen times while *mens* is referred to six times. However, a closer appraisal of Augustine's life reveals that preaching had, by this point, become a major part of his regular routine. Though they would not be completed for several years, Augustine had begun composing his *Enarrationes in Psalmos* the previous year, in 392. During their preparation and delivery they would have had a formative

---

25. These include *mor.*; *lib. arb.*; *imm. an.*; *quant.*; *mus.*

26. These include *Gn. adv. Man*; *mag*; *uera rel.*, and *div. qu.*

27. James O' Donnell, *Augustine, Sinner & Saint: A New Biography* (London: Profile Books, 2005), 37.

28. Harrison, *Rethinking Augustine's Early Theology, an Argument for Continuity* (Oxford: Oxford University Press, 2006).

29. Brown, *Augustine of Hippo* (London: Faber & Faber, 2000).

influence on Augustine, and they displayed a considerable weighting towards *cor*, mentioning *cor* 2,079 times and the *mens* only 310 times.

When eventually published, Augustine's other sermons revealed that this emphasis was carried across into the rest of his preaching, with the *Sermones* containing only 644 mentions of *mens*, but 2,013 occurrences of *cor*. From these figures, we may conclude that the *Confessiones* display a fresh focus on the *cor* as opposed to *mens*, not because that text in itself represents a revolution in Augustine's theology, but because over the previous few years he had, in his preaching of the Psalms and other Scripture passages, been affected with a view of interiority which favored the *cor*. The Scriptures, mediated to Augustine through the preaching experience, were the formative influence in shaping Augustine's outlook on the *cor*.

We know that Augustine meditated on passages on which he was going to preach, and shared with his congregation that which caught his attention as significant. He could refer to sermons as authoritative proclamations on theological issues, as seen in a letter mentioning some of his sermons in a manner which shows he viewed them as equivalent in authority to his Anti-Arian writings. Sending a few sermons to an enquirer was sufficiently important to make Augustine pause in writing *De Civitate Dei*.[30] He viewed the task of preaching as central to his ministry. All this being the case, it is understandable that his sustained engagement with Scripture through preaching would impact him noticeably. Preaching would have shaped Augustine during the times he prepared, delivered and edited his material.[31] That the *Sermones* and *Ennarationes* were not actually published till later dates has perhaps been the reason scholars occlude their influence and think that the *Confessiones* are the first major work to reveal a major interest in the *cor*.

For the purpose of our study, it is worth noticing that the commonality between the *Ennarationes*, *Sermones*, and *Confessiones* is that they all represent sustained engagement with Scripture. That Augustine's interest in the *cor* as the centre of interiority developed at the time it did, and is revealed in these particular works, supports our claim that Augustine's use of interiority and temporality in his preaching arose out of his use of Scripture. Attributing the progress to Augustine's sustained engagement with Scripture through preaching is a more moderate vision of Augustinian development than that critiqued by Carol Harrison, and it is reconcilable with the earliest usage of

---

30. *Ep.* 23A.3 (CSEL 88, 123).

31. Before death he completed the editing of the sermons on the Psalms, but did not manage to finish the process for the *Sermones*.

cor. It is also historically plausible in that both preaching and a related focus on Scripture are developments Augustine himself noted; in 391 c.e., he wrote to Bishop Valerius requesting time for a retreat to study Scripture more closely; in light of the importance of preaching, Augustine viewed this as requisite to his ordained ministry.[32]

Augustine's realization of the *cor's* importance gave him a powerful tool in preaching. The *cor* was used as a transformative tool of analysis; that is, it was a tool which helped him study, examine, and expose the behavior of listeners. The very act of doing so was transformative, as it involved exposing the *cor's* desires to God's Scripture and Spirit. Thus, for example, when Augustine offers to help listeners discern whether or not they are Pharisees, he urges them to trace the fruit in their lives back to the root: the *cor*.[33]

The *cor* is revealed in actual behavior.[34] All actions should be analyzed not merely in the context of what people would like them to be perceived as, but in the context of the desires that gave them birth. Such a probing analysis exposes the deepest nature of people to themselves and God, and is a crucial element of the transformative process Augustine envisioned his preaching as facilitating. Augustine, as a preacher, was enthusiastic to subject his own heart publicly to the kind of analysis he enjoined upon others. Thus, on one occasion he mentioned that a preacher could easily become proud because of his enjoyment of a special seat in church. He recognizes that the heart must be exposed and considered carefully. Although Augustine encourages all to do this, he accepts that it is not a task a human can do unaided: "For this one has accused their heart. He could not be an accuser of the heart, unless he were an inspector of the heart."[35]

In this quotation, Augustine argues that only God can accuse the heart, for only God can see the heart. Yet Augustine's exposure of this spiritual interior reality does have a transformative effect, for to desire to trace actions back to the *cor's* desires, and to accept one's inability to do so, places a listener in a position of dependence upon God. In this particular sermon, that is precisely the logic which Augustine follows, as he teaches that the heart is shut up in its love of temporal things unless God removes its veil to see clearly.

32. *Ep.* 21.3 (CSEL 34, 1).

33. *s.* 74.4 (PL 38, 473).

34. *s.* 74.5 (PL, 38 474).

35. "Hic enim cor eorum accusauit, accusator autem cordis esse non posset, nisi cordis inspector." *s.* 91.5 (PL 38, 569).

HIERARCHICAL ORDERING

Means and ends were an issue of discussion in Greek philosophy from Plato onwards. Aristotle applied the distinction to human relationships and Cicero contrasted *honestum* and *utile*.[36] Against that backdrop, Augustine made the distinction between *uti* and *frui* a mainstay of his theological thought:

> We may reasonably say that in the early to mid 390s the contrast of use and enjoyment has become a locus upon which many elements in Augustine's thought converge.[37]

In general, Augustine held to a hierarchical view of reality: God, angels, men, women, animals, and finally, inanimate creation. Such a view has implications for the importance one should attach to each part of the hierarchy. When Augustine says that only God is to be enjoyed and all other things are to be used, he makes explicit that his hierarchical view of the universe has pointed implications for interior desires and loves.

Augustine's *uti/frui* distinction shows that he was not interested in defending an ordered universe simply for the sake of order; he wished to help people themselves become ordered. That necessitated a focused concern for the internal desires. An ethic which focuses on what one should value can easily become preoccupied with the external nature of things. An ethic like Augustine's, shaped by use and enjoyment, is more concerned to measure the extent and depth of internal loves. His violation of Kant's moral imperative, to never to treat people as means, may appear unreasonable to modern readers.[38] However, Augustine was attempting to ensure that people would not place excessive weight of expectation and hope upon created things. Only God can be loved as the final eternal unchanging ultimate. To treat a person as if they can take the place of God would in fact not be truly loving to God or the person concerned:

> The language of *uti* is designed to warn against an attitude towards any finite person or object that terminates their meaning in their capacity to satisfy my desire, that treats them as the end of desire, conceiving my meaning in terms of them and theirs in terms of me.[39]

36. Henry Chadwick, "Frui – Uti," in *Augustinus-Lexikon*, ed. Cornelius Mayer (Basel: Schwabe, 2004), 71–75.

37. O'Donovan, "Usus and Fruitio in Augustine, De Doctrina Christiana 1," *Journal of Theological Studies* 33, no. 2 (1982): 361–97, 383.

38. *doctr. Chr.* 1.21 (SIM 40).

Augustine's distinction between use and enjoyment remained an important part of his outlook through his life. Its importance serves to highlight the considerable value he placed on the interiority as the place of regulating and measuring the appropriate depth of love.

DEFINING INTERIORITY

Our consideration above of four major features of Augustine's theological enterprise (self-reflection, the Inner Teacher, the heart, and hierarchy) suggests that, in order to understand Augustine, we need to reckon with the important role interiority had in his theology. It has been observed that "it is philosophically difficult to speak of interiority in light of the weight of outside."[40] Despite the weight of outside, we must reckon with the importance of Augustine proclaiming "my weight is my love."[41]

Our definition of interiority needs to be general enough to encompass the broad range of concepts outlined above, and yet must be sensitive to the emphases which Augustine made. As a first step towards definition, when we speak of interiority, we are doing so in distinction from exteriority. This does not mean we are dismissing the external world, or presenting a solipsist Augustine. It does not suggest that there is no relation between interiority and exteriority. However, if interiority is to mean anything, it must represent a genuine concern with that which is in distinction from the exterior world. Our definition must then go beyond a mere lexical search for Latin words associated with interiority. As we have demonstrated, Augustine's interest in interiority is seen not merely by the appearance of words, such as *intus*, but also in concepts such as the Inner Teacher.

Each of the four broad concepts treated above make contributions that should nuance our definition of interiority. Thus, the nature of Augustine's self-reflection in the *Confessiones* demands that an Augustinian definition of interiority posits an interior reality which is created to be not in isolation, but intimate relationship to God. Indeed, the interior is that which is most congenial to communion with the divine. The motif of an Inner Teacher reminds us that the interior is where God communicates and reveals truth to a person. Thus, the interior can be acted upon by God. The importance of the heart suggests that our definition of interiority must take account of its desirous,

39. Williams, "Language, Reality and Desire in Augustine's *De Doctrina*," *Literature and Theology* 3 (1989): 138–50, 140.

40. Dorothea Olkowski and James Morley, ed. *Merleau-Ponty: Interiority and Exteriority, Psychic Life and the World* (New York: State University of New York Press, 1999), 25.

41. "Pondus meum amor meus." *conf.* 13.10. (CCL 27, 246)

longing nature. Augustine's use of hierarchical ordering, and his distinction between "use" and "enjoyment", imply that the interior may be evaluated and assessed as to the worthiness of its desires.

Building upon our earlier discussion of *De Doctrina* and these leading themes, we may posit a definition of interiority which seeks to do justice to the various motifs and constructs which played a part in Augustine's conception of interiority. In short, interiority may for the purposes of our book be defined as the inner realm of desirous longing, evaluation and prayer.

It is hoped that this definition of interiority is broad enough to include the various ways in which Augustine approaches it, but specific enough that it encompasses the distinctively Augustinian flavor of his methodology in general, and his preaching in particular.

Temporality

In order to appreciate Augustine in an appropriately balanced manner, it is important to see that his focus on interiority is related to a concern for temporality. So for example, in the following quotation, interiority and temporality are both present:

> Therefore in all these things only those should be enjoyed, which we mentioned as eternal and unchanging; the others however should be used, that we may be able to come through to the fruition of the former.[42]

Augustine's concern with enjoyment is interior, but its coming to fruition is temporal. It is typical of Augustine's theological method and his preaching that interiority is not considered in isolation from, nor opposition to, temporality.

Paul Ricoeur has commented on the relationship between temporality and interiority in Augustine:

> On the one hand, his reflections on time place him... in what I characterised as the school of inwardness. . . . On the other hand, it is theology that is asked to interpret historical time.[43]

---

42. "In his igitur omnibus rebus illae tantum sunt quibus fruendum est, quas aeternas atque incommutabiles commemorauimus; ceteris autem utendum est, ut ad illarum perfructionem peruenire possimus." doctr. Chr. 1.20 (SIM 40).

43. Paul Ricoeur, *Memory, History, Forgetting*, (Chicago: University of Chicago Press, 2004), 356.

Exploring how temporality and interiority are related in Augustine's preaching is a major goal of our book. As a step towards analysing the sermons, we will outline several major aspects of Augustine's theology which contribute to his concern with temporality. These motifs will then be used to construct a definition of temporality which will aid us in our study of his preaching.

CREATED MATTER

The *Sermones*[44] may be added to the five larger works[45] of Augustine in which he wrestled with scripture's teaching on creation. Through these years of interpretation Augustine developed his theological views. Stimulated by opposition to Manichaeism, he came to hold a more positive view of created matter than he is often credited with. Since his reputation for denigrating the physical is usually linked to his views of sex, it is instructive to note Augustine's affirmation of the goodness of creation in that context. *De Continentia* was referred to by Possidius as a "sermo"[46] and was most likely written in 418–420.[47] With the intention of teaching Christians how to resist sexual (and other) temptations, Augustine encourages a positive view of created matter:

> Indeed the body is certainly different by nature from the soul, but it is not alien to human nature. For the soul does not consist of body. But nevertheless a person consists of soul and body: and when God frees someone, he frees the whole person.[48]

A positive view of created matter undergirded Augustine's preaching and enabled him to preach about the concerns of temporal life, for example, wealth, old age, marriage tensions, health and apathy.[49] Augustine's affirmation of created matter was a development beyond Neo-Platonism. In and of itself, the reality and goodness of creation does not encompass Augustine's conception of temporality; it is merely a pre-requisite. Other conceptions related to time and narrative are necessary additions.

44. *s.* 1 (CCL 41); 212 (SC 116); 214. (RB 72).

45. *Gn. adu. Man.*; *Gn. litt. imp.*; *conf.* 11–13; *civ. Dei.* 11; *Gn. litt.*

46. Possidius, *Life of Augustine* (PL 46, 2.207).

47. David G. Hunter, "The Date and Purpose of Augustine's *De Continentia*," *Augustinian Studies* 26 (1995): 7–24.; Michael R. Rackett, "Anti-Pelagian Polemic in Augustine's *De Continentia*," *Augustinian Studies* 26 (1995): 25–50.

48. "Corpus quippe ab anima est quidem natura diuersum, sed non est a natura hominis alienum. non enim animus constat ex corpore; sed tamen homo ex animo constat et corpore: et utique deus quem liberat, totum hominem liberat." cont. 26 (CSEL 41, 175).

49. *s.* 68.11 (MA 11); 81.8 (PL 38, 504); 152.4 (PL 38, 821); 255.3 (PL 38, 1187); 87.15 (PL 38, 538).

TIME

In *Confessiones*, Augustine realizes that time, though often measured and discussed, is difficult to define.[50] For our purposes, three aspects of his method of enquiry are helpful. First, the nature of time is closely related to God's nature. Augustine's response to those who think that created matter must be everlasting is to complain "those who are saying these things do not yet understand you."[51] Second, Augustine is above all not primarily concerned with a theoretical definition of time, but rather, with finding meaning in successive events. Interpretation rather than measurement or definition motivates him. In his attempts to measure time, he is exploring time's nature with the hope of bringing coherence and meaning to life's events. There is existential angst as Augustine bemoans the lack of understanding he feels "I have fallen apart in times, of which order I do not know."[52] Third, when attempting to find meaning in time Augustine turns to consider words, to their speaking, hearing, and singing. When singing one senses the distension of time as words and notes are remembered and expected.[53] Planning to speak for a long time drives Augustine to consider the internal sensation of time.[54]

Augustine's use of words to explore time is suggestive of his appreciation of the power of words to interpret reality. When seeking to understand the nature of creation, Augustine realizes that the words of Moses can give him answers. However, even when he understands the language, there is still the need of an interior ability to know that the words understood are true.[55] As he affirms the ability of words to bring meaning to temporal events, Augustine recognizes the need for an interior insight that goes beyond the naked word.

The opening words of *De Civitate Dei* similarly contrast time with eternity: "The most glorious city of God whether in these times, when it sojourns among the wicked, living by faith, or established in that seat of eternity."[56] From this quotation we see that the "temporum" are but one stage of God's city's existence. Tracing the journey of God's city through time to eternity was one of the great aims of this work. If *Confessiones* evidence Augustine's interest in the personal interior existence, *De Civitate Dei* affirms that his interest in temporal

---

50. *conf.* 11.17 (CCL 27, 202).

51. "Qui haec dicunt, nondum te intellegunt." *conf.* 11.13 (CCL 27, 200).

52. "At ego in tempora dissilui, quorum ordinem nescio." *conf.* 11.39 (CCL 27, 215).

53. *conf.* 11.40 (CCL 27, 215).

54. *conf.* 11.36 (CCL 27, 213).

55. *conf.* 11.5 (CCL 27, 196).

56. "Gloriosissimam ciuitatem dei siue in hoc temporum cursu, cum inter impios peregrinatur ex fide uiuens, siue in illa stabilitate sedis aeternae." *civ. Dei.* 1.Praef. (CCL 47, 1)

matters extends to the broader canvas of Rome, the church and the world. Williams highlighted the importance of time, saying "central to nearly all of Augustine's theology is the assumption that we think about God and speak to God only from our setting: within time."[57]

JOURNEYING

Augustine describes this life as a journey travelled by the affections.[58] As the image of a journey is developed, it begins to transpire that he sees the voyage of Christians towards Heaven as being intimately tied to the movement of God to Earth in the incarnation. Speaking of God's wisdom, Augustine says in *De Doctrina*, "Therefore since [wisdom] himself is the homeland, he also made himself the way for us to the homeland."[59] Thus, there is a twofold journey in Augustine's theology. The incarnation is a journey which enables the Christian to travel towards Heaven.

This has at least two implications for Augustine's interest in temporality. First, the vision of the Christian journeying through life demands a certain mindset towards the things of this temporal world. They are to be used to help along the way, but should not become an all absorbing distraction. Second, the two-fold journey suggests that the temporal plane is established upon and affirmed by the incarnation. In a sense "Augustine can speak only from temporality stabilized by the incarnation—which integrates time and eternity".[60] Such insights begin to suggest the central importance of the incarnation in relating the temporal world to the eternal.

In preaching, Augustine could develop his image of a journey in the most vivid manner, perhaps in no more vivid way than when he spoke of this life as a journey of never-ending walking, which results in us all dying of tiredness.[61] His focus on the incarnation is particularly pronounced at those liturgical seasons which highlighted it, namely the sermons preached to celebrate the birth of John the Baptist and those delivered at Christmas.

DEFINING TEMPORALITY

These three aspects of Augustine's theology can contribute to understanding Augustine's approach to temporality. The purpose of formulating such a

57. Rowan Williams, "Augustine and the Psalms." *Interpretation* 28, no. 1 (2004): 17–27. 23.

58. *doctr. Chr.* 1.16 (SIM 36).

59. "Cum ergo ipsa sit patria, uiam se quoque nobis fecit ad patriam." *doctr. Chr.* 1.11 (SIM 30).

60. Calvin L. Troup, *Temporality, Eternity and Wisdom: The Rhetoric of Augustine's Confessions* (Columbia: University of South Carolina Press, 1999), 104.

61. *s.* 305A.8 (MA 1, 63).

definition of temporality is to better understand the specific aspect of Augustine's life which is the focus of our study: his preaching. This being the case, it is instructive to note that the context of preaching itself, the liturgical calendar, has a bearing upon temporality. Time, conceived of abstractly, is most naturally considered in terms of past, present and future. Indeed this is part of Augustine's exploration in *Confessiones*. However, temporality in the context of a liturgical calendar has different, more theological referents:

> The liturgical calendar creates a form into which eternity is invited... Through the calendar, what is past is not lost and what is future can be grasped. The annual calendar provides markers in the sea of undifferentiated time that gives time shape and punctuation.[62]

Therefore, it is significant that many of Augustine's sermons were given in the context of special days such as Ascension, Christmas or martyrs' memorials. The regular liturgical context of gathering, singing, and the Eucharist impacted the reception of the sermon. The liturgical context reminds us that Augustine's preaching involved an interpretation being placed upon the time of listeners. Lives were being read in the light of Scripture's narrative; people were being drawn into the story of God's people. Augustine's meditations on a passage of Scripture were shared in preaching, and applied to the people who listened. Narratives, rather than abstract philosophical truths, were encountered and interpreted. In this sense, temporality was a key hermeneutical assumption of Augustine's approach to preaching. Stock has observed that Augustine's concern for narrative in his other writings also undergirded his spiritual ministrations:

> Augustine situates his soliloquies within a pair of narrative contexts: these are concerned, in the *Confessions* and *The City of God* respectively, with his personal life history and with the history of civilization as recounted in ancient writings and the Bible. His spiritual exercises thus become part of a temporal scheme.[63]

In preaching, Augustine was concerned with temporality in that he helped people interpret their created lives as part of the Bible's narrative. Augustine viewed life as a race which must be run: nobody can opt out and stand still

62. Randi Rashkover and C.C. Pecknold, eds., *Liturgy, Time, and the Politics of Redemption* (Grand Rapids: Eerdmans, 2006), 117.

63. Stock, *Augustine's Inner Dialogue*, 230.

in the race towards death.[64] Preaching Scripture was an opportunity for him to offer people a richer, more fulsome, narratival view of the race. Lives and relationships were part of a good creation, ordered as a journey viewed through the narrative of Scripture. The idea that narratival approaches can be drawn into people's interiors has been observed:

> In Augustine's view, narrative thinking has its basis in a sequence of sounds or images impinging on the senses, which subsequently pass through the *sensus* interior to the mind.[65]

This approach to temporality may have resonances with Neo-Platonic attitudes to improvement and order, but in the final analysis, "the notion of this future itself as well as the possibility of an ordering of the present from the standpoint of an absolute future, is quite uncharacteristic of Stoicism as well as Neo-Platonism."[66] It would appear then that, while granting Neo-Platonism its appropriate place in Augustine's formation, we are correct to give Scripture the leading role in shaping his approach to temporality.

In view of Augustine's theology and assumptions, we may offer a definition of temporality, namely, the successive flow and teleological development of God's plan for creation from beginning to consummation. This definition highlights that, in Augustine's view, present, created reality must be interpreted in the light of God's future plans for it. Matter is affirmed as a good creation, but it cannot be understood in a way which ignores its fundamentally "journey-shaped" nature.

The term "teleological" attempts to preserve this concept. The teleological purposes of God are in the future, but they are part of the interpretation that needs to be brought to bear upon present experiences within time. Our definition does not mean that only the beginning and end of creation matter; there are developments which occur between these poles: people are born, sins are embraced, Christ becomes incarnate. These, and myriad other events, happen and possess significance. Recognizing that there is change and development in our relationships is a basic part of our care of and attention to others.[67] The point is that when temporality is given a key role in interpreting these encounters, they gain their meaning from their place within the

---

64. *civ. Dei.* 13.10 (CCL 48, 391).

65. Stock, *Augustine's Inner Dialogue*, 181.

66. Hannah Arendt, *Love and Saint Augustine* (Chicago: University of Chicago Press, 1996), 41.

67. Soskice, Janet. "Love and Attention," in Michael McGhee, ed., *Philosophy, Religion and the Spiritual Life* (Cambridge: Cambridge University Press, 1992), 59–72, on p. 71.

interpretive framework which is accorded weight. In the case of Augustine's preaching, this authoritative role is taken by Scripture.

Scripture

Scripture was immensely important to Augustine and was formative in shaping both the content and style of his writings: "Two-thirds of the Biblical text could be assembled from his works. The importance of Scripture for Augustine can hardly be exaggerated."[68] Augustine's *Sermones* are a special instance of his writings, in which the formative influence of Scripture is actually increased, as compared to other parts of his corpus. This is due to the way he composed a sermon, the way he used Scripture while preaching, and the assumed doctrinal convictions which were at work. Our book will show that the reason Augustine was concerned with interiority and temporality in his preaching was that he used Scripture in an attempt to change people. Williams notes that Augustine felt we need an address from outside ourselves: "Augustine presents us with a self constructed in and only in contingency, and intelligible only as responding to address from beyond itself."[69]

Scripture addresses sermon listeners from "beyond". Therefore, Scripture ought to be held in a position of prime importance when approaching Augustine's understanding of preaching, even as we utilize terms such as "interiority" and "temporality" to explicate his assumptions. If this is done then neither the task of comprehension nor selection of terms ought to be problematic. As Stock reasons:

> It is important not to separate Augustine's conception of the inner life from its Christian theological background... he begins almost all his reflections on interiority with the close examination of a specific situation.[70]

That is to say, the interaction between interiority and temporality is often present in Augustine's theology. To maintain such a "Christian theological background" and "specific situation", we can note some of the interplay between scripture and the hermeneutical keys of interiority and temporality in a sample sermon. When preaching about the woman who suffered a discharge

68. Mervin Monroe Deems, "Augustine's Use of Scripture," *American Society of Church History* 14, no. 3 (1945), 189.

69. Rowan Williams, "Know Thyself: What Kind of Injunction?" in *Philosophy, Religion and the Spiritual Life*, ed. Michael McGhee , 211–27, on p. 223.

70. Stock, *Augustine's Inner Dialogue*, 53.

of blood,[71] Augustine opens by challenging his listeners to consider if they are the true church, whether they are wheat or tares. The distinction will be made upon the basis of the interior, with the distinguishing feature of the true believer found in the heart: "Truly all who draw near in such a way, that they do not draw near with the heart, he counts as chaff and tare."[72] On this basis, Augustine insists that hearers recognize the importance of their interiority and examine their motivations for coming to church carefully.

When he comes to preach on the passage, Augustine works with both interior and temporal concerns. He emphasizes that God can heal ailments; this affirms the temporal, in that it means God is changing the trajectory of the woman's life. However, he argues that the temporal healing of the woman was in order to alert people to God's desire to heal the interior. He mentions, wryly, that the disease of bloody discharge is terrible when it occurs in the body but "a disease of the heart is more to be avoided."[73] Therefore, Jesus healed the exterior body in order to encourage an interior desire for the heart's healing: "And it is necessary that he should heal internally, who also healed outside so that to be healed interiorly may be desired."[74]

In this case, the temporal healing serves mainly to highlight the superior importance of the interior and Jesus' ability to heal it. However, there are several comments in the sermon which show Augustine is also pondering wider temporal concerns. Thus, he suggests the woman represents the Gentile church,[75] since she encountered Jesus en route to a synagogue leader, and is accosting Jesus in a similar way to the woman in Mark 7. Making this allegorical connection led Augustine to a reflection of a temporal nature. He concluded his sermon by describing the Gentile church before it believed the Gospel, that is, before it had received the apostolic ministry of Paul.[76] As he reflected on the passage of time, the spread of the church and its temporal existence, Augustine argued that prior to believing the Gospel the Gentiles were like the doctors who tried ineffectually to heal the woman: they were obsessed with the physical and

---

71. *s.* 63A (MA 1, 317).

72. "Omnes uero qui sic accedunt, ut corde non accedant, paleam et zizania numerat." *s.* 63A.1 (MA 1, 317). By 1 b.c. the letter "z" had been adopted into Latin for spelling Greek words subsumed into the language.

73. "Morbus plus in corde uitandus." *s.* 63A.2 (MA 1, 318).

74. "Et opus est ut intus sanet ille, qui propterea foris sanauit, ut intus sanare desideraretur." *s.* 63A.2 (MA 1, 318).

75. *s.* 63A.2 (MA 1, 318).

76. *s.* 63A.3 (MA 1, 319).

were unable to see the need for interior healing. One of the greatest temporal developments in Scripture is the spread of the Gospel from Jews to Gentiles.

Thus Augustine's sermon affirms the priority of interior healing. Such healing is, however, demonstrated in a temporal healing, and gives rise to a meditation on the temporal developments of the Gentile nations as they were impacted by the Gospel's spread. One gets the sense that Augustine is playing with the passage, probing it to find meaning which can be preached. As he does so he is drawn towards the two central aspects of his preaching methodology: a concern for the interior and temporality. His goal is very much to impact and change his listeners. He calls on them to believe and be healed as the woman was; he wants them to touch Jesus by faith. As we continue to explore the *Sermones*, we will consider the extent to which the main driving force behind Augustine's use of interiority and temporality was not merely his desire to change listeners, but his determination to do so by means of using Scripture.

Augustine affirmed the truthfulness of Scripture in the most stringent terms possible. The nature of Augustine's doctrinal convictions about the accuracy of scripture are eloquently described in Costello's doctoral thesis:

> The inerrancy of Scripture is, therefore, a dogmatic principle which we are to bring with us to the reading, investigation and study of scripture. And it is one which serves to guide St. Augustine himself in all his attempts to reconcile and harmonize the statements of the four Evangelists.[77]

In numerous places, Augustine emphasized that he viewed Scripture as his supreme authority. It should be trusted before human reason or cognition, and is truthful in all that it states.[78] This aspect of Augustine's legacy has led to modern scholars focusing on him as a key figure in debates about contemporary applicability of terms such as infallibility and inerrancy.[79] Augustine not only affirms much of the content of the dogmatic terms; when stating that Scripture is completely free from error, he uses the word from which inerrant is derived:

---

77. Charles Joseph Costello, "St. Augustine's Doctrine on the Inspiration and Canonicity of Scripture" (The Catholic University of America, 1930), 31.

78. E.g. *Ep.* 82.3 (CSEL 34, 2), *s.* 162C.15 (DOLBEAU 55), *c. Faust.* 11.5 (CSEL 25, 1:320), 26.7 (CSEL 25, 1:735), *cons. Ev.* 3.9 (CSEL 43, 278).

79. For summary of scholarship see R.L. Peterson, "To Behold and Inhabit the Blessed Country: Revelation, Inspiration, Scripture and Infallibility. An Introductory Guide to Reflections Upon Augustine, 1945–80," in *Biblical Authority and Conservative Perspectives: Viewpoints from Trinity Journal, Biblical Forum Series*, ed. Douglas Moo, (Grand Rapids: Kregal Publications, 1997).

"errasse."[80] Augustine's affirmations of Scripture's truthfulness are implications of his strong rejection of the possible ethical probity of ever lying.[81]

While Augustine did indeed affirm the inerrancy of scripture, and in that sense Woodbridge[82] rather than McKim[83] may be said to have interpreted most accurately Augustine's teaching, our book may yet have something to add to the debate. The significant point, overlooked too often, is that while affirming inerrancy, Augustine often approached Scripture in ways which modern dogmaticians would say is inconsistent with holding to inerrancy; most well-known would be his allegorical interpretations. We could add to that his preference for ecclesial consistency over the most up-to-date scriptural translation.[84] We may conclude that a simple affirmation of Scripture's truthfulness falls short of a full representation of Augustine's doctrine of Scripture.

The *Sermones* add an existential and congregational aspect to Augustine's approach to scripture. There have been exhaustive searches of Augustine's corpus which collect together every relevant statement he made on his view of Scripture's nature. As David Kelsey has shown,[85] there is considerable value in exploring not only what a theologian says about their doctrinal view of Scripture, but also how they actually use Scripture. Preaching is a form of theological discourse which especially demands such an inductive approach. When we study how Augustine actually used Scripture in preaching, we find a preacher concerned primarily with the task of drawing people into the depths of the scriptural narrative. An infallible understanding of the facts contained in Scripture would fall far short of the warm, heartfelt sense of intimacy with God which Augustine's handling of Scripture aimed to inculcate. Our study adds to the debates about Augustine's view of Scripture by suggesting that to appreciate his doctrine of Scripture, we must spend time observing how he actually used

---

80. *Ep.* 82.3 (CSEL 34, 2:354).

81. Paul J. Griffiths, *Lying: An Augustinian Theology of Duplicity* (Grand Rapids: Brazos Press, 2004); Wayne Grudem, "Why It Is Never Right to Lie: An Example of John Frame's Influence on my approach to Ethics,"in *Speaking the Truth in Love: The Theology of John Frame*, John J. Hughes, ed., (Phillipsburg: P&R Publishing, 2009), 778–801.

82. John D. Woodbridge, *Biblical Authority: A Critique of the Rogers/McKim Proposal* (Grand Rapids: Zondervan, 1982).

83. Jack Bartlett Rogers/Donald K. McKim, *The Authority and Interpretation of the Bible: An Historical Approach* (London: Harper & Row, 1979).

84. *Ep.* 28.2 (CSEL 34, 1:105); 71.3–6 (CSEL 34, 2:250); 82:34–35 (CSEL 34, 2:385); *civ. Dei* 18.43 (CCL 48, 638).

85. David H. Kelsey, *The Uses of Scripture in Recent Theology* (London: SCM Press, 1975), 2, 3, 4, 152, 210.

it in preaching. Our aim in doing so should be to penetrate to the underlying assumptions and concerns which shaped Augustine's approach to Scripture and preaching. As outlined above, we intend to do so by utilizing interiority and temporality as hermeneutical keys.

ALTERNATIVE INTERPRETATIONS

We wish to show the value of the terms we have selected as our hermeneutical keys by comparing our interpretation of Augustine to that of three other modern writers. For this purpose we have selected Coleen Hoffman Gowans, Paul Ricoeur and Charles Taylor. When each of these alternatives are examined, it may be seen that our approach has both validity and value.

COLEEN HOFFMAN GOWANS

The only published doctoral thesis on the doctrine in Augustine's *Sermones* is the substantive contribution from Gowans.[86] There has been more research produced on the closely related *Enarrationes*, for example the unpublished thesis of Robert Dowler.[87] Since Gowans has been the first to publish on the *Sermones* as a corpus of doctrinal literature, she focuses on some of the leading themes of Augustine. For example, she correctly delineates the central position that is taken by the *cor*, writing, "The *Sermones ad Populum* of Augustine of Hippo clearly reveal his understanding of the *cor* as the centre of identity."[88] She devotes a chapter to the community within which the *Sermones* were preached,[89] and defends the value of reading the *Sermones* as a body of work.[90] These key insights will form an important part of our investigation, and Gowans' study is a helpful introduction.

Hopefully however, our research can bring a doctrinal precision to the interpretation of the *Sermones* that is lacking in Gowans' thesis, for she selects only one theme as the key to the *Sermones*, anthropological identity:

---

86. Coleen Hoffman Gowans, *The Identity of the True Believer in the Sermons of Augustine of Hippo, a Dimension of His Christian Anthropology* (New York: Edwin Mellen Press, 1998)..There is another unpublished doctoral thesis which contains analysis of Augustine's Sermones. This is discussed in our conclusion.

87. Robert Dowler, "Songs of Love: A Pastoral Reading of St Augustine of Hippo's Enarrationes in Psalmos," (PhD diss., Durham University, 2006)

88. Gowans, *The Identity of the True Believer*, 3.

89. Gowans, *The Identity of the True Believer*, 161–210.

90. Ibid., 8–12.

My thesis is that the sermons of Augustine of Hippo present his anthropology in action. Careful examination of the sermons reveals the way in which Augustine defines the true believer.[91]

This approach, though correct insofar as it goes, is not sufficient to explain the full sweep of Augustine's preaching.[92] It is intended that our approach of considering not only interior identity, but also temporality, will have more explanatory power than that which attempts to view all the material through the one lens of identity.

Gowans's interpretation appears to be rather static when compared to the dynamic actually at work in Augustine's preaching. That is to say, Augustine was doing far more than holding up a mirror to identity[93] or asking "who is the true believer?"[94] He was seeking to change people. Doing so would involve creating new believers, and molding the interior and temporal lives of those who had begun the journey. Identity is certainly a major part of the hermeneutical key to Augustine's preaching, but we suggest it is too passive and limiting a concept to capture the full dynamic of change which Augustine sought to serve. Also absent from Gowans's approach is any examination of Augustine's secular career as an orator, which we would contend is crucial to appreciating the nature of the beliefs he brought to the task of preaching. The dynamic of change he sought to engender in listeners was one that had dramatically altered him, and this demands to be given more weight in an interpretation of the *Sermones*. It is hoped that our study interprets Augustine and his preaching by extending and developing the work of Gowans beyond the parameters of her thesis.

PAUL RICOEUR

The central thesis of *Time and Narrative* is that narrative enables humans to interpret and form themselves and their temporal existence:

> Time becomes human time to the extent that it is articulated in a narrative way; by contrast the narrative is significative to the extent that it outlines the characteristics of temporal experience.[95]

---

91. Ibid., 2.

92. For insightful material on the significance of desire for God in Augustine's anthropology, see David H. Kelsey, *Eccentric Existence: A Theological Anthropology*, 2 vols., vol. 1 (Louisville: Westminster John Knox Press, 2009), 32.

93. Gowans, *The Identity of the True Believer*, 13.

94. Ibid., 243.

The first volume of *Time and Narrative* opens with an exploration of Augustine's discussion of time in *Confessiones*. Ricoeur suggests that Augustine attempted to understand time with no regard for narrative. Aristotle, treated in the following chapter, presented narrative plot with no concern for time. These two different entry points to the hermeneutical spiral which Ricoeur wishes to travel contribute the motifs of temporality and narrative. As Ricoeur considers the approach Augustine took to temporality, he convincingly shows that Augustine internalized and psychologized time. Augustine knew that a skeptical posture to time was wrong instinctively, for he could speak of the past, present and future. However, to answer the question of what time is was problematic. The solution devised by Augustine was to reject the idea that time is an external, measurable movement, and to posit instead an internal distension of the soul. Past is present to the soul as memory, future as anticipation and present as attention. In effect there is a threefold present:

> The invaluable findings of Saint Augustine, in reducing the extension of time to the distension of the soul, is to link this distension to the faultline that does not cease to penetrate to the heart of the triple present: between the present of the future, the present of the past and the present of the present.[96]

Throughout the first volume of *Time and Narrative*, Ricoeur hints at his dissatisfaction with Augustine's approach to time. He suggests that Augustine had to pay the price of ever-increasing *aporiae* for advancing his argument. In his final volume Ricoeur explicitly states that he finds Augustine's approach to be unconvincing, saying, "The major failure of Augustine's theory is to have not succeeded to substitute a psychological conception of time for a cosmological conception."[97] Ricoeur recognizes that Augustine wrote of temporal time and cosmological time, and astutely points out that the internalized psychological approach for which Augustine settles leaves a gulf between the two. Narrative is that which enables Ricoeur to bring order and reconciliation to the discordance.

At least three points of importance for our book may be gleaned from Ricoeur's interpretation of Augustine. First, it is reassuring and stimulating to note that he works with very similar interpretive motifs to us. The central terms of his investigation, time and narrative, approximate our usage of temporality.

95. Paul Ricoeur, *Temps et Récit*, vol. 1, *L'ordre Philosophique* (Paris: 1983), 17.

96. Ibid., 41.

97. Paul Ricoeur, *Temps et Récit*, vol. 3, *L'ordre Philosophique*, 19.

Further, Ricoeur shows that in Augustine's psychological approach to time he interiorized it. Ricoeur does not major on an explicit development of interiority in *Time and Narrative*, but it is clear that his third level of mimesis, refigurement, is something that must occur at a deep interior level of identity. The narrative refiguring of temporal identity is something for which humanity cries out for with a deep longing:

> We tell stories because in the end human lives need and deserve to be told. This comment is most relevant when we evoke the necessity of keeping the history of the victors and the defeated. All of the history of suffering cries for vengeance and is a story worth telling.[98]

As his explanation of refigurement greatly concerns interiority and identity, we may appreciate that Ricoeur used similar terms to us in his philosophical investigations. First, that he found Augustine's views of time inadequate does not detract (neither in our view nor his) from the promise that these terms of investigation hold. Second, it is only reasonable to note that Ricoeur's aim in *Time and Narrative* is not primarily to interpret Augustine. Ricoeur recognizes this and notes that a further context of reading beyond the eleventh book of *Confessiones* is required.[99] For his purposes, that wider context of interpretation is Husserl and Heidegger.

Appropriate as this may be for the thesis of *Time and Narrative*, in our study, we aim to focus more on exposing the shape of Augustine's own presuppositions and assumptions. We seek to do so by letting *De Doctrina Christiana* inform our hermeneutical keys, and testing them in case studies drawn from the *Sermones*. That being the case, our argument differs from Ricoeur in focus, not principle. That is to say, we would contend that in the preaching of Augustine we find much that supports Ricoeur's framework, but for Augustine it was not narrative in general which changed people, but Scripture in particular.

Third, Ricoeur's thesis is congenial and stimulating in that his analysis of how narrative interprets and reforms temporal identity coheres with much that we will suggest about the way in which scripture impacts people. The dynamism of interaction between narrative and identity, together with the projection of oneself into a narrative, are central features of Ricoeur's work which we hope to see exemplified in Augustine's preaching.

---

98. Ricoeur, *Temps et Récit*, 2:115.

99. Ricoeur, *Temps et Récit*, 1:11.

In summary, there is much to commend Ricoeur's general approach to identity, temporality and narrative. Where we differ from him we remain indebted to him. The points of divergence are more due to our research being specifically on Augustine's preaching than any substantive disagreement with his contribution. Elsewhere, Ricoeur highlights the significance of temporal development between the Old and New Testaments:

> A contrast is set up between the two Testaments, a contrast which is at the same time a harmony by means of a transfer... The event becomes advent. In taking on time, it takes on meaning.[100]

CHARLES TAYLOR

That the modern person struggles with his or her identity is a leitmotif of Charles Taylor's writing. The modern world developed "the ideal of the disengaged self, capable of objectifying not only the surrounding world but also his own emotions and inclinations, fears and compulsion, and achieving thereby a kind of distance and self-possession which allows him to act "rationally."[101] An important factor in the development of a disengaged self was insufficient attention to interior desires and loves:

> Moral philosophy has tended to focus on what it is right to do rather than on what it is good to be, on defining the content of obligation rather than the nature of the good life; and it has no conceptual place left for the notion of the good as the object of our love.[102]

Taylor insists that modern calls to abandon interpretive frameworks are futile, saying "Doing without frameworks is utterly impossible for us . . . [It] would be tantamount to stepping outside what we would recognize as integral, that is, undamaged personhood."[103] In line with our interpretation of Augustine, Taylor suggests that a narrative framework which is linked to temporality offers the best hope of securing meaningful interior identity. Thus he notes "my self-understanding necessarily has temporal depth and incorporates narrative."[104] Taylor sees Augustine as an important instance of narrative shaped identity

100. Paul Ricoeur, "Preface to Bultmann," in Don Ihde, ed., *The Conflict of Interpretations: Essays in Hermeneutics* (London: Routledge, 2004), 379–80.

101. Charles Taylor, *Sources of the Self: The Making of the Modern Identity* (Cambridge: Cambridge University Press, 1989).,21.

102. Ibid., 3.

103. Ibid., 27.

104. Ibid., 50.

being communicated; Augustine's *Confessiones* are, in effect, a life being transformed by a new narrative.[105] People are constituted in such a way that the interiority invites earnest enquiry: "we are creatures with inner depths; with partly unexplored and dark interiors."[106]

Thus the lines of Charles Taylor's investigations complement our interest in discerning the relationship between identity and temporality in Augustine. When writing about him, Taylor offers comments on both interiority and temporality. The former is developed in his earlier work, the latter in his most recent. As regards interiority in Augustine, Taylor begins his interpretation by stating that Augustine recognized "the whole moral condition of the soul depends ultimately on what it attends to and loves."[107] The way a person's loves are changed lies in an inward turn:

"The road from lower to higher, the crucial shift in direction, passes through our attending to ourselves as inner... inward lies the road to God."[108] The reason that Augustine urges an inward turn is that God himself is the means by which one sees and understands. God is "for us primarily the basic support and underlying principle of our knowing activity. God is not just what we long to see, but what powers the eye to see."[109] Reflecting on the interior process of knowing as enabled by God is what Taylor designates a "turn to radical reflexivity."[110] Such an inward turn is the crucial step towards God, which enables interior loves to be reordered. Much of Taylor's narrative of philosophical history takes its cue from Augustine's own inward turn which he sees in secularised forms, for example in Foucault's admonition to take care to oneself.[111]

The inward turn, as Taylor outlines it, is valuable as an attempt to explain the significance of interiority in Augustine. However, as Taylor introduces the theme of blindness, he raises further unresolved questions about the nature of Augustine's view of interiority. The capacity to see has, for Augustine, been lost: "This must be restored by grace. And what grace does is to open the inward man to God, which makes us able to see that the vaunted power is really God's."[112] How God thus acts upon the interior is unanswered by Taylor's

---

105. Ibid., 97.
106. Ibid., 111.
107. Ibid., 128.
108. Ibid., 129.
109. Ibid., 129.
110. Ibid., 131.
111. Ibid., 130.
112. Ibid., 139.

interpretation of Augustine. It is our hope that a study of Augustine's preaching will offer further insight.

Over time, Taylor maintained the structure of his interpretation of Augustine. However he has recently added a concern for temporality. He argues that the Christian conception of temporality evolved slowly, but is best seen in Augustine: "with him eternity is reconceived as gathered time."[113] By this, Taylor means that people should resist the temptation to divinize their "little parcel of time" and accept Augustine's insight that "rising to eternity is rising to participate in God's instant."[114]

It is highly significant for the purposes of our study that reflection on the value of Augustine's view of temporality leads Taylor to investigate the value of liturgy:

> The church, in its liturgical year, remembers and re-enacts what happened *in illo tempore* when Christ was on earth. Which is why this year's Good Friday can be closer to the crucifixion than last year's mid-summer day. And the crucifixion itself, since Christ's action/passion here participates in God's eternity, is closer to all times than they are in secular terms to each other.[115]

Taylor's perception of a link between Augustine's approach to temporality and liturgy suggests that there may be particular value to considering temporality in Augustine's liturgical preaching.

Augustine features as a key figure in Taylor's philosophy. In light of this, it is surprising that he may underestimate the importance of Augustine in his narrative. We see this when he writes about the ordinary aspects of daily life. He posits that the significant point at which ordinary life became central to cultural thought was the Reformation, writing "the entire modern development of the affirmation of ordinary life was, I believe, foreshadowed and initiated, in all its facets, in the spirituality of the Reformers."[116] Many agree with Taylor's focus on the Reformation. However, the fact that the Reformers viewed themselves as attempting to recover something that had been obscured suggests there may have been an earlier precedent. Some have traced a focus on ordinary life to the New Testament,[117] while others have seen it coming to the fore in Augustine's ministry.[118] In missing this aspect of Augustine's theology, Taylor is

---

113. Charles Taylor, *A Secular Age* (Cambridge: Belknap Press, 2007), 56.

114. Ibid., 56.

115. Ibid., 58.

116. Taylor, *Sources of the Self: The Making of the Modern Identity*, 218.

following the well-trodden path of focusing on his more philosophical writings and neglecting his preaching. It is to correct this imbalance in our portrait of Augustine that we have focused our book upon the *Sermones*. Thus interiority, temporality, narrative, liturgy and ordinary life are also explored by Taylor in ways which recommend further analysis of Augustine's preaching.

CONCLUSION

This chapter has outlined the doctrinal contours of the terms upon which our interpretation of Augustine's preaching is constructed. Our claim is that Augustine preached with a particular regard to interiority and temporality, because he wished to use Scripture to change listeners. We have provided definitions of interiority and temporality, our two hermeneutical keys. These speak to the issues raised by pagan rhetoric, and draw together relevant wider themes from *De Doctrina* and Augustine's theology. We have outlined how parts of these themes have been addressed by other modern commentators. The helpfulness of our terms as interpretive tools will be seen as we use them to explore some themes of Augustine's preaching. Within this chapter, we have constructively explored one sermon and highlighted the formative role of Scripture. It is hoped that, as our argument is developed, it will be found sufficient to provide a coherent interpretation of Augustine's preaching.

117. Erich Auerbach, *Mimesis: The Representation of Reality in Western Literature* (Princeton: Princeton University Press, 1953), 44.

118. R.A. Markus, "Augustine: In Defense of Christian Mediocrity," in *The End of Ancient Christianity* (Cambridge: Cambridge University Press, 1998); Henry Chadwick, "Augustine," in *The Cambridge History of Early Christian Literature*, ed. Young, Ayres and Louth, 340.

5

Case Study: Riches and Money

And may you await the last day safely: truly rich, inwardly rich.[1]

Our three case study chapters aim to explore inductively themes which were of particular importance in Augustine's preaching. It is hoped that these studies deepen the conclusions drawn in our book, and provide the reader with something of the experience of reading through Augustine's *Sermones*. This chapter shows that riches and money hold a position of particular importance in Augustine's sermons. The use he makes of financial riches arises from his appreciation of interiority and temporality. After an inductive presentation of the ways in which Augustine handles the topic of finances throughout his *Sermones*, the act of almsgiving and two sermons of particular relevance will be treated in detail. Initial conclusions are then drawn about the significance of temporality and interiority, insofar as this can be inferred from the specific issue of riches.

THE IMPORTANCE OF RICHES IN AUGUSTINE'S PREACHING

Like any bishop, Augustine was concerned with the relationship between finances and the church's ministry. Hence, he was happy preaching at the dedication of new church buildings.[2] Understandably, when doing so, he thanked the congregation for their fundraising.[3] If this were the only mention of riches in Augustine's *Sermones*, we could conclude that his concern with finances was merely ecclesiastical and bureaucratic, but this is far from the case. It has been noted that "Augustine's many homilies on this issue provide a

---

1. "Et diem nouissimum securi expectetis: uere diuites, intus diuites."*s.* 299E.5 (MA 1, 556).

2. *s.* 336 (PL 38, 1471); 337 (PL 38, 1475); 338. (PL 38, 1478)

3. *s.* 337.1–2 (PL 38, 1475); 5 (PL 38, 1477).

rudimentary theology of wealth".[4] It is striking how frequently Augustine turns to the issue of finances and riches when preaching.

The *Corpus Augustinianum Gissense* enables statistical analysis of Augustine's corpus. This reveals that 38.73% of Augustine's uses of Latin words (including all cognates) concerning wealth occur in his sermons. This figure has been given excluding "*ops*", as the word group can refer to wealth, but more frequently suggests power. This occurrence is remarkably high, as the *Sermones* comprise only 1.19% of the words in Augustine's corpus. Thus, the distribution of words is not reflective of the length of the *Sermones*. If one considers three commonly used words—*cor*, *peccatum* and *animus*—it is found that their percentage occurrence in the *Sermones* are lower than the words concerned with riches. Statistical analysis shows that riches and money were treated by Augustine in his preaching more frequently than elsewhere.

The importance of riches in Augustine's sermons cannot be explained merely by assuming that he was interested in helping listeners manage their personal finances. The high level of concern with riches is not simply a sermonic focus on ethical behavior. When the references to riches are explored, it is discovered that they are part of Augustine's rich tapestry of theological reflection that went beyond surface appearances to reveal the interiority and temporality of riches. Riches were conceived as a key theological metaphor, which he used to relate interiority and temporality, and to shape his method of preaching Scripture.

ORIENTATION TO RICHES

Augustine does teach from passages of Scripture which speak of riches, and in doing so, he gives ethical and practical advice on how to approach finances.[5] However, such direct expositional instances account for only a fraction of the high frequency of financial themes in his sermons. Even when he does offer what could be termed ethical advice about financial affairs, in *s.* 239.5, for example, he moves from specific warnings against extortion in daily life to a financial view of God and the Christian life:

> Be a usurer, spend what you may recoup. Do not be afraid that God might judge you a usurer. Absolutely, absolutely be a usurer. But God says to you, 'What do you want?' Do you want to be a usurer?

---

4. Boniface O.P. Ramsey, "Wealth," in *Augustine through the Ages*, ed. Allan Fitzgerald (Grand Rapids: Eerdmans, 1999), 878.

5. See, for example, *s.* 85 (PL 38, 520).

What is it to do usury? To give less, and to get more. 'Behold, give
to me,' God says to you, 'I receive less, and I give more.' What [do I
give]? A hundred-fold, and eternal life.[6]

Augustine refuses simply to tell his congregation that he disapproves of usury.
Instead, he subverts the normal view of usury, of the Christian life, and of
God by showing how God himself practices subversive, radical usury: God
gives more than he takes. Augustine demonstrates his appreciation of financial
imagery as a tool to re-envision God and life.

His appreciation of the value of financial imagery is also seen in that he can
shift from a passage entirely unrelated to finance, and use a passage or imagery
about riches in order to explain it. Thus, when preaching in celebration of
the birthdays of Peter and Paul[7], the reading is John 21. This introduces the
theme of the apostles' love, manifest in Peter's case by his feeding of the Lord's
sheep, but 2 Timothy 4:1–2 is brought in to show that Paul was concerned to
encourage others to endure suffering and to preach the word despite opposition.
Temporality is then discussed in typically Augustinian terms:

Whatever sweet thing this life can hold, it is not paradise, it is not
heaven, it is not the kingdom of God, it is not the company of angels,
it is not the fellowship of those citizens of the heavenly Jerusalem.
May the heart be carried upwards, may earth by spurned by the flesh.
The Lord has taught us to scorn transitory things, and to esteem
eternal things.[8]

Augustine warms to his theme and turns to one of his favorite images: that of
a doctor. The doctor has drunk the cup of suffering for us and can be trusted
to prescribe nothing that is not good for us. He could easily have ended his
sermon there, but instead adds a conclusion which is full of financial imagery.
2 Timothy 4:8 mentions a crown, which Augustine expands by suggesting that
Paul used financial language intentionally:

6. "Faenerator esto, eroga quod recipias. Noli timere, ne te faeneratorem iudicet deus. Prorsus, prorsus
esto faenerator. Sed deus tibi dicit: quid uis? Faenerare uis? Quid est faenerare? Minus dare, et plus
accipere. Ecce mihi da, dicit tibi deus: ego accipio minus, et do plus. Quid? Centuplicia, et uitam
aeternam." s. 239.5 (PL 38, 1128).

7. s. 299A.1 (DOLBEAU 511).

8. " Quidquid potest habere dulce ista uita, paradisus non est, caelum non est, regnum dei non est,
societas angelorum non est, consortium illorum ciuium supernae Hierusalem non est. Sursum cor feratur,
terra carne calcetur. Docuit nos dominus contemnere transitoria, diligere aeterna."s. 299A.2 (DOLBEAU
512).

> It [The Scripture] does not say: 'He gives,' but, 'He will repay,' and
> if he will repay it, he was owing it. I absolutely dare to say, if he will
> repay it, he was owing it. Had he borrowed anything of ours, that he
> should owe it? He owes a crown, he repays a crown, but he was not
> made a debtor by borrowing from us, but by his own promise.[9]

In this quotation Augustine expected his listeners to be surprised at his claim
that God owes them anything. He knew how to subvert his normal teaching on
grace to good effect, with usury employed as a subversive presentation of grace.

Financial language can sometimes, as in the above passage, involve
focusing on a scriptural word and developing it at length, or it can involve
allegorizing a financial reference, as in his explanation of Jesus' commandment
not to carry a purse. This is taken to mean that the Spirit's gift of wisdom should
not be stored away in a purse, but spread abroad liberally.[10] Peter's words about
vows concerning money can be likewise applied to vows about virginity.[11]
Augustine fears his listeners deceive themselves over riches: "Do not be thrifty
with passing treasures, with vain treasures. Do not increase your money under
the guise of piety. [You say], ,I am saving for my sons.' That's a big excuse."[12]

He is realistic about financial temptations. Since "one delights in great
riches,"[13] he knows listeners will be tempted "to commit fraud for money."[14]
As a bishop with involvement in civil matters, Augustine arbitrated disputes
between people. In one such case, a Christian was accused of theft by another
Christian. Augustine rebuked the thief for thinking that it would be easy to
steal from a believer, because Augustine was in the habit of telling people who
were stolen from to "redeem the time" (Eph. 5:16) by accepting their losses and
not pursuing the matter legally. Augustine's response was to close his sermon
with an ominous temporal financial warning: "But perhaps you are laughing
at this, because you are snatching money. Laugh, Laugh, and scorn: I may
pay out, he will come to pay back."[15] This quotation is an example of a way

9. " Non ait: dat, sed: reddet; si reddet, debebat. Prorsus audeo dicere: si reddet, debebat. Et numquid
mutuum acceperat, ut deberet? Debet coronam, reddit coronam, non factus debitor ex mutuo nostro, sed
ex promisso suo." *s.* 299A.2 (DOLBEAU 512).

10. *s.* 101.6 (SPM 1, 49).

11. *s.* 148.2 (PL 38, 799).

12. "Noli parcere thesauris caducis, thesauris uanis. Noli sub imagine pietatis augere pecuniam. filiis
meis seruo: magna excusatio."*s.* 9.20. (CCL 41, 146) The image of treasure is also applied in *s.* 339.4 (SPM
1, 115) to the scriptures which Augustine enjoys reading for his pleasure, but finds terrifying when read
as preparation to teach others.

13. "Delectat pecuniae magnitude." *s.* 39.1 (CCL 41, 489).

14. "Facere fraudem ut acquiras pecuniam." *s.* 32.15 (CCL 41, 405).

Augustine used temporality to engage with the topic of riches. The future temporal judgment would be an accounting at which listeners' financial actions would be weighed. Awareness of the temporal future ought to impact present attitudes and behavior.

Riches, however, are not of absolute value: "Faith is better than gold, and faith is better than silver, than wealth, than estates, than family, than riches."[16] Despite his warnings against riches, Augustine does not think material wealth itself is evil: "May things not be eliminated from human affairs: let there be things, and let there be a use of good things."[17] He noted that Paul "accused desires, not means."[18] Gold and silver are explicitly affirmed by Augustine as good because they can be used to do good things. Financial greed is a bad thing, but it is not the worst sin, lying.[19]

Bad methods of getting riches do not sully their value: "Therefore those of you who have [things] by [doing] evil, from now on do good [with them]."[20] They can, for example, be used to buy a person out of slavery.[21] However one must not overvalue their power, for though they can do good, riches can neither cleanse sin[22] nor make you good: "Gold exists, silver exists; it is good, not because it makes you good, but because you can do good with it."[23] The right use of money is determined, rather, by the interior desires and loves: "Nobody can live well, who does not love well. May gold be eliminated from human things: to the inmost may gold be present, to test human things."[24]

And so, riches act as a test of the interior. We suggested in our initial definition of interiority that it is that inner realm of desirous longing, evaluation

15. "Sed hoc forte rides, quia pecuniam rapis. Ride, ride, et contemne: ego erogem, ueniet qui exigat." s. 167.4 (PL 38, 910).

16. "Melior est fides quam aurum, et melior est fides quam argentum, quam pecunia, quam praedia, quam familia, quam diuitiae." s. 159.3 (PL 38, 869).

17. "Non tollantur res de rebus humanis: sint res, et adsit usus rerum bonarum." s. 311.11 (PL 38, 1417).

18. "Cupiditates accusauit non facultates." s. 39.3 (CCL 41, 489).

19. s. 148.1 (PL 38, 799).

20. "Ergo qui habetis de malo, facite inde bonum." s. 113.3 (PL 38, 649).

21. s. 134.3 (PL 38, 650).

22. Ibid.

23. "Aurum est, argentum est; bonum est, non quod te faciat bonum, sed unde facias bonum." s. 61.3.(PL 38, 410).

24. "Non faciunt bonos mores, nisi boni amores. Tollatur aurum de rebus humanis: imo adsit aurum, ut probet res humanas." s. 311.11 (PL 38, 1417). The first clause of this quote is literally, "[People] do not make good customs, except for good lovers." I have rendered it more loosely, with "live" and "love", to preserve Augustine's play on the verbal similarity between *mores* and *amores*.

and prayer. The above quotation suggests that such interiority may be refined and tested by riches: riches have a spiritual, interior impact. In light of the temporality of a future second death, Augustine urges listeners not to fear barbarians stealing money or property; the money necessary to survive the second death is *iustitia*: "You do not lose justice against your will; it abides in the inmost treasure house of the heart."[25]

As a pastorally sensitive preacher, Augustine not only located the true problem of riches in the interior desires and wrong temporal uses, he identified with the weaknesses he pointed out in others. With a rhyming rhetorical flourish, Augustine declared even himself to be a debtor "not of riches, but of sins."[26] This rhyme is of particular interest since "peccatorum" is such a well-known Augustinian term. That such a famous word is linked to money by means of a rhetorical phrase reminds us that Augustine's theology was shaped not only by heresies refuted, by philosophy studied, and by the Scriptures, but also by his oratorical desire to present theology in pleasing verbal forms. That such rhetorical concerns fashioned his theology is one of the values of a theological investigation of his preaching.

The real problem lies not in riches themselves, but inside those who desire and use them wrongly:

> You want to have gold and silver? Look I say this: It's good, but only if you have used it well; but you do not use it well, if you are bad. And through this, gold and silver to the bad is bad, to the good is good: not because gold and silver makes them good, but, because it comes to good people, and is turned to good use.[27]

To the person focused on saving and hoarding wealth, Augustine asks, "What are you to do? The enemy is not outside snatching, but is inside ruining."[28] There is a way to use finances well: Augustine commends investing in the heavenly treasure house.[29] Listeners may be tempted to trust their soul in the heavenly treasure house, but their gold to the ground or a slave. Augustine warns people considering such an approach to remember that there is no more

25. "Iustitiam non amittis inuitus; in thesauro cordis intimo manet." *s.* 344.4 (PL 39, 1513).

26. "Non pecuniarum, sed peccatorum." *s.* 56.11 (RB 68, 33).

27. "Aurum et argentum habere uis? ecce et hoc dico: bonum est, sed si bene usus fueris; bene autem non uteris, si malus eris. Ac per hoc aurum et argentum malis malum est, bonis bonum est: non quia eos bonos facit aurum et argentum, sed, quia bonos inuenit, in usum bonum conuertitur." *s.* 72.4 (DOLBEAU 123).

28. "Quid facturus es? Non est foris hostis auferens, sed est intus absumens." *s.* 86.8 (PL 38, 527).

29. *s.* 18.3 (CCL 41, 246).

trustworthy person than Christ, and that the slave may cheat you: "How much better also (to entrust) your gold to him, to whom (you entrust) your soul?"[30] To the person who is sad because he or she has lost money, Augustine uses the surprising image of dung. He reflects, "I see dung, I enquire where."[31] That dung is good in the right place, but bad in a wrong place. If the sadness felt is due to the loss of money, then this sadness is like dung in the wrong place: it damages. On the other hand, the sadness of a prayer longing for mercy would be like good dung: appropriate mournfulness.

Financial imagery is used in extended treatments of the atonement. So the blood of Jesus is more valuable than gold or silver. As a slave would not be entrusted with sheep who were of greater financial value than the slave could afford to replace (with his "*peculium*"—private property) should harm come to them, so Jesus had to have the financial resources to pay for his sheep.[32] Jesus is addressed "O good merchant."[33]

"But the redeemer has come, and the deceiver is beaten."[34] Augustine observed. He continues:

> To pay our price he stretched out his cross, like a mousetrap. He planted there, as if bait, his own blood. The former one [the devil] had power to shed that blood; he was not worthy to drink it. And since he shed the blood of one who was not a debtor, he was commanded to release the debtors.[35]

Edmund Hill writes that the image of a mousetrap baiting the devil is "one of Augustine's favorite, more grotesque metaphors for explaining how Christ's death has delivered us from the devil's clutches."[36] However, it should be noted that the image is applied to the cross in only four sermons.[37] In the other four sermons in which the metaphor features, the mousetrap represents temptations

---

30. "Quanto melius illi et aurum tuum, cui et animam tuam?" *s.* 345.3 (MA 1, 204). The verb "commendo" is present in the previous sentence.

31. "Stercus uideo, locum qaero." *s.* 254.4 (RB 79, 65).

32. s. 296.4 (MA 1, 403).

33. "O bone mercator " *s.* 130.2 (PL 38, 726).

34. "Sed uenit redemptor, et uictus est deceptor." *s.* 130.2 (PL 38, 726).

35. "Ad pretium nostrum tetendit muscipulam crucem suam: posuit ibi quasi escam sanguinem suum. Ille autem potuit sanguinem istum fundere, non meruit bibere. et in eo quod fudit sanguinem non debitoris, iussus est reddere debitores." *s.* 130.2 (PL 38, 726).

36. Augustine, *Sermons*, ed. John Rotelle, vol. 3.4, *The Works of Saint Augustine, a Translation for the 21st Century* (New York: New City Press, 1992), 315.

37. s. 130.2 (PL 38, 726), 134.6 (PL 38, 745), 263.2 (MA 1, 508), 265D.5 (MA 1, 662).

to listeners.[38] The word "*muscipula*" is used in the Vulgate translation of Wisdom 14:11–13, quoted by Augustine in the recently discovered *s.* 360A.6. Though the term is absent from Psalm 140:5 (Psalms 139:6, Vulgate), Augustine uses it in a gloss when he quotes from the Psalm in *s.* 16A.10. Thus, while the image was applied to the cross, where it has financial connotations, it was just as common in preaching for Augustine to use it of temptations facing believers. In doing so, he followed the Vulgate's lead; Hill, thus, appears to overstate his case.

Augustine accepted that he preached to listeners, but reflected, "However inwardly where nobody sees, we are all listeners: [it is] inwardly in the heart, in the mind, where he teaches you, he who persuades you to praise."[39]

The theme of Jesus being the Inner Teacher is a well-known feature of Augustine's theology. But less frequently observed is the way in which he could combine financial imagery with this theme of interiority. With reference to the preceding exhortations to allow the Word to bear fruit inwardly, Augustine warns, "We [bishops] are able to spend the church money, the tax-collector will come."[40] The implication is that Augustine sees interior riches impacting external financial actions. Further, he interprets riches in light of the coming temporal return of God to judge; the future temporal consummation ensures interior listening is not performed in a vacuum, but with purpose. As we see, Augustine utilizes financial imagery to describe the impact his listeners could have on him: "I want to have joy from your good works, not money. For it is not he who lives well, who makes me rich. And yet let him live well and he does. My riches are nothing if not your hope in Christ."[41]

Thus, Augustine used the metaphor of riches as an image of the relationship between preacher and listeners. Since so much of Augustine's preaching involved a hermeneutic of interiority and temporality, it is fitting that he made so much use of a concept such as riches, which could be related to both interiority and temporality. Since our book suggests that Scripture motivated this hermeneutic of interiority and temporality, we will now consider some of the *Sermones* in depth. Following the logic of some actual *Sermones* is an

---

38. *s.* 57.9 (*Homo sp.* 420), 216.6 (PL 38, 1080), 16A.10 (CCL 41, 226), 360A.6 (DOLBEAU 237).

39. "Intus autem ubi nemo uidet, omnes auditores sumus: intus in corde, in mente, ubi uos docet ille, qui uos admonet laudare." *s.* 179.7. (PL 38, 970)

40. "Nos pecuniam dominicam erogare possumus: ueniet exactor." *s.* 179.7 (PL 38, 970).

41. "De bonis operibus uestris gaudium uolo habere, non pecuniam. Non enim qui bene uiuit, diuitem me facit. Et tamen bene uiuat et facit. Diuitiae meae non nisi spes uestra in Christo." *s.* 232.8 (SC 116, 274).

inductive method which will highlight how deeply Augustine felt his preaching to be shaped by Scripture.

Interiority and Temporality of Riches in Sermon 177

In this longer than usual sermon, Augustine uses 1 Timothy 6:7–19 to explore the theme of riches. As he does so, he uses interiority and temporality to establish his theological insight. This sermon deserves analysis because of the way riches are treated throughout the sermon, with aspects of temporality and interiority producing a vision of the Christian experience which is saturated with financial theologizing.

The issue presented in the passage is "avarice: may it be accused, not defended."[42] Avarice, Augustine argues, is attacked in talk but protected in behavior. Secular philosophers, orators, poets and historians speak against avarice, but cannot escape it themselves. In the opening of his sermon, Augustine portrays secular writers as men who speak against avarice but cannot avoid its grip on their hearts. By presenting the issue in this way, he is effectively dismissing pagan teachers as (by his definition) liars: to lie is to speak words that do not reveal the heart's intentions. People who speak against avarice, while feeling its grip, suffer what Augustine elsewhere calls a "duplicitous heart."[43] Augustine later raises the issue of lying; when he does so, he focuses attention on the heart, asking, "Are you not accused by your very heart inside you? Why do you lie?"[44]

Augustine ponders what is distinct from pagan wisdom in the Scripture's teaching on avarice. He encourages that "if we take notice, we learn something which belongs only to the school of Christ."[45] Augustine intrigues by saying that which many have said about the Scripture: it urges us to be content with what we have, and to remember our mortality. Likewise, he says that many have told us the root of evil is avarice, and since people outside the church have spoken against avarice, there is a danger of thinking too highly of them; in reality, "piety's stability is far away from their chattering cheeks."[46] The unique contribution of piety is emphasized: "This firstly we ought to understand and hold on to- we do that which we do because of God." *s.* 177.2 (SPM 1, 64).[47]

---

42. "Auaritia: accusetur, non defendatur." *s.* 177.1 (SPM 1, 64).

43. "Duplex cor." mend. 1.3 (CSEL 41, 415).

44. "Ipso corde intus non accusaris? Quare mentiris?" *s.* 177.5 (SPM 1, 67).

45. "Si aduertamus, aliquid quod proprium non habet nisi schola Christi." *s.* 177.2 (SPM 1, 64).

46. "Longe est a crepantibus buccis soliditas pietatis " *s.* 177.2 (SPM 1, 64). Hill fails to translate *pietatis* as a genitive, missing the idea that piety itself has a quality of stability.

47. "Hoc primitus discernere et tenere debemus propter deum nos facere quod facimus."

Augustine continues comparing pagan to Christian teaching on avarice by warning:

> Indeed it is obscene, and hugely scandalous and grievous, if idol worshipers are found to be the conquerors of avarice, and the worshiper of the only God is overcome by avarice, and becomes avarice's slave, whose is the blood of Christ.[48]

He explains what it means to do whatever we do for the sake of God, holding a Christian theological appreciation of temporality. Initially, this might appear to be a normal use of his common journey metaphor:

> With the desire of him [Christ] all things are devalued; let not those things among which we are born be born in us, because on account of him we are reborn. Let these things be for our necessary use, not for love's affection: they may be like a traveller's stable, not like a landlord's estate. Recover yourself and move on. You are making a journey, attend to where you are going, for great is he who came to you.[49]

However, the temporality about which Augustine is preaching is not simply the progression of time towards a future moment, as this would have no greater power over avarice than the teachings of pagan writers. Augustine is affirming a distinctively Christian journey, a theological temporality unique to the school of Christ:

> Therefore one thing is the journey of mortality, another thing is the journey of piety. The journey of mortality is common to all who are born, the journey of piety is not common to all: indeed the former way all who are born walk: the latter way not unless they have been reborn.[50]

48. "Turpe est enim, et nimium pudendum et dolendum, si cultores idolorum inuenti sunt auaritiae domitores, et cultor dei unius ab auaritia subiugetur, et fiat auaritiae mancipium, cuius sanguis Christi fit." *s.* 177.2 (SPM 1, 64).

49. "Huius desiderio uilescant omnia; nec nata nobis sint inter quae nati sumus, quia propter illum renati sumus. Sint haec ad necessitatis usum, non ad caritatis affectum: sint tamquam stabulum uiatoris, non tamquam praedium possessoris. Refice te et transi. iter agis, adtende ad quem uenis, quia magnus est qui ad te uenit." *s.* 177.2 (SPM 1, 64).

50. "Aliud est ergo iter mortalitatis, aliud iter pietatis. Iter mortalitatis commune est uniuersis nascentibus, iter pietatis non commune est omnibus: illud enim ambulant omnes nati: istum non nisi renati." *s.* 177.3 (SPM 1, 66).

The contrast between the journey of mortality and piety is emphasised by the rhyming couplets, underlined in the Latin; the rhetorical power of Augustine's spoken Latin is apparent. Without script or rote memorization, his meditations naturally expressed themselves in oratory of rhyme and concise contrasts. Thus, Augustine uses all the tools at his disposal to compel listeners to flee avarice, including commonalities and distinctions to secular philosophy, Scripture quotations and secular oratory, common metaphors, and distinctively Christian theology.

Augustine presents temporality so to impact the interiority of listeners. Riches are reframed and reordered in light of Christian temporality, to develop a hunger for interior riches: "these riches are interior."[51] God's Word comes to the rich to make them inwardly rich: "The word of God finds you rich outwardly, it makes you rich inside, accept what is said to the rich."[52] Love, faith, and hope all find their interior locus in the heart. It is there that money exerts power through love: "If with the love of money you desire to bind your heart, you are planting for yourself many sorrows."[53] Faith is the key which opens the heart to true riches: "the heart is opened with the key of faith."[54] Hope is to be fixed not on riches but God: "there fix your hope, there fix the anchor of your heart."[55] The image of an anchor is developed here in terms of the danger of storms, the fear of shipwreck and the need to moor oneself securely. This said, it may be granted that Augustine's purview is not just the heart but includes other aspects of the interior, for example the conscience: "fortify the interior strong-box, that is, the conscience."[56] The temptation as one journeys temporally is to let the heart desire riches which should be passed over in preference for God. External riches weigh us down, but it is not only external riches that create difficulties; there is a negative internal principle at work also, which is avarice:

> Money burdens you on this road, and after this road avarice burdens you. For avarice is the uncleanness of the heart. You take nothing from this world, which you have loved: but you take the error, which

---

51. "Hae diuitiae intus sunt." *s.* 177.4 (SPM 1, 66).

52. "Verbum dei te foris diuitem inuenit, intus diuitem fecit, accipe quae diuitibus dicta sunt." *s.* 177.7 (SPM 1, 68).

53. "Si pecuniae amore cor alligare uolueris, inseris te doloribus multis." *s.* 177.3 (SPM 1, 66).

54. "Aperit cor clauis fidei." *s.* 177.4 (SPM 1, 66).

55. "Ibi fige spem, ibi anchoram cordis tui." *s.* 177.8 (SPM 1, 70).

56. "Muni arcam interiorem, hoc est, conscientiam." *s.* 177.4 (SPM 1, 66).

you have loved. If you continually love the world, he who made the world, he does not find you clean.[57]

Avarice, here defined as filthiness of the heart, is an interior sinfulness with temporal consequences. As avarice dirties the heart, it creates a disordered love that is preserved beyond the end of the temporal journey: God will not find a heart of avarice to be clean. The irony is obvious: by loving money, which you cannot take beyond this life, you sully your heart with avarice, the filth of which will be seen by God at the end of the journey. Avarice is not merely an interior matter; it is an interior twisting of temporal loves that has temporal consequences. As Augustine comments wryly, the burden becomes even heavier at the road's end.

Augustine risks using the illustration of slavery: "Indeed cupidity makes you a slave, love makes you free."[58] In light of the power of cupidity to enslave, he controversially approves of slaves (metaphorically) escaping: "In this case, if you do not wish to be a slave, become a fugitive."[59] The freedom which should be sought is avarice not for money, but for God. Avarice is as insatiable as "dropsy."[60] The more water you drink the more you feel you need. Money functions as the temporal manifestation of interior endless desire. As such it functions well as an illustration of one of Augustine's grand themes – the endless desire and thirst for God. With the ironical linguistic shift of the orator, Augustine suggests that avarice should be felt not towards money, but God:

> God the Father and Son and Holy Spirit [is] everything. Rightly he alone suffices. If we are avaricious, may we love him. If we desire riches, may we desire him. Only he will be able to satisfy us.[61]

Augustine would have known that the Latin word for "avarice" was ordinarily a covetous desire for money, as used for example by Cicero. Though occasionally used by Virgil without moral reproach, and by Plautus of food, applying it to a lust for God is distinctively Augustinian. It may appear that when patristic

---

57. "Premit te in hac uia pecunia, et post hanc uiam premit te auaritia. Auaritia enim cordis est immunditia. Nihil tollis de hoc mundo, quod amasti: sed tollis uitium, quod amasti. Si perseueranter amas mundum, qui fecit mundum, non te inuenit mundum." *s.*177.3 (SPM 1, 66). Note Augustine's poetic use of *mundum* to mean both "world" and "clean".

58. "Seruum autem te facit cupiditas, liberum caritas." *s.* 177.3 (SPM 1, 66).

59. "In hac causa, si non uis esse seruus, esto fugitiuus." *s.* 177.3 (SPM 1, 66).

60. "Hydropsis." *s.* 177.6 (SPM 1, 68).

61. "Omnia deus pater et filius et spiritus sanctus. Merito solus sufficit. Si auari sumus, ipsum amemus. Si opes desideramus ipsum desideremus. Solus nos satiare poterit." *s.* 177.9 (SPM 1, 70).

writers use money as a metaphor for the Christian life, they are utilizing an overly rationalistic transactional view of God's relationship with people. Indeed, in his financial conclusion to this sermon, Augustine appears to do just this. Christians are described as merchants who give what is temporal for that which is eternal:

> The exchange is of such a kind, my brothers, as our trade. What do we give, and what do we receive? We give what we cannot take with us, even if we desire to, so why does it perish. Let the lesser thing be given, that the greater may thereby be found. We give earth and receive heaven; we give temporal things, we receive eternal things; we give rotting things, we receive immortal things; at the last we give what God has given, and we receive God himself.[62]

However, it should be remembered that Augustine's description of avarice is the theological context for these financial images. The use of money in his preaching was thus not primarily transactional and rationalistic, but desirous and heart-centered. The temporal image of money opens a window on the interior desires and invites journeying listeners to reflect whether they will lust for temporal or eternal riches. As Augustine concludes his sermon with an exhortation based on Hebrews 13:5, it is the God who keeps his promises, satisfies avarice, and welcomes us as debtors who takes central place:

> If a man were to promise, you would believe; God promises, and you doubt? He has promised, he has written, he has made a pledge: be secure. Read what you are holding, you hold God's pledge, you have held him as a debtor, whom you have petitioned to loosen your debts.[63]

In summary, it may be observed that this exploration of *s.* 177 highlights how Augustine both used interiority and temporality to interpret riches, and used

---

62. "Talis est ista mutatio, qualis, fratres mei, nostra mercatio. Quid damus, et quid accipimus? Hoc damus quod nobiscum ferre non possimus, etsi uellemus, quare ergo perit? Hic quod minus est detur, ut quod est maius ibi inueniatur. Damus terram, et accipimus caelum; damus temporalia, accipimus aeterna; damus putrescentia, accipimus immortalia; postremo damus quod dedit deus, et accipimus ipsum deum." *s.* 177.10 (SPM 1, 71).

63. "Homo si promitteret, crederes; deus promittit, et dubitas? Promisit, scripsit, cautionem fecit: esto securus. Lege quod tenes, cautionem dei tenes, ipsum debitorem tenuisti, a quo tua debita relaxari petisti." *s.* 177.11 (SPM 1, 72).

riches to interpret interiority and temporality. Both aspects of his preaching were driven and given shape by the text of Scripture which he preached.

INTERIORITY AND TEMPORALITY OF RICHES IN SERMON 299E

It appears that, halfway through this sermon, Augustine abruptly introduces the topic of riches by way of a meditation on the Rich Man and Lazarus in Luke 16. Augustine "proceeds on what seems to be an entirely new tack."[64] However, the apparent shift of focus fits with our claim that interiority is related to temporality. The setting of the sermon is a memorial of martyrs, and Augustine suggests that if pagan lovers are willing to die for their love, Christian lovers have greater motivation to suffer loss for love, since death removes what the pagan loves but gives God to the Christian:

> And if this salacious love has persuaded lovers, that they may suffer bravely many things for their own frivolities and faults, and those who ambush another's modesty see no danger; how much braver they should be in the love of God, who love him from whom they cannot be separated, alive or dead? [...] In fact the salacious lover fears to confess, the lover of God fears to deny. So let us choose love, brothers, in which we may live innocently, and die securely.[65]

Such encouragement to choose the correct love is set within a temporal frame. Death is the temporal reality which brings the nature of our love to light "by dying we come through to what we love."[66] Compared to the more philosophical presentation of time in *Confessiones*, the sermonic treatment is practical and focused on daily life. Augustine asks listeners to count the years left of life on their fingers, challenges them to keep an appointment they missed earlier in the day, and wonders if years to be lived are added or subtracted from life. This is an existential, sermonic treatment of time, aimed at forcing listeners to embrace a due sense of temporality. Less philosophical than the better known passages it may be, but as Augustine uses the subjunctive (*ames*) to evoke a

64. Augustine, *Sermons*, ed., Rotelle, vol. 3.8, *The Works of Saint Augustine, a Translation*, 270, footnote 6.

65. "Et si hoc amor lasciuus persuasit amatoribus, ut pro suis nugis et delictis multa fortiter patiantur, nec periculum ullum ante oculos ponunt, qui alieno pudori insidiantur; quanto debent esse fortiores in caritate dei, qui illum diligunt, a quo et uiuentes et morientes separari non possunt? [...] Denique amator delicti confiteri timet, amator dei negare timet. Eligamus ergo amorem, fratres, in quo innocenter uiuamus, et securi moriamur." *s.* 299E.1 (MA 1, 550).

66. "Moriendo ad quod amamus peruenimus." *s.* 299E.1 (MA 1, 551).

sense of possible loves, it is no less poetic: "You might love, you might not love, whatsoever you love is fleeing away: it flees, you cannot hold on to what you love. The years march on, time declines, what remains is short-lived."[67] In terms of appreciating the impact of this presentation of temporality, it is also interesting to note also that Augustine prefers to address the crowd of listeners in the second person, suggesting individual immediacy.

This discussion of temporality and death is aimed at making the congregation love God rather than other things. Those who think the martyrs pitiable, "for they did not have the eyes of faith, so they were not able to foresee that which was promised."[68] The whole first half of the sermon represents temporality as to set the stage for Augustine's introduction of Luke 16; as he turns to the passage, he raises the prospect of a future beyond the grave, exhorting "as long as it is necessary that the flesh is here, let the heart be there: all will be there, if the heart is there."[69]

Thus, the theme of temporality unites the setting and material preceding the mention of Luke 16. In doing so, it lays the theological foundation for Augustine's approval of interior riches. Augustine sets the agenda for the theological investigation which takes up the rest of his sermon by stating that the damnation of the rich man and salvation of the poor man have nothing to do with their financial status: "However it is not riches being accused in the rich man, nor poverty praised in the poor man; but in the former impiety condemned, in the latter one piety praised."[70] Augustine represents a listener objecting to this interpretation, arguing that it is obvious riches are what is condemned in Luke 16. The sharpness of Augustine's response, and appeal to his interpretative authority, suggests that, if this was an imaginary interlocutor, it was one which accurately summed up the unconvinced views of some listeners: "If I cannot prove it from this passage of the evangelist, may nobody listen to me."[71]

In this phrase, we see the mingling of Ciceronian prosecution technique with distinctively Augustinian homiletics. While Cicero would appeal to character witnesses or evidence, Augustine appeals to the passage from which

67. "Ames, non ames, fugit quod amas: fugit, nec tenes quod amas. Anni accedunt, aetas deficit, quod restat breuiatur." *s.* 299E.1 (MA 1, 551).

68. "Oculos enim fidei non habebant, ideo ad ea quae promissa erant prospicere non ualebant." *s.* 299E.2 (MA 1, 552).

69. "Quamdiu necesse est ut hic sit caro, ibi sit cor: totum ibi erit, si cor ibi est." *s.* 299E.3 (MA 1, 553).

70. "Non utique in diuite diuitiae sunt accusatae, nec in paupere laudata paupertas; sed in illo damnata impietas, pietas autem in isto laudata." *s.* 299E.3 (MA 1, 554).

71. "Ego si non ex ipso euangelii capitulo probo, nemo me audiat." *s.* 299E.3 (MA 1, 554).

he preaches. The problem to be solved is in the passage, and so is the evidence for an authoritative interpretation. In one moment, Augustine both asserts and moderates his authority. He will prove his theological view, but unless that can be done on the basis of the Scripture itself, he believes he is not worth listening to.

Two points are made by Augustine to defend his interpretation. First, he argues that Luke 16:25 suggests that the Rich Man did not believe he could have good things beyond the temporal goods of this mortal realm: "You had your good things in your life: what you believed in is finished, so the good things which are better you have not accepted; because while you were below, you refused to believe them."[72] The only good that can be possessed is that which is believed. Augustine must have seen that his interpretation was not winning the listeners: "Maybe we are accusing this rich man, and we are understanding our own reading instead of father Abraham's."[73] Unsurprisingly, he had further proof from the passage that his interpretation was correct. He pointed to the reference to Moses, the Prophets and a possible resurrection: "It is done, it is fulfilled: they did not hear Moses and the prophets, they despised the risen Lord."[74] In this way, Augustine established that the Rich Man's fault was not his money, but his refusal to believe or listen.

Augustine felt that his interpretation was proven: "We have proved, convincingly I believe, that it is not riches accused in the rich man, but impiety."[75] Still, he perhaps felt the smart of listeners challenging his interpretation and so urged people to "hear the greater instruction."[76] The second proof that it was not riches condemned in the Rich Man was simply that the person welcoming Lazarus into heaven was Abraham, a very wealthy man! Augustine gives every impression of enjoying announcing the ironic proof of his interpretation: "Read in the book of Genesis of Abraham's riches, gold, silver, cattle, family: Abraham was rich. Who accuses a rich man? A rich man received the poor man."[77] Augustine did not take such trouble proving

72. "Bona tua in uita tua percepisti: finitum est quod credidisti, ideo bona quae meliora sunt non accepisti; quia cum esses in inferioribus, ea credere noluisti." s. 299E.3 (MA 1, 554).

73. "Forte accusamus istum diuitem, et sensum patris Abrahae pro nostro captu interpretamur." s. 299E.4 (MA 1, 555).

74. "Factum est, impletum est: Moysen et prophetas non audierunt, resurgentem dominum contemserunt." s. 299E.4 (MA 1, 555).

75. "Probauimus, quantum arbitror, non in diuite illo diuitias accusatas, sed impietatem." s. 299E.5 (MA 1, 556).

76. "Audi maius documentum " s. 299E.5 (MA 1, 556).

77. "Lege in libro Geneseos diuitias Abrahae, aurum, argentum, pecora, familiam: abundabat Abraham. Quid accusas diuitem? Diues suscepit pauperem." s. 299E.5 (MA 1, 556).

his interpretation merely to establish his authority and insight; the issues of avarice, temporal loves and secular views of riches were raised earlier in the sermon. These issues were not ignored as Augustine concluded; the pertinent question to address remained: how had Abraham possessed his riches so as to enter heaven?

Augustine's answer is that Abraham had what the poor man also had—"interior riches."[78] Interior riches are explored by means of a meditation on inheritance. People save money for their children because they love the person saved for more than the money. Abraham proved he has interior riches because he loved neither external riches nor his son more than God; he was willing to obey God and sacrifice his son when so commanded. Augustine's congregation would be familiar with many of the scriptural narratives, and so he was able to invite some theological reflection by asking the listeners to imagine what would happen if the rich young ruler in Matthew 19 had in fact been Abraham: would he have departed sadly from Jesus?

Drawing on scriptural texts, vivid scenes, and financial inheritances, Augustine evocatively appeals for people to "distribute earnings, order love."[79] True interior riches are enjoyed when love is rightly ordered, and when riches are not held in greater esteem than the inheritor—or giver. As Augustine evaluates interior loves and riches, the temporal is still formative. We should possess whatever we can rightly, so as to "await the last day securely: truly rich, inwardly rich."[80] Augustine engages temporal and interior, preaching a delightfully practical and gracious financial ethic: we ought to be rich "outwardly as you are able, inwardly as you have been commanded."[81] In summary, we may observe that Augustine's sermon delved into the narrative of Scripture. Our detailed consideration of s. 299E has shown the way in which Augustine used his hermeneutic of interiority and temporality to preach Scripture, and used Scripture to expound upon interiority and temporality.

ALMSGIVING: INTERIORITY LIVED OUT IN TEMPORALITY

Peter Brown has demonstrated that bishops' oratory exerted considerable influence by way of promoting almsgiving.[82] Augustine's *Sermones* testify to

---

78. "Interiores diuitiae." *s.* 299E.5 (MA 1, 556).

79. "Distribue merita, ordina amorem." *s.* 299E.5 (MA 1, 556).

80. "Diem nouissimum securi expectetis: uere diuites, intus diuites." *s.* 299E.5 (MA 1, 557).

81. "Foris ut potueritis, intus ut iussi fueritis." *s.* 299E.5 (MA 1, 557).

82. Peter Brown, *Power and Persuasion in Late Antiquity: Towards a Christian Ethic* (Wisconsin: University of Wisconsin Press, 1992).

the enthusiasm with which Augustine spoke up for the practice. Almsgiving was mentioned in a number of classical Christian sources: saints' lives, pastoral treatises, letters, monastery records, and secular honors. However, the preeminent place for promoting and encouraging almsgiving was the sermon:

> Sermons were the most important way in which promoters of almsgiving advanced their cause. Preaching was regarded as the basic way in which Christian teaching, moral and doctrinal, was communicated to the faithful.[83]

Finn concludes that almsgiving is present to a greater or lesser degree in one-fifth of Augustine's sermons,[84] making it a theme of greater prominence than others more traditionally associated with Augustine, such as asceticism or virginity. Nine sermons are mainly focused on encouraging almsgiving,[85] and in many others, it features as a major theme or passing comment.

Augustine's preaching on almsgiving relates directly to our study in three ways. First, almsgiving was an issue which in several ways permitted him to step existentially into the issue of finances and riches. When he preached about almsgiving, he was not a distant observer or disinterested encourager; Almsgiving functioned within the temporal framework of church discipline and general Christian ethics, which Augustine held as one of his chief episcopal responsibilities. He most likely drew his own personal payments from the same fund which he used to relieve the poor. This can be surmised from the way in which he asked people to not give money directly to clergy but rather to donate it to the main collection, which could then be divided out among any who had need.[86] Augustine linked both himself and his preaching with almsgiving: "Today we have our fellow paupers eating, and with them kindness is to be shared: however the dishes for you are these words of mine."[87] He did not see himself as telling the listeners to feed the poor but represented himself as one of those who gave. Almsgiving was an act in which preacher and congregation acted together. Indeed, in this quotation, we see Augustine seize upon almsgiving as an illustration of the task of preaching itself. In all these

---

83. Richard Finn, *Almsgiving in the Later Roman Empire: Christian Promotion and Practice*. Oxford Classical Monograph Series (Oxford: Oxford University Press, 2006), 313–450, on p. 137.

84. Ibid., 150.

85. *s.* 61 (PL 38, 409), 86 (PL 38, 523), 113 (PL 38, 648), 164A (RB 66, 156), 350B (RB 77, 326), 350C (REAug 28, 1982: 253–54), 367 (PL 39, 1650), 389 (PL 39, 1701) and 390 (PL 39, 1705).

86. *s.* 356.13 (SPM 1, 140).

87. "Pascendos habemus hodie compauperes nostros, et cum eis communicanda est humanitas: uobis autem fercula mea uerba ista sunt." *s.* 339.4 (SPM 1, 115).

ways almsgiving was a financial act which Augustine not only encouraged, but which he represented as an existential experience that the preacher himself entered into. He oversaw it, depended upon it, identified with it and preaching was an expression of it.

Second, almsgiving was an exterior expression of interior riches. Almsgiving was frequently held out by Augustine as the ideal of practical behavior. Preaching which focused on interior desires and realities was not restricted to the interior, and was not in conflict with concrete external suggestions and expressions. The theological presentation of almsgiving in Augustine's sermons begins to reveal the connections between external actions and interior desires. Most strikingly he warns that in the opposite situation to almsgiving, where a person tries to take somebody's money, the bad external action has an internal effect: "For he tries to hurt him outside, he destroys himself inside."[88] The attempt to steal from another person wounds the thief internally. But the internal realm of desires and spirit is not a hermetically sealed unit but can be affected by external actions. Still, one may not understand the nature of self-inflicted internal harm: "Interiorly he is an enemy to himself, because he hates another. But since he does not feel the evil it does to himself, he is furious at the other."[89]

Since almsgiving was an exterior expression of interior riches, Augustine saw no conflict between focusing on the internal and directing the external. He warned against creating an idol in the heart: "Do not paint God like that to yourself, do not put in the temple of your heart such an idol."[90]

This was part of the theological foundation for urging listeners to give alms in the same sermon. The internal "tablets of the heart"[91] were of great concern to Augustine, but his focus there did not preclude external guidance and direction. He reminded listeners that the coming mercy which they hoped for was related to their internal riches of mercy: "Concerning this coming mercy, your treasure is in your heart: there you display yourself before the face of God."[92] The interior person is visible to God and will be examined at a future judgment.

---

88. "Illum enim laedere conatur extrinsecus, se uastat intrinsecus." *s.* 82.3 (PL 38, 507).

89. "Intus enim sibi ipse inimicus est, qui odit alterum. Sed quia non sentit quid sibi mali faciat, in alterum saeuit." *s.* 82.3 (PL 38, 507).

90. "Noli tibi talem pingere deum, noli collocare in templo cordis tui tale idolum." *s.* 113.2 (PL 38, 649).

91. "Tabulis cordis " *s.* 113.2 (PL 38, 649).

92. "Ad hanc eleemosynam impendendam thesaurus tuus in corde tuo est: ibi te explicas coram deo." *s.* 259.4 (PL 38, 1199).

Third, almsgiving was ultimately encouraged on the basis of Augustine's full vision of the temporal sweep of time. It would be a distinguishing mark of those on the Lord's right hand at the final judgment. Augustine frequently sought out a mystery or problem in Scripture—attacking it would be the central thrust of the sermon. In one sermon, the problem to be solved in this way is why on judgment day, God is satisfied only to mention acts of giving as the mark of the redeemed. Obviously, there were other good acts performed and other forms of virtue. The reason Augustine adduces is that acts of giving can redeem acts of sin, not in a mechanical fashion, but as part of the mark of a genuinely changed life. Giving to the poor in this time enables people to transfer their earthly riches to heavenly riches.[93]

Thus, the relationship between internal and external in almsgiving helps us begin to discern the link between internal and temporal in Augustine's thought. Temporality motivates and shapes almsgiving. This almsgiving can be construed as internal or external. The internal giving reveals the giver to God; the external flows from the interior and is a basis for future temporal judgment. The interior and temporal are not entirely disparate; through almsgiving, one can transfer value from this present life to the interiority, which will be assessed in the future heavenly life.

The Temporality and Interiority of Riches

The goal of this chapter has been to explore Augustine's preaching on riches, that we might continue to delineate the nature of his views on temporality and interiority. The purpose of this and the two subsequent case study chapters is to offer an inductive and exploratory reading of key themes, viewed through the hermeneutical keys of interiority and temporality.

The first point we can make on the basis of our inductive study is that a survey of Augustine's preaching on riches suggests that temporality and interiority are indeed related in his theological assumptions. Augustine frequently moves in his thought, analysis, and application between the poles of interiority and temporality. He can be presented as the mystical, psychologically introverted, reflective philosopher of the soul. He can also be viewed as philosophizing about, and pastoring on the basis of, the nature of time and penning an apologia of God's City developing through time. In all these things, Augustine can appear as the theologian of interiority or temporality. Our study leads us to urge that he is better understood when his presentations of interiority

---

93. *s.* 389.4 (RB 58, 46); 114A.3–4 (MA 1, 234).

and temporality are appreciated as closely related and interconnected, as seen in his treatment of riches, one of the most preached about themes in his *Sermones*.

Second, interiority and temporality are not only related; they impact each other. Interior desires lead to exterior actions in the temporal plane while the shape of temporality shapes interiority. It is possible to order giving temporally so that it results in interior riches. Interior riches lead to commendation from God at the future, temporal judgment.

Third, interior riches are more valuable than earthly riches, gained and held only for a brief stage of temporality. Augustine sees true riches as residing in the interior person rather than one's pocket or bank balance. Riches received in the present moment of temporality ought to be used with the cultivation of interior riches in view

Fourth, it does not follow that present temporal riches are therefore insignificant or sinful. They are a blessing from God, not only in so far as they can lead to interior prosperity, but also in the tangible good riches can bring to people over time. The giving of alms is not only for the interior riches of the giver; it is genuinely intended that alms help the recipient in their temporal journey.

Fifth, sin affects riches, and does so primarily in the interiority of people. The corroding effect of sin distorts desires, and makes people prefer the less valuable temporal riches over internal riches. The sin of avarice inflicts the hearts even of those who see it to be wickedness.

Sixth, riches in temporal life have value not only for what they can do in temporality; they have value as a temporal expression of interiority. Money is more than just coinage and more than merely a means of exchange. Riches are a temporal expression, revealer, and conduit of interior desires. Since this is the nature of riches, it makes sense that the right ordering of interior desires for riches requires a reorientation to the full Christian temporal vision. When temporality is limited only to the present, apart from future judgment and past creation, then riches become an expression of a temporality in which the agent is autonomous. Adrift from all temporal moorings aside from oneself and one's own desires, the only recourse is to the dissatisfaction of avarice. Money, due to its liquidity and fluidity, is particularly suited in its nature to becoming a substitute for God who shapes a larger temporal universe.[94] If only God can satisfy the restless Augustinian heart, it is understandable how money can appear as a God-like imitator.

---

94. Philip Goodchild, *Theology of Money* (London: SCM Press, 2007), 219.

Seventh, Augustine's use of interiority and temporality to preach the true nature of riches suggests that there is a certain obscurity or hiddenness to true value. Riches appear to be so quantifiable, so discrete and manageable. In Augustine's preaching, we are invited to look beneath the surface, to explore the mystery of true value. Interiority and temporality in their full nature are not immediately visible to the naked eye. As Augustine struggled to understand himself and time, interiority and temporality stand as invitations to step into a view of reality which has intrigue, mystery and depth. Such a theological posture lends itself to preaching which beckons listeners to have a fresh look at life, God and the world; all is not what it appears to be. There is a need for faith, with understanding coming to those who believe. Consequently, it may be that Augustine's use of interiority and temporality fits with his view of the centrality of faith in epistemology.

Eighth, these observations about the nature of riches in Augustine's preaching go some way towards justifying his frequent use of riches as a metaphor for the flourishing Christian life. Experiencing the wholesome reality of Christian living for Augustine has much to do with rightly ordering and reconciling our interiority with temporality as it is understood in the fullness of God's plans. This being the case, financial riches are constituted in their nature as to be peculiarly suited to portraying such an existence. Money itself is a temporal expression of interiority and has the ability to link the interior with the temporal. What better sermon illustration could there be to help people reorder and reconnect their own interiority with God's plans for temporality?

Conclusion

This chapter has been the first of three inductive exploratory chapters. We have explored the *Sermones* of Augustine in depth and in broad compass, with the aim of elucidating interiority and temporality in regard to riches. We have established that there is a link between interiority and temporality in Augustine's approach to the issue. We have suggested that Augustine's hermeneutic both flows from his attempt to preach Scripture, and is deepened by his engagement with Scripture. A fuller analysis of the nature of this relationship and its significance for preaching in particular will be attempted after we explore how interiority and temporality function in regard to some other key themes of Augustine's preaching: death and resurrection (chapter 6) and relationships (chapter 7).

6

Case Study: Death and Resurrection

If you are dreading death, love the resurrection.[1]

Augustine's preaching does not merely make frequent reference to death and resurrection: it is saturated with a thorough-going emphasis upon the end of mortal life. A case study upon this theme of death and resurrection permits us to examine how Augustine appealed to interiority and temporality when applying Scripture to this important concern. It is our intention in this chapter to expose the methods Augustine used in a way which demonstrates empathy for his approach. Just as we have selected the topic of death and resurrection because it is so prevalent in his preaching, so the aspects of that preaching which we will consider aim to be representative of Augustine's practices. Our intention is that the form of exploration be shaped by the content. In that sense, our study will be appropriately inductive.

Jesus' Death

The death of Jesus was the means by which God overcame death. Augustine was concerned to proclaim the full reality of what happened on the cross: "God died, that he might make compensation in a certain kind of divine exchange, that humanity might not see death. So Christ is God, but he did not die in the aspect by which he was God."[2] Not shying away from the bold claim that God died on the cross, Augustine is careful to explain in what sense this ought to be understood. In the incarnation, "he put on what he was not, he did not lose what he was."[3] The humanity which he assumed enabled God to experience death through the person of Jesus. Augustine was clearly determined to preach

---

1. "Si expauescis mortem, ama resurrectionem." *s.* 124.4 (PL 38, 688).

2. "Mortuus est deus, ut compensatio fieret caelestis cuiusdam mercimonii, ne mortem uideret homo. Deus enim Christus, sed non ibi mortuus ubi deus." *s.* 80.5 (PL 38, 496).

3. "Assumpsit enim quod non erat, non amisit quod erat." *s.* 80.5 (PL 38, 496).

that God died, and when he did so, he wished to explain in what sense the immortal God could die. Augustine agonized over the conundrum: how could he who cannot suffer or die be killed?[4]

Defense of orthodoxy, however, was only part of the preacher's interest; Augustine desired to present the death of Jesus in such a way that the implications for listeners were made clear. The crucial point he highlighted, then, was that the death of Jesus was the means of killing death itself, saying, "The immortal one put on mortality, that he might die for us, and by his death kill our death."[5]

With the aim of persuasion and exhortation, Augustine followed such presentations of the death of Jesus with invitations to confession: "First confess, that you may prepare a dwelling place for him whom you are calling upon."[6] Such language echoes that of *Confessiones*: "I will always confess to him . . . who lives in us."[7] In this way, we see that Augustine's preaching of the death of Jesus aimed to provoke a reaction in a manner which complements the responsive nature of *Confessiones*.

Consistent with our study, it is Scripture which shapes the way Augustine presents Christ's death. The death of Christ is situated in the temporal narrative of Scripture; two examples of this may be considered. First, the figure of Elisha is said to enact prophetically Jesus' overcoming of death.[8] Augustine suggests that the way Elisha conformed his body to the shape of the dead boy's form was a prophecy of Jesus conforming himself to mortals through the incarnation. Second, he preached about Moses' rod which was turned into a snake, arguing that the snake represents mortality, since in Eden it was the snake who offered death to Eve.[9]

By ascribing to the snake these various significations, Augustine establishes his proclamation of Jesus's death within the temporal narrative of scripture: "He was robed in mortality, which he also fixed to the cross."[10] Thus, the putting on of mortality is not simply a philosophical notion or an atemporal concept; the scriptural setting gives it a temporal signification. Similar links are made elsewhere when Augustine notes that as a woman seduced Adam into death, so

4. *s.* 375B.4 (MA 1, 25).

5. "Immortalis suscepit mortalitatem, ut moreretur pro nobis, et morte sua occideret mortem nostram." *s.* 23A.3 (CCL 41, 322).

6. "Primo confitere, ut pares habitationem ei quem inuocas." *s.* 23A.4 (CCL 41, 323).

7. " Semper confitebor illi . . . qui habitat in nobis." *conf.* 13.15 (CCL 27, 250).

8. *s.* 26.11 (CCL 41, 355).

9. *s.* 6.7 (CCL 41, 65).

10. "Mortalitate indutus est, quam et fixit in cruce." *s.* 6.7 (CCL 41, 65).

a woman proclaimed Jesus' resurrection.[11] The Scriptures performed a greater role in Augustine's preaching than merely illustrating truth; he could quote Luke 16:31 and John 5:46 to show that failure to believe in Jesus' resurrection was the result of not believing the Scriptures.[12]

Augustine preached that God sovereignly planned the death of Jesus.[13] The interior intentions and desires of Judas were sinful, while the intentions of God were praiseworthy. Judas was a murderer; God a liberator. As he focused on interior desires to exonerate the morality of God, Augustine presented the death of Jesus in a temporal setting in order to impact the interiority. As he argues at the end of one sermon on the death of Jesus, "For neither, as some think, is the old man the body, and the new man the soul. Rather the body is the exterior man, the soul the interior. This old and new pertain to the interior."[14]

In Jesus, Augustine saw the relationship between interiority and temporality manifested. He preached that as Jesus suffered he had the Holy Spirit to "renew the interior."[15] This inner renewal enabled Jesus to see his sufferings with all the meaning that the wider temporal narrative of scripture invested in them: "Observing with the interior eyes of faith, [he saw] how great a price of temporal things he would be paying for future life."[16] In Augustine's preaching, the death of Jesus is proclaimed in a manner aimed towards changing listeners' interiors. Augustine sought to achieve this by presenting Jesus at the center of a temporal narrative: the narrative of Scripture.

DEATH

Augustine affirmed in his preaching such doctrinal claims as death being the just punishment for sin.[17] Though such theological interpretations were assumed in his preaching, the two main ways in which Augustine preached on the topic of death were on the imminence of death and the example of martyrdom. These two approaches account for the vast majority of Augustine's mentions of death and mortality in the *Sermones*. Temporality and interiority guided his handling

---

11. *s.* 45.5 (CCL 41, 519).

12. *s.* 41.4 (CCL 41, 499).

13. *s.* 8.15 (CCL 41, 92).

14. "Neque enim, ut nonnulli putant, uetus homo corpus est, et nouus homo anima; sed corpus exterior homo est, anima interior. In interiore agitur haec uetustas et nouitas." *s.* 218A.3 (RB 84, 262).

15. "Interiorem renouaret." *s.* 70.2 (PL 38, 443).

16. "Intuens interioribus et fidelibus oculis, quanto pretio temporalium emenda sit futura uita." *s.* 70.2 (PL 38, 443).

17. *s.* 26.10 (CCL 41, 355).

of these themes as he sought to use Scripture to change listeners. Each of these two aspects of Augustine's preaching on death will be considered.

IMMINENCE OF DEATH

Throughout Augustine's preaching, he pays due regard to the temporal movement of God's plans. This aspect of his hermeneutic is particularly marked by his treatment of death. The fulfilled predictions recorded in Scripture are presented as evidences that God will bring to pass the final part of his plans: "All which has been predicted of the church, we see fulfilled. Is it only the day of judgement which will not come?"[18]

The illustration of a legal judge is used to emphasize the significance of God's warning of the future judgment. A human judge simply hands down a sentence; God warns of his future condemnation so that the prediction may be heeded and the judgment avoided.[19] Augustine used other illustrations to show that God did indeed want people to live and escape condemnation. On one occasion, he acted out a scene in which he played the role of a doctor visiting an elderly patient. He invites listeners to imagine themselves as a son of the patient. Playing the part of the doctor, Augustine warns the child that his father will die if he falls asleep. He then pictures the son constantly nagging at his father to keep him awake. The father may find it troubling, but the son persists since he desires that his father live. Augustine argues that in the same way, the Lord is urging listeners to not go to sleep, because he wants them to live.[20]

For those who ignore the route of escape, the fear of death "is a daily winter."[21] Though it is certain that all people will die, the precise time of each person's death remains a mystery. When preaching on Sirach, Augustine argued that this is a blessing to us, as it urges us to take every day seriously.[22] This has particular implications for those with responsibilities in the church; bishops will be judged on whether they have cared for the sheep.[23] Given the short span of a human life, whenever death might arrive it cannot be far off for any individual listener.[24]

---

18. "Omnia quae ante praedicta sunt de ecclesia, uidemus inpleta. Solus dies iudicii non est uenturus?" *s.* 22.4 (CCL 41, 294).

19. *s.* 47.4 (CCL 41, 573).

20. *s.* 40.6 (SPM 1, 117).

21. "Hiemps cotidiana est." *s.* 38.7 (CCL 41, 481).

22. *s.* 39.1 (CCL 41, 489).

23. *s.* 46.2 (CCL 41, 529).

24. *s.* 64A.1 (MA 1, 310).

The temporal movement towards death is inevitable and relentless: "For from when we are born, it is inevitable that we die."[25] Stoics such as Cicero also wrote about the temporal approach of death. What distinguishes Augustine's preaching on the topic is his emphasis that it is sin which gives specific reason to fear death and future judgement. He pictures this life as a tiresome dinner party, writing "Nobody can excuse himself from this grievous party. What Adam has handed over must be drunk."[26] The sin of Adam means that all subsequent people face death and judgment. However, sin is particularized in individual lives, and in various ways. In one developed treatment of this aspect of sin, Augustine preached that there are three kinds of sinners, each corresponding to a different dead person who was raised to life by Jesus in the Gospels.[27] The daughter of a synagogue ruler was dead in her house; the dead young man whose mother was a widow, was being carried from his home to a grave; Lazarus was actually in his tomb. Augustine highlights the location of each corpse: in the home, on the way to a grave and in the tomb. Each corresponds to a state of sin. The first state corresponds to a person who has conceived of sin in his or her heart but not yet acted upon the desires, the second to a person whose inner desires have been made public by action, and the third to one who through habit has become so used to sin that it is defended and reveled in.

This sermonic use of the three corpses draws together the aspects of Augustine's hermeneutic that we are highlighting in his preaching. The temporal inevitability of death and its approach is emphasized in the sermon. Augustine is bringing the Gospel narratives to listeners' attentions so as to warn them of their own deaths. Individual lives also follow a temporal development between birth and grave; sin runs a course through a life, a course which may be charted and described in the same way: from desire, to consent and action, to habit and death.

Charting this temporal movement requires bringing peoples' interiority to the foreground. The first step in the process is an interior one: the sin in the heart which is desired and loved secretly. The interior sinful desire is sufficient justification for death. Carrying the desire through to action actually provides grounds for some hope for a sinner; as Augustine reasoned, one could be rebuked for a public sin, and then perhaps respond by turning to God. The preeminent danger of acting sinfully is that refusal to turn from sin leads to the tomb of *consuetudo*: habit. Buried in one's habit of sin, a person has little

25. "Nam ex quo nascimur, necesse est ut moriamur." *s.* 77.14 (PL 38, 489).

26. "Ab isto molesto conuiuio nemo se excusat. Bibendum est quod propinauit Adam." *s.* 60.2 (RB 58, 37).

27. *s.* 98.4–5 (PL 38, 593).

hope: "That heavy stone put on the tomb, is the hard force of habit. The soul is squeezed by it; permitted neither to rise up nor to breath."[28] *Consuetudo* "is built on the human mortality which is the result or effect of Adam's sin."[29]

As Augustine sought to warn of the impending temporal threat of death, he exposed the interior desires which could grow through consent and action into habit. It is important for our book to observe that just as it is scripture which drives Augustine to explore interiority and temporality, so it is Scripture that he uses to expose the same themes. Augustine found that Scripture taught him both about the sin of Adam and the subsequent sinning of his descendants. His allegorical use of the three corpses in the Gospels aimed to draw listeners into their own personal experience of Jesus' resurrection power. Augustine wanted people to see themselves in the Gospel narrative, to sense their need of Christ's resurrection power: "So then beloved, may we so listen to these things, that those who live, may live on; that those who are dead, may come to life."[30]

By this point in his sermon, it is clear that Augustine has in mind not only the future day of resurrection, but also a present experience of inner spiritual resurrection that anticipates this. He aims to utilize scripture in preaching so that listeners' interior desires and temporal destinations are transformed. He preaches about death with particular regard for interiority and temporality. This he does because he aims to use Scripture to change his listeners.

The *animus*, or soul, was a topic Augustine frequently discussed. Outside the *Sermones*, it is usually aspects of the soul's creation and nature which concern him, due to his personal experience and rejection of Stoic and Manichean beliefs. The former held that all real substances, including God and the soul, are bodily; the latter thought the soul to contain sparks of the divine, imprisoned in bodies. It is not surprising that Augustine's wrestling with Scripture led him to focus on such issues as the soul's incorporeality, about which he wrote to Jerome.[31] So significant was Augustine's acceptance of the soul's incorporeality that Teske can claim "in the West there was no concept of God's or the soul's spirituality until the time of Augustine."[32] The main problem which pressed

28. "Moles illa imposita sepulcro, ipsa est uis dura consuetudinis, qua premitur anima, nec surgere, nec respirare permittitur." *s.* 98.5 (PL 38, 593).

29. Allan Fitzgerald, "Habit," in *Augustine through the Ages,* ed., Allan Fitzgerald (Grand Rapids: Eerdmans, 1999) 410.

30. "Haec ergo, carissimi, sic audiamus, ut qui uiuunt, uiuant; qui mortui sunt, reuiuiscant." *s.* 98.7 (PL 38, 595).

31. *Ep.* 166 (CSEL 44, 545).

32. R.J. Teske, *To Know God and the Soul: Essays on the Thought of Augustine* (Washington: Catholic University of America Press, 2008), 201.

upon Augustine once he accepted the soul's incorporeal nature was how the soul originated in such a way that a baby could be saved by God's grace from Adam's sin only through baptism. However, in the *Sermones*, Augustine posed the question of whether the soul could die, or if it was immortal. Reflection upon the soul's future provides further striking examples of his focus upon interiority and temporality in preaching. Again, considering the possible death of the soul represents an important strand of his sermonic treatment of interiority and temporality.

Augustine preached that a believer who faced physical persecution could take comfort from the fact that a torturer could harm only the body, not the soul: "Indeed brothers, the soul is regarded as immortal, and it is immortal following its own certain kind of way."[33] Yet, Augustine felt driven by Scripture to restrict the meaning of the immortality of a soul, since in 1 Timothy 6:16, immortality is ascribed to God alone. As Augustine reflects upon the significance of this verse,[34] he goes further: "The soul is able to die, it is able to be killed. It is certainly immortal. Look at what I dare to say—it is immortal and able to be killed. I said this since it is a certain kind of immortality."[35]

Augustine's hierarchical view of the universe is crucial to understanding his view of the possible death of a soul: God gives life to the soul and the soul gives life to the body.[36] The ability to move parts of the body indicate that the soul is able to enliven the body, but it does not demonstrate that God is giving life to the soul. The body dies when it is separated from the soul that gives it life; the soul dies when it is separated from God by sin or unbelief. As such, Augustine preaches a grotesque vision of living bodies animated by dead souls:

> So wonderful a thing is the soul, that it is able to maintain bodies in life though it is itself dead. So great a thing is the soul, so excellent a creature, that it is able to enliven a body though it is itself dead.[37]

Few aspects of Augustine's reflections highlight more clearly the importance of interiority than his bold claims about the possibility of dead souls animating

33. "Etenim, fratres, anima immortalis perhibetur, et est immortalis secundum quemdam modum suum." *s.* 65.4 (PL 38, 428).

34. 1 Tim 6:16 is also used in *De trin.* 1.2 (CCL 50, 29) to make the same qualification about the soul. The point is not there developed in the detail with which it is pursued in *s.* 65 (PL 38, 426).

35. "Anima potest mori, potest occidi. certe immortalis est. Ecce audeo dicere, et immortalis est, et potest occidi: et ideo dixi quoniam est quaedam immortalitas." *s.* 65.3 (PL 38, 428).

36. *s.* 65.5 (PL 38, 428).

37. "Tanta enim res est anima, ut idonea sit uitam praestare corpora etiam mortua. Tanta, inquam, res est anima, tam excellens creatura, ut idonea sit etiam mortua carnem uiuificare." *s.* 65.6 (PL 38, 429).

living bodies, which leads to the exhortation, "the soul is dead without God. Every person without God has a dead soul. You mourn the deceased: mourn rather the sinner, mourn the wicked, mourn the faithless."[38]

Augustine's preaching on the soul's death reveals a concern for interiority and temporality. The former, he explores the innermost reality of what lies within a body; the latter, he explores as he seeks to prepare listeners for the inevitably of approaching death. In line with our research, the reason Augustine makes such bold claims is that he wishes to use Scripture to change people. To do so, he must ensure that his views of the soul conform to Scripture.

It is striking how he reasons with his listeners from Scripture in s. 65. At point after point, he blocks off possible avenues of misunderstanding with a Scripture, or points another way forward with a different scripture. We have already noted above how 1 Timothy 6:16 was pivotal to his reflections. In addition, he quoted Matthew 10:28 to prove that the soul may be killed in general, and 1 Timothy 5:6 and Wisdom 1:11 to show that sin specifically kills the soul, even while the body lives. Scripture was Augustine's guide and tool as he probed interiority and temporality with the aim of changing people.

EXAMPLE OF MARTYRDOM

A considerable number of Augustine's *Sermones* which are focused on death were preached in memory of, and on the topic of, martyrdom. One of the most striking examples of his allegorical exegesis was a sermon on the woman in Proverbs 31, whom he interpreted throughout to be the church, mother of the martyrs.[39] On the festivals of martyrs, it was common to read or sing accounts of their deaths in addition to Scripture. Occasionally, this practice was explicitly mentioned in the sermon.[40] These martyrs were usually Christians persecuted for their refusal to deny Christ, but also included the Maccabees, whom Augustine commended as having died for Christ in their devotion to the Mosaic Law.

These figures may not have concurred, but Augustine was happy to claim "So the Macabees are martyrs of Christ."[41] Such subsuming of the Maccabean Martyrs into the Christian fold may lend support to Boyarin's insight that Christian martyrdom developed in ways more intertwined with Jewish martyrdom than commonly noted.[42] Ironically, one of the classic historical

---

38. "Animam mortuam esse sine deo. Omnis homo sine deo mortuam habet animam. Plangis mortuum: plange peccatorem magis, plange impium, plange infidelem." *s.* 65.7 (PL 38, 430).

39. *s.* 37.1 (CCL 41, 446).

40. *s.* 275.1 (PL 38 1254), 276.1 (PL 38, 1255), 280.1 (PL 38, 1281).

41. "Machabaei ergo martyres Christi sunt." *s.* 300.6 (PL 38, 1379).

studies of martyrdom posits the Donatists as a more natural heir of the Macabees.[43]

Scripture moderates, informs, and shapes Augustine's attitude to martyrdom, causing him to take umbrage with listeners who remembered martyrs inappropriately. Drunken parties were preached against,[44] as was worshiping the dead heroes: "And now, beloved, we do not have our martyrs as gods, neither do we revere them as gods."[45] If forced to choose, Augustine was of the view that the martyrs found drunken revelry in their honor to be less offensive than worshiping them.[46] But Scripture informed his insistence that the martyrs were not to be worshiped. One passage he utilized to make this point was the story in Acts 14 of Paul and Barnabas being shocked at people treating them as gods.[47]

Sometimes, his desire to let Scripture shape his view of martyrdom led him to make what must have seemed shocking comments about the sufferings, and he was not above attempting to use Scripture to provoke listeners. One such example was his use of Psalms 2, which permitted him to paint a gory picture of the arena in which martyrs were being torn limb from limb, and then ask what the different reactions were of those in both the amphitheater and Heaven to the violent scenes. His answer was that the crowds watching the violence shouted and roared, but that God laughed at the spectators—not in amusement but derision.[48]

The scriptural expectation that a Christian should imitate Jesus prompted Augustine to suggest that the martyrs too should be imitated.[49] This may at first seem like a call to superhuman virtue, but it was precisely the opposite in Augustine's view. Due to the temporal connection between martyrs and Christians, it is easier to imitate them than Christ, since the martyrs shared common human Adamic flesh with listeners.[50] The martyrs were caught up in a flow of events which followed from Adam's sin; furthermore, both martyrs

---

42. Daniel Boyarin, *Dying for God: Martyrdom and the Making of Christianity and Judaism* (Stanford: Stanford University Press, 1999), 93.

43. W. H. C. Frend, *Martyrdom and Persecution in the Early Church: A Study of a Conflict from the Maccabees to Donatus* (Oxford: Blackwell, 1965), 562.

44. *s.* 273.8 (PL 38, 1251).

45. "Et tamen, carissimi, nos martyres nostros . . . pro diis non habemus, non tanquam deos colimus." *s.* 273.7 (PL 38, 1251).

46. *s.* 273.8 (PL 38, 1251).

47. *s.* 273.8 (PL 38, 1251).

48. *s.* 280.2 (PL 38, 1281).

49. *s.* 284.6 (PL 38, 1292).

50. *s.* 273.9 (PL 38, 1252).

and listeners are part of the same body of Christ: the church.[51] Thus, a common temporal origin, nature, and unity suggested to Augustine that imitation of the martyrs was not only desirable, but feasible.

Nevertheless, an obstacle presented itself: how could listeners imitate the martyrs when the Roman state was not persecuting the church? Augustine's solution was to present the martyrs for imitation, with an explicit focus on interiority rather than exterior concerns. This manifested itself in three principal ways. Martyrdom was configured with an emphasis upon interiority, first of all, by preaching the possibility of interior martyrdoms that did not involve actual physical violence and persecution. The most evocative and pastorally insightful of these interpretations was Augustine's comment that many suffered martyrdom as they died peacefully in bed, holding on to faith in God as they died: "Therefore many undergo martyrdom on a bed, a great many."[52]

Augustine's interiorizing of martyrdom had a pastoral application. The ordinary peaceful death of a believer could be viewed as being at one with the lauded martyrs who went before; the ordinary believer could take his or her place with the greatest martyr. He went on to develop this theme by saying that the same devil who persecuted martyrs with violence persecutes dying believers with doubts that their prayers would go unheard.[53] As persecution was made interior, unity with the earlier martyrs was forged and a spiritual imitation became possible.

While the state may cease persecution, the devil never stops.[54] The sin of anger may be a persecutor.[55] Augustine's interiorizing of martyrdom stands in marked contrast to the views of Origen, found in his "Εἰς μαρτυριον προτρεπτικος."[56] In that treatise, Origen comes close to encouraging believers to seek out physical martyrdom. Augustine, by contrast, explicitly stated that Christians should not seek or hope for persecution; the daily temptations of life are a sufficient arena within which to imitate martyrs.[57]

Interior martyrdom was possible not only in the case of dying a peaceful death. With astonishing self-deprecation, Augustine is recorded as stating that even an overly long sermon can be a form of martyrdom:

51. *s.* 280.6 (PL 38, 1283).

52. "Multi ergo ducunt martyrium in lecto: prorsus multi." *s.* 286.7 (PL 38, 1300).

53. *s.* 286.7 (PL 38, 1300); 305A.5 (MA 1, 59).

54. *s.* 94A.2 (MA 1, 252).

55. *s.* 315.9–10 (PL 38, 1430–1431).

56. Origen, *An Exhortation to Martyrdom*, in *Origen: Classics of Western Spirituality*, ed. Rowan Greer, (New Jersey: Paulist, 1979), 41–80.

57. *s.* 318.3 (PL 38, 1439).

We have heard a long reading, brief is the day. And now with a long sermon I should not hold your patience. I know you have listened patiently, and by standing and listening like martyrs you have suffered.[58]

However, set against that comment (and lest we devalue the place he gave to preaching), on a different occasion Augustine noted that the listeners were restless and said that though some would like the sermon cancelled, he would preach out of deference to the martyr. He prayed that God would ensure the timing of the sermon would be such that listeners would not be bored.[59]

The second way in which Augustine interiorized martyrdom was by theologizing that it was the cause, not the punishment, which made one a martyr. The understandable emotional empathy for martyrs, as well as the fact that Donatists presented themselves as persecuted martyrs, drove Augustine to develop a method of distinguishing between orthodox and Donatist martyrs. He preached, "It is clear that it is not endurance which makes them victors, but justice: since martyrs are distinguished by the cause, not punishment."[60] This insight placed the focus upon the interior concerns, beliefs, and interpretations of events held by martyrs. It was an attempt to justify not only his dismissal of Donatist martyrs, but also God's approval of orthodox martyrs. God could be said to take pleasure in martyrdom, not because he sadistically enjoyed suffering, but because he rejoiced in the causes for which his martyrs died.[61]

The third way in which Augustine interiorized martyrdom was by urging listeners to copy the martyrs' interior valuations. This coheres with our observation that interiority is best understood as the realm which includes the faculty of evaluation. The martyrs valued Christ, and the future life, as being of greater worth than the world and their earthly life; the cause which could identify a true martyr flowed from godly interior concerns. Pleasure and pain motivate; the former attracts, while the latter incites fear.[62] The martyrs were attracted to God more than the world, and feared Hell more than earthly suffering. As usual, Augustine utilized Scripture's temporal narrative

---

58. "Longam lectionem audiuimus, breuis est dies: longo sermone etiam nos tenere uestram patientiam non debemus. Nouimus quia patienter audistis, et diu stando et audiendo tanquam martyri compassi estis." s. 274 (PL 38, 1253).

59. s. 305A.1 (MA 1, 55).

60. "Scilicet ut uictores non tolerantia faciat, sed iustitia: quoniam martyres discernit causa, non poena." s. 275.1 (PL 38, 1254). See also s. 325.2 (PL 38, 1096), 94A.1 (MA 1, 265).

61. s. 285.2 (PL 38, 1293).

62. s. 283.1 (DOLBEAU 196, 1).

as the setting within which interior desires were appealed to. Thus, Hell was introduced as a future suffering more worthy of fear than present earthly persecution. On another occasion, he could describe the martyrs as setting one interior delight against another:

> Any time the holy martyrs were thinking about that delight, then all the evil and bitter and harsh things were becoming worthless. It was delight against delight; it was delight against sorrow.[63]

Thus Augustine's interiorizing of martyrdom enabled him to make pastoral use of the martyrdom accounts, distinguishing orthodox sacrifices from Donatist. In many ways, his interiorizing was an attempt to normalize and democratize martyrdom. That which was often portrayed as the summit of Christian spirituality was actually, when viewed from the perspective of interior valuations, merely an outworking of the normal Christian life.

Perhaps one of the most surprising ways Augustine applied this framework of thought was to pagans. His focus upon interior desires led him to argue that even pagans live lives of martyrdom; believer and unbeliever can say Romans 8:35 of themselves. However whilst the former dies every day for Christ, the latter dies for money: "They themselves are able to say of money that which the martyrs say of wisdom."[64] Augustine utilized Scripture's temporality to interiorize martyrdom in listeners. This was his normal practice, but it is particularly noteworthy that he approached the task of preaching on martyrdom in this way since, as noted above, there were readings of the accounts of martyrs' sufferings included in services. It is striking that Augustine makes only passing reference to the details of the narratives which were read, sometimes referring to them only to encourage listeners to focus upon fostering a different reaction than that of those who originally witnessed the sufferings. Augustine knew that the detail and gore of martyrdom narratives could move people's emotions. Nevertheless, his preferred method for enabling deep heart change was the opening up of the Scripture narrative.

One doctoral thesis has observed that the narrative of Scripture has a particular relevance to Christian martyrdom:

---

63. "Martyres sancti quando illam delectationem cogitabant, tunc illis mala omnia et acerba atque aspera uilescebant. Erat delectatio contra delectationem: erat delectatio contra dolorem." *s.* 284.4 (PL 38, 1290).

64. "Possunt et ipsi dicere pecuniae quod martyres sapientiae." *s.* 299F.5 (PLS 2, 791).

> Martyrdom, as an expression of Christian discipleship is a performance of Scripture as a witness to Jesus as the Son of God and Lord of all. Hence, scripture ought to have particular prominence and authority in any theological account of martyrdom. More than this: a reading of the canonical scriptures which highlights their salvation-historical—and so Christological—shape is the appropriate complement to the subject at hand, because theological reflection on martyrdom has always cast itself as imitative of, and indeed generated by, the death of Jesus Christ. This means that typological readings will have a particular (though not singular) prominence in this discussion.[65]

Jensen here intuits correctly that there is a constitutive relationship between martyrdom and Scripture's temporality. Augustine's focus upon Scripture, rather than the martyrdom, may appear to be a shying away from the nature of martyrdom, but in actuality, it was essential to foster a genuine appreciation of what it meant to die for the faith.

Scripture was used to shape views of martyrdom by drawing attention to martyrs in scripture. John the Baptist was utilized,[66] though Stephen was a particular favorite. Stephen's death could be preached on at length, since the actual account of his martyrdom was in Scripture. Augustine pointed out that a focus on Stephen had a practical aspect; canonical Scripture was more readily available than the accounts of other martyrs.[67] Augustine found significance in Stephen's Greek name meaning a crown.[68] When preaching on Paul, Augustine would frequently remind listeners that the Apostle had persecuted Stephen.[69] He suggested that Saul held the garments of others so that he could throw stones with all their hands rather than just his own. The change wrought in Paul by Jesus was acted out by Augustine in dramatic form, emphasising that God could save not just martyrs but persecutors.[70]

Augustine sought to position Stephen's martyrdom within the temporal narrative of Scripture; he related the birth and death of Jesus to the death of

---

65. Michael Jensen, "I Wish to Be What I Am: Martyrdom and the Self in Theological Perspective" (DPhil, Oxford University, 2008), 76. Edited version available as Michael Jensen, Martyrdom and Identity: The Self on Trial, (London: T&T Clark, 2010).

66. s. 94A (MA 1, 265).

67. s. 315.1 (PL 38, 1426).

68. s. 299C.1 (MA 1, 521).

69. s. 278.1 (PL 38, 1268), 279.1 (PL 38, 1275), 298.1 (SPM 1, 95).

70. s. 299.6 (PL 38, 1370).

Stephen.[71] All of these points in Scripture are marked by liturgical festivals, drawing the church into a recapitulated experience of the events thus celebrated. That Stephen was ordained a deacon may also be a part of his experience with which some listeners would identify.[72] Those who follow Stephen's example can look forward to a future experience of the crown with which he was crowned.[73] The temporal development of Stephen's life, as a part of the scriptural narrative, is something into which listeners can step and make their own; Augustine encouraged this in his preaching. If the example of Jesus loving his enemies appears to be beyond listeners' ability, perhaps Stephen, a weak human, can be imitated.[74]

Unsurprisingly, there were many points which Augustine held in common with the vast majority of the church. For example, he officially repudiated the practice of voluntary martyrdom.[75] However, we have seen that Augustine's use of Scripture when he preached on martyrdom drove him to be particularly concerned with interiority and temporality. This led him to the opposite position from many others who revered Christian martyrdom. In sum, Peter Brown's description that "the heroism of the martyrs had always been treated as a form of possession, strictly dissociated from normal human courage", could not be applied accurately to Augustine's preaching.[76] As we argued above, Augustine preferred to see the martyrs as people similar to his listeners, and he so appealed to temporality and interiority as to urge feasible, normal imitation of their desires.

RESURRECTION

The resurrection will bring about momentous changes in the experience of believers. Among other things, Augustine preaches that there will be neither sin[77] nor works of mercy.[78] The connections Augustine perceived between the future resurrection of all people and the past resurrection of Jesus creates particularly close links between interiority and temporality. We shall first delineate these connections with particular reference to several of the major

71. s. 314.1 (PL 38, 1425).

72. s. 315.1 (PL 38, 1426).

73. s. 314.2 (PL 38, 1426).

74. s. 382.3 (RB 80, 204).

75. G.E.M. De Ste. Croix, *Christian Persecution, Martyrdom & Orthodoxy* (Oxford: Oxford University, 2006), 160.

76. Peter Brown, *The Cult of the Saints* (London: SCM Press, 1981), 79.

77. s. 131.7 (PL 38,732).

78. s. 11.1 (CCL 41, 161).

sermons on resurrection, and then explore more of the way this was worked out in preaching Scripture by referring to the Easter sermons.

INTERIORITY AND TEMPORALITY IN RESURRECTION

Particularly close links between interiority and temporality are seen in the way Augustine highlights a relationship between the resurrection of Jesus and that of other people. The resurrection of Jesus was temporal; it was part of God acting in conformity with his successive plans for the universe. The physicality of Jesus' resurrection was part of this temporal action. Crucially, for Augustine, the temporal resurrection of Jesus aimed at drawing believers into their future temporal resurrection, through an interior transformation.

A connection between Jesus' temporal resurrection and the disciples' interior hearts may be seen. As Augustine argues, "Indeed he judged it to be profitable for his own disciples, that his scars might be preserved. This was to heal the wounds in the heart. What wounds? The wounds of unbelief."[79] The temporal act of resurrection was performed in the manner it occurred so as to heal hearts of the interior wound of unbelief. Jesus' eating of food is likewise taken by Augustine to be part of the same movement from temporal to interior.[80] The apostles who believed in Jesus' resurrection were able to preach the word of Christ's resurrection.[81] This preaching led to the spread of the Christian church, which as the body of Christ, is itself a worldwide visible portrayal of the resurrection.[82]

The interior impact of Jesus' temporal resurrection is further developed by Augustine. Belief in this word preached is itself an interior resurrection: "This is a resurrection of minds, this is a resurrection of the interior man, this is a resurrection of the soul."[83] Whether or not a person has experienced the interior resurrection of belief determines the end of their future temporal resurrection: "Whoever rises in soul, rises in the body to life. Those who do not rise in the soul, rise in the body to punishment."[84] Thus, we see that Augustine shapes his

79. "Hoc enim discipulis suis expedire iudicauit, ut cicatrices eius seruarentur, unde cordis uulnera sanarentur. Quae uulnera? uulnera infidelitatis." *s.* 116.1 (PL 38, 657).

80. *s.* 116.2, 3 (PL 38, 658–59).

81. *s.* 116.3 (PL 38, 659).

82. *s.* 116.6–7 (PL 38, 659–61).

83. "Haec resurrectio mentium est, haec resurrectio interioris hominis est, haec resurrectio animae est." *s.* 127.7 (PL 38, 709).

84. "Qui resurgit in anima, resurgit in corpore ad uitam: qui non resurgit in anima, resurgit in corpore ad poenam." *s.* 127.8 (PL 38, 710).

conception of resurrection around a movement between temporal and interior resurrection.

Consistent with our book, this use of temporality and interiority is aimed at changing listeners. Augustine exhorts: "Believe! Because if you believe this, you soul will be made to rise. And if your soul is made to rise now—the hour will come, and is now—then at that time your body will rise for your good."[85] In this exhortation, he uses John 5:25 to demonstrate his belief in an interior soul resurrection prior to the future bodily resurrection. Another verse he uses to show this is Ephesians 5:14.[86] Consistent with our book, Augustine appreciates that he is using Scripture to change his listeners. As he asks God to open listeners' hearts to believe in Jesus' resurrection, he quotes Luke 24:45, seeing himself as a preacher who proclaimed Jesus' resurrection, having had his own heart healed through faith. Augustine opened up the Scriptures in such a way that listeners could be caught up in the scriptural narrative which had so impacted the preacher.

His use of Scripture and the dynamic of preacher/listener when preaching the resurrection is captured well by one scholar:

> The sermon initiates a toto-christological spiritual exercise whose stretching and straining actualizes the death and resurrection of Jesus in the people's consciousness. The work of interpreting Scripture was especially apt for this.[87]

We may summarize Augustine's use of interiority and temporality with regard to resurrection as follows: Jesus is resurrected temporally, so that the apostolic witnesses may believe and be healed interiorly. This leads to the word being preached. When the word is heard and believed, people experience an interior resurrection. The ability to believe in Jesus' resurrection arises from that act occurring temporally, as part of God's ongoing teleological plan. At a future time, all people will be temporally resurrected. Those who have experienced a prior interior resurrection will be resurrected to the good. Those who have not believed, and so have not been resurrected interiorly, will be raised to punishment.

---

85. "Crede: quia si credideris hoc, tunc suscitabitur anima tua. Et si suscitabitur anima tua nunc; ueniet hora, et nunc est [John 5:25], tunc bono tuo resurget caro tua." s. 127.15.

86. s. 127.7 (PL 38, 709).

87. Michael Cameron, "Totus Christus and the Psychagogy of Augustine's Sermons," *Augustinian Studies* 36, no. 1 (2005), 69.

PREACHING THE RESURRECTION TO TEACH BELIEVERS

Sermones 361 and 362 are among the longest recorded in the *Sermones*. Their extraordinary length appears to be because they were preached with the particular aim of instructing believers. Ordinarily, Augustine preached as if there were a number of unbelievers, and even heretics, among his listeners. However, on these two occasions, he seemed to be aware that his listeners were more uniformly Christian. He acknowledges their shudder at the mention of those who deny the resurrection.[88] He suggests that there are two main questions to ask concerning resurrection: will it happen, and what will it be like?[89] When speaking to unbelievers, it is necessary to show that it will happen, but since Christians all believe the resurrection, only the second issue is of interest to them. Augustine states that in view of the belief of his listeners, there may be no need to focus on the first issue.[90]

Augustine's unusual certainty about the believing composition of his congregation may suggest that he was preaching to a group of presbyters or deacons. The listeners are those who have a higher than normal interest in the Scriptures.[91] He mentions that it is winter[92] and that he is preaching because there is some kind of pagan festival happening.[93] At one point, he uses an illustration of being trodden upon in a crowd.[94] He says that he has used the illustration before, suggesting that he is not travelling away from Hippo, but is speaking to those to whom he preached regularly. It would appear that he saw the need and opportunity to teach and train believers about the resurrection. The unusual length of these sermons was because they were part of Augustine's training program for believers which went beyond his usual pattern of preaching.

The first sermon focused on the reality of the resurrection. Augustine said he would speak about this despite his listeners being believers. He says that he will do this because there are pagans and weaker Christians who constantly threaten to undermine the beliefs of those present:

---

88. *s.* 361.1 (PL 39, 1599).

89. *s.* 361.3 (PL 39, 1600).

90. *s.* 361.3 (PL 39, 1600).

91. *s.* 361.4 (PL 39, 1600).

92. *s.* 361.10 (PL 39, 1604).

93. *s.* 361.19 (PL 39, 1610). Since it was winter, the festival could have been either *Saturnalia* at the start of the year, or February's *Parentalia* celebration of the dead.

94. *s.* 361.14 (PL 39, 1606).

> For I consider none of you here now to be pagan, rather all are
> Christian. Yet pagans and mockers of the resurrection do not cease
> daily to mutter in Christian ears: let us eat and drink, for tomorrow
> we die. [1 Cor 15:32].[95]

He gives an example of the kind of muttering which could undermine Christian
belief. He claims that some say Jesus may have been resurrected, but that was
due to his great power and superiority over others; no such hope could be
entertained for his followers.[96] Augustine noted that all he was saying was
preached with the aim of enabling his listeners to give an answer to those who
deny the resurrection.[97]

While s. 361 focused upon the reality of the resurrection, s. 362 picks up
on the issue which more ordinarily concerns believers directly: the nature of the
resurrection. It seems that the second part of this teaching program was given a
short time after the first. Augustine notes that he has selected suitable readings
to facilitate his aims.[98] His opening remarks about Scripture are consonant with
our claim that it is Scripture which lies behind his hermeneutic of interiority
and temporality. He draws attention to the fact that it is the Scriptures which
assure us of that which lies ahead and also emphasizes that the promises of
Scripture must be taken into the heart.[99] Having thus mentioned the need of
interior appropriation, he then highlights the need to appreciate the temporal
nature of this process. Familiar metaphors of journey, exile, and homeland are
used to convey temporality.[100]

As the sermon develops, interiority and temporality are the lenses through
which he sees the nature of resurrection. Augustine realizes that his emphasis
on interiority may be misleading, especially as he notes that many others have
thought that the resurrection would be a merely interior resurrection of the
soul. In s. 229J.1, he notes this as a central belief of the Manichees. He affirms
that the resurrection is essential to Christian belief, and that the appropriate
question is not whether bodies will be raised, but what kind of bodies they will

---

95. "Nam neminem hic paganum nunc esse arbitror, sed omnes christianos. Pagani uero et irrisores
resurrectionis quotidie in auribus christianorum immurmurare non cessant: manducemus et bibamus; cras
enim morimur" s. 361.4 (PL 39, 1600).

96. s. 361.14,15 (PL 39, 1606–7).

97. s. 361.18 (PL 39, 1609).

98. s. 362.1 (PL 39, 1611).

99. s. 362.2 (PL 39, 1612).

100. s. 362.4 (PL 39, 1613).

be.[101] Temporality and interiority are utilized by Augustine in his answer to this enquiry.

Temporality is affirmed in his central argument that there is a link between the resurrection of Jesus and that of Christians. He preaches, "I say this, what we ought to hope for in the resurrection of the dead is that which has been expressed in our head, that which has been expressed in the body of our Lord Jesus Christ."[102] The link between the resurrections means that Augustine's way of enquiring into the kind of bodies with which believers will be raised will involve studying the scriptural record of Jesus' resurrection. Thus, for example, he considers whether or not we will eat food in resurrected bodies.[103] His enquiry leads him to conclude that Jesus ate food in his resurrected state, not because he needed to, but with the aim of showing his disciples that his body was real; in this sense, the body of resurrected believers will be similar to that of angels.

The point is important to Augustine: Christ's solidarity with the Christian in participation in the experience of embodiment does not end with his earthly body, but persists as a model and guarantee of the resurrection body.[104] The importance of this link was that it opened up to Augustine a means of investigating the nature of believers' resurrected bodies. Reflection upon the scriptural record of Jesus' resurrection led to insights into the wider resurrection of Christians. The temporal connection between each event facilitated understanding; however, it must be noted that, as our book suggests, it was Scripture which ultimately permitted these temporal links to be explored.

As Augustine made the case for temporal links between resurrections, he did not omit his emphasis upon interiority. For the foundation of building towards the resurrection is laid "if Christ has taken first place in the heart."[105] Thus, his treatment of resurrection in these sermons is consistent with our conclusions. His hermeneutic of interiority and temporality is the grammar of his preaching and this is due to his use of Scripture. The fact that Scripture drove and shaped his approach to the issue meant that, as he outlined his answers to the questions raised, Augustine felt obliged to highlight possible difficulties with the Scripture. For example, he paused in the middle of preaching to ask whether

---

101. *s.* 362.6 (PL 39, 1614).

102. "Illud dico, hoc nos sperare debere in resurrectione mortuorum, quod expressum est in capite nostro, quod expressum est in corpora domini nostri Iesu Christi." *s.* 362.10 (PL 39, 1616).

103. *s.* 362.11–12 (PL 39, 1617–19).

104. Margaret Miles, *Augustine on the Body*, vol. 31, *American Academy of Religion Dissertation Series*, ed., H. Ganse Jr. Little (Missoula: The American Academy of Religion, 1979), 119.

105. "Si primum locum in corde Christus obtinuit." *s.* 362.9 (PL 39, 1616).

1 Corinthians 15:50 contradicted the conclusions he drew from the temporal link between the resurrections of Christ and Christians.[106] Incidentally, it may also be noted that these two sermons should be given high priority in any consideration of Augustine's theology of the resurrection, though, were one to explore this more widely, many parts of his corpus would need to be consulted. That said, it is difficult to see why two long sermons given with the aim of training Christians to think scripturally about the resurrection ought not to take a central place in such an endeavor.

PREACHING THE RESURRECTION AT EASTER

Over eighty resurrection-themed sermons are recorded as having been preached by Augustine during Easter celebrations.[107] The liturgical setting affected his attempt to use Scripture to change people via a focus on interiority and temporality in various ways. Augustine did not preach on baptism or the Eucharist in a systematic manner, but the links made in his Easter sermons to these sacraments and the liturgical context offer tantalizing glimpses into his appreciation of them. Easter Day was the normal point in the liturgical calendar to be baptized. Thus, much that happened had a focus on those who were being presented for baptism: the *competentes*.

Prior to being *competentes*, they had been *catechumens* for several years. As such, they listened to Augustine's preaching and learned how to live the Christian life. Those deemed ready for baptism were then designated *competentes*, and spent Lent fasting and listening to preaching on the Lord's Prayer and Creed. The lengthy fast was broken on Holy Thursday. Since they did not wash during Lent, the *competentes* also washed at the baths. As Augustine noted, this avoided them giving offense to the senses.[108]

On Good Friday the passion was read and the rest of the church began a new fast with the *competentes*. The Easter Vigil, or Holy Night, began at sunset on Saturday. The whole congregation kept vigil throughout the night. At various points, Augustine would make a brief sermon, or a candidate for baptism would recite the Creed.[109] One of the recorded sermons preached before the Creed was recited; we know this to be from early in Augustine's career, since in it he refers to himself as a priest.[110]

---

106. *s.* 362.13–15 (PL 39, 1619–21).

107. A classic example is *s.* 219 (PL 38, 1087).

108. Ep. 54.10 (CSEL 34, 2).

109. *s.* 59.1 (SC 116, 186).

110. *s.* 214.1 (RB 72, 14).

During the Easter Vigil, the church was lit throughout the night. Augustine noted that this, together with the crowds and singing, meant that neighbouring pagans were angry at being kept awake. Keen to capitalize theologically from the disturbance caused by his church, he preached, "So on this night, both the hostile world and reconciled world keep vigil. One keeps vigil to praise the doctor who set it free. The other keeps vigil to blaspheme the judge by whom it is condemned."[111]

This is a striking example of the liturgical event dominating Augustine's concern in preaching. He recognizes that even those present at the vigil may not be taking the significance into their hearts, so he urges them to celebrate both outwardly and inwardly.[112] Usually in his preaching, Augustine reserved such language for the insight he draws from Scripture. However, in his preaching during the vigil, his approach appears at first examination to be different. The liturgical setting comes to dominate the horizon of his preaching.

In the Easter Vigil preaching, Augustine gave short sermons[113] which reflected upon metaphors associated with the liturgical ceremony: sleeping, keeping watch,[114] and light and darkness.[115] Various parts of Scripture were quoted by way of meditating on the theme. In this way, the liturgical event became the focus of the sermon. The actual practice of keeping vigil was presented by Augustine as having apostolic warrant on the basis of 2 Corinthians 11:27;[116] the Vulgate spoke of Paul being "in vigiliis multis". In context, the passage was not actually a command to imitation from Paul, but the regular appeal to the verse by Augustine serves to demonstrate how far the actual nature of a vigil itself dominated his preaching when they occurred.

The crucial question for our investigation is whether a liturgical celebration such as this, dominating a sermon as it does, militates against our conclusions. Was Augustine backing away from using Scripture to change people through a focus on interiority and temporality? He thought the Easter Vigil to be the most important of all vigils: the mother of all holy vigils.[117] Was it weighty enough an occasion to overwhelm his normal beliefs about preaching?

111. "Uigilat ergo ista nocte et mundus inimicus, et mundus reconciliatus. Uigilat iste, ut laudet medicum liberatus: uigilat ille, ut blasphemet iudicem condemnatus." *s.* 219 (PL 38, 1088).

112. *s.* 219 (PL 38, 1088).

113. One exception to this in *s.* 223A (MA 1, 11), which begins with a broken promise of brevity.

114. *s.* 223B.2 (MA 1, 456).

115. *s.* 222 (PL 38, 1091).

116. *s.* 219 (PL 38, 1087), 221.2 (SC 116, 212).

117. *s.* 219 (PL 38, 1087).

It may be suggested that, while the liturgical setting certainly impacted Augustine's preaching, he still approached the situation with the same undergirding theological assumptions which we have seen elsewhere. He explained the liturgical celebration in terms which showed that his goal was still to use Scripture to change listeners; delineating temporal connections and appealing to interiority remained crucial to this endeavor. Having argued that it is essential that people remember what happened in the past, Augustine preached:

> This is where such great solemnity of this night is relevant, where by keeping vigil it is just as if we are re-enacting the resurrection of the Lord by the remnants of thought. Thinking truly we confess it happened only once.[118]

Augustine is arguing that the Easter Vigil permits the church to re-enact the resurrection of Jesus in a way which both helps the past event be remembered, and which makes clear that the past event did in fact occur only once. The determination to preserve the historical particularity of the event being celebrated contrasts with the vague participation or repetition posited by pagan celebrations such as the resurrection festivals of Osiris. It was Augustine's intention that the sermons at the Easter Vigil should explain the liturgical event in such a way as to impress upon listeners that they were supposed to be entering more deeply into a remembrance of the past events recorded in Scripture.

Numerous portions of Scripture were read at the vigil.[119] When they were read, Augustine wanted listeners to enter more deeply into the narrative, to sense themselves becoming part of the story. All the while, the historical particularity was preserved by the fact that there was clearly only one time at which Jesus actually rose from the dead. Thus, for example, Augustine carefully blends the experience of the disciples keeping watch with that of listeners: "Beloved brothers, since this night we are celebrating a vigil in which we recollect our buried Lord, may we keep vigil for a time, during which that one slept for us."[120] The distinction between past and present is clear, yet

---

118. "Ad hoc pertinet noctis huius tam praeclara solemnitas, ubi uigilando tanquam resurrectionem domini per cogitationis reliquias operemur, quam semel factam cogitando uerius confitemur." *s.* 220 (PL 38, 1089).

119. *s.* 223A.1 (MA 1, 11).

120. "Quia hac nocte, carissimi fratres, qua sepultum recolimus dominum, uigilias celebramus, eo tempore uigilemus, quo pro nobis ille dormiuit." *s.* 223B.2 (MA 1, 456).

listeners are invited to *recolere* the past event in such a way that they experience its reality afresh; temporal connections are being made between listener and past event that permit a deeper entering into the Scriptures, all the while safeguarding historical particularity. Augustine wanted the liturgical celebration to bring scriptural events deeper into a listener's interiority, without collapsing the one into the other. Past and present became one in his preaching without becoming indistinguishable. In this way, his Easter Vigil preaching may be seen to be consistent with his approach on other occasions. His goal is still to use Scripture to change people. The liturgical celebration makes a temporal connection between present and past, done in order to make the past event penetrate listeners' interiority more deeply: "The truth declares that in reality it happened once, this frequent celebrating renews solemnity in pious hearts."[121]

Just before dawn on Easter Sunday, the *competentes* processed with Augustine to the baptistry, singing Psalm 41.[122] Erwan Marec's archaeological work has revealed that the baptistry stood apart from the basilique of the main church and was decorated with detailed mosaics. One of these portrayed the serpent tempting Eve in Eden.[123] Those newly baptised were now referred to by Augustine as *infantes*.[124] The *infantes* were dressed in white linen,[125] a veil[126] and sandals[127] that kept their feet from touching the ground. They would then participate in their first Eucharist as the sun rose on Easter Sunday. After this, they would depart, only to return later in the day for a further Eucharist. Augustine warns the *infantes* not to get drunk since they have to return for the second service.[128]

This second service was an opportunity to give them more teaching on the significance of the Eucharist, when would go through the Eucharistic liturgy in detail.[129] In opposition to Donatist tendencies Augustine emphasized that the

---

121. "Quod enim semel factum in rebus ueritas indicat, hoc saepius celebrandum in cordibus piis solemnitas renouat." *s.* 220 (PL 38, 1089).

122. *en. Ps.* 41.1 (CCL 38, 459).

123. Erwan Marec, *Monuments Chrétiens D'hippone Ville Épiscopale De Saint Augustin* (Paris: Arts et Métiers Graphiques, 1958), 103–5, 108–9.

124. Their baptism was very much an opportunity for Augustine to preach to them. See Everett Ferguson, *Baptism in the Early Church: History, Theology, and Liturgy in the First Five Centuries* (Grand Rapids: Eerdmans, 2009), 794.

125. *s.* 120.3 (PL 38, 677), 223.1 (PL 38, 1092).

126. *s.* 376A.1 (PL 39, 1669). Augustine's passing reference to the wearing of a veil is the only patristic comment on this practice.

127. Ep. 55.35 (CSEL 34, 2). Augustine here expresses disapproval for the various traditions of clothing that had developed around the rituals.

128. *s.* 225.4 (PL 38, 1098).

sacrament made partakers into one body that holds together in love.[130] The bread and wine were the sacrament of unity.[131] He was so keen to emphasize that the communicants are changed into one body that he developed the imagery by suggesting that the Holy Spirit's heat bakes the Christians into one loaf of bread.[132] Easter Sunday was a very busy day for Augustine; his use of the word sacrament to refer to so many aspects of the day suggests something of its hectic nature:

> Today we owe a sermon at God's altar, to the infants, on the sacrament of the altar. We have explained to them the sacrament of the Creed; what they should believe. We have explained the sacrament of the Lord's Prayer; how they should pray. And we have covered the sacrament of the font and baptism.[133]

In another sermon Augustine refers to the prayer in the liturgy as a distinct sacrament,[134] and he also refers to the kiss of peace as a sacrament.[135] Through all this Augustine maintained his concern for interiority. People were being exhorted to lift their hearts to God; in the end it is only God who enables this.[136] When each sacrament was experienced, partakers were to pay attention to their interior reality. Thus, for example, when giving each other the kiss of peace care was to be taken that they did not imitate Judas, who kissed with his lips but set a trap in his heart.[137]

Temporality was highlighted in ways which built upon the liturgical link with the past highlighted above. Augustine drew people deeper into the temporal narrative of Scripture by pointing out that the Eucharist was really a Christian Passover.[138] The Jews still clung to the shadowy symbols of the Old

129. *s.* 229.3 (MA 1, 30), 229A.3 (MA 1, 463).

130. *s.* 227 (SC 116, 234), 229.1 (MA 1, 29).

131. *s.* 229A.2 (MA 1, 463).

132. *s.* 229.1 (MA 1, 29).

133. "Sermonem ad altare dei debemus hodie infantibus de sacramento altaris. Tractauimus ad eos de sacramento symboli, quod credere debeant: tractauimus de sacramento orationis dominicae, quomodo petant; et de sacramento fontis et baptismi." *s.* 228.3 (PL 38, 1102).

134. *s.* 227 (SC 116, 234).

135. *s.* 229.3 (MA 1, 30).

136. *s.* 227 (SC 116, 234).

137. *s.* 229.3 (MA 1, 30).

138. *s.* 229C.2 (MA 1, 692).

Testament,[139] while the Christians were celebrating that to which the prophets pointed.[140]

The initiation continued through the following week, during which the *infantes* would remain in their baptismal clothes, stand apart from the congregation and listen daily to Augustine preach. These sermons were aimed at building up confidence in the resurrection. Consequently, the nature of faith in the resurrection was a key theme; Christians believe in Jesus' resurrection through the scriptures despite not having seen the event.[141] Indeed, it is better to touch Jesus by faith than in the flesh.[142] Throughout the week, Augustine invited people to step deeper into the temporal movement of Scripture. For example, he expanded upon the idea that Jacob's wrestling prefigured both the Jewish rejection and acceptance of Christ;[143] the number of fish caught in John 21 represented the fulfillment of the Law by the gift of the Holy Spirit.[144]

Eventually, on the Octave, the Sunday after Easter, the *infantes* dressed in normal clothes and mingled with the other Christians. They listened to further sermons which emphasized important points such as the harmony between the resurrection accounts[145] and the physical reality of Jesus' resurrection.[146] In all of this, Augustine utilized the Easter liturgical season to preach in a manner which, though it can be differentiated from his normal practice, was in reality consistent with the undergirding assumptions we have been explicating in our study. At a time of year reverenced by the Church as the most important moment in the liturgical calendar, it is unsurprising that Augustine permitted the liturgical setting to come to the foreground in his preaching. Augustine's goal remained changing people through using Scripture; his method continued to be highlighting interiority and temporality. Utilizing the liturgical season as he did suggested to people that their own temporal experiences were rooted in the temporal narrative of Scripture. The events of the past were not distant and unconnected to their daily lives; they were part of the temporal movement which God controlled and interpreted through Scripture. Charles Taylor has pointed out that secularity has much to do with suggestion to people that they exist only in one ordinary version of temporality. On the other hand, as Taylor

139. *s.* 229C.1 (MA 1, 691).

140. *s.* 228B.1 (MA 1, 18).

141. *s.* 229F.1 (MA 1, 471).

142. *s.* 229K.1 (MA 1, 483).

143. *s.* 229F.2 (MA 1, 472).

144. *s.* 229M.2 (MA 1, 490).

145. *s.* 236A.1 (PLS 2, 1074), 240.1 (PL 38, 1130).

146. *s.* 237.1 (SC 116, 280).

notes, "The Christian liturgical year draws on this kind of time-consciousness, widely shared by other religious outlooks, in re-enacting the founding events of Christ's life."[147] Such a re-enacting was precisely what Augustine sought to do in his Easter preaching, and his use of the liturgical season was consistent in its underlying aims with the rest of his preaching.

CONCLUSION

One of the benefits of having this case study as part of our investigation is that it permits us to consider key aspects of Augustine's preaching from multiple perspectives. In this chapter, we have explored the themes of death and resurrection from various angles that attempt to represent fairly Augustine's preaching. As we have examined Augustine's preaching on death and resurrection, we have again found that interiority and temporality repeatedly surface as important aspects of the way he approached the themes. He aimed to change listeners through exposing them to Scripture. A hermeneutic which appealed both to interiority and temporality was the means he utilized to do this.

---

147. Taylor, *A Secular Age* (Cambridge: Belknap Press, 2007), 195.

7

Case Study: Relationships

Most importantly, my brothers, attend to the faithfulness of your sons, that those you have faithfully spoken for may be baptized.[1]

The people listening to Augustine preach were varied in age, gender, and status; Augustine mentions in a letter that both sexes listen to the Scripture reading in church together.[2] Part of the value of the *Sermones*, then, is their ability to portray something of what Augustine thought about ordinary human relationships. Especially since he died before editing them, the *Sermones* offer a vivid portrait of one of the great theologians preaching in a way which he hoped would enable ordinary listeners to make sense of their lives in light of God's revelation.

This chapter aims to explore some of the places where Augustine offered explicit comment upon the relational commitments of listeners: children, parents, married partners, slaves, and friends. Augustine's preaching to these relational categories of people will be set in the context of his wider theological writings, as appropriate. For example, his preaching to children may be explicated by consideration of his views on infant baptism, and his preaching on marriage is connected to his views of women.

It is hoped that this extended case study gives a sense of the sweeping breadth of application Augustine made in his preaching to these relational categories. As with the other case studies, this one aspires to give readers something of a sense of what it is like to listen theologically to Augustine the preacher. As we so listen, we shall find that Augustine dealt with the various relationships about which he preached in a manner consistent with what we

---

1. "Maxime, fratres mei, filios uestros fideles adtendite, quos fidedixistis ut baptizarentur." *en. Ps.* 50.24 (CCL 38, 616).
2. *Ep.* 28.2 (CSEL 34, 1).

have discovered elsewhere. Namely, he utilized a hermeneutic of interiority and temporality in order to let Scripture impact and change listeners.

CHILDREN

Augustine famously drew theological lessons from observation of infancy.[3] People of all ages were present when Augustine preached, including young children. Mindful of the range of life from womb to adulthood in his congregation, Augustine preached about and to children in a manner which emphasized interiority and temporality. Jesus Christ was born a baby. Augustine drew attention to this and highlighted that our journey from childhood to maturity ought to have a relationship to his, saying, "We have the baby Christ, may we grow up with him."[4]

Augustine here pictures not merely an imitation of Christ, but our being present with him. Christ would be with children from life's beginning to end. The image of growing up with Christ captures Augustine's focus upon temporality. A less temporally concerned preacher may only use the baby Jesus as a model of virtue to be imitated, but Augustine presents him as one with whom to grow up, journeying together through the temporal nature of life.

EXHORTING CHILDREN

In *Sermone 391*, Augustine addresses children directly for the majority of his time preaching. His listeners are young, but sufficiently mature to comprehend his words.[5] He starts by framing youthfulness with the temporal context of what happens before and after: being a baby and elderly person. Augustine accepted that babies could not be tempted to sin via their own understanding, but he thought they could be tempted through their parents: "He is already able to be tempted, indeed if not yet within his own mind, nevertheless within the mind of his own parents or whatever people, in whose hands he is being nourished—situated in his weakness."[6]

---

3. Daniel A. Dombrowski, "Starnes on Augustine's Theory of Infancy: A Piagetian Critique," *Augustinian Studies* 11 (1980), 125–33.

4. "Ecce habemus infantem Christum, crescamus cum illo." *s.* 196.3 (PL 38, 1020).

5. There is some doubt about the authenticity of *s.* 391 (PL 39, 1706–9). The Maurists accepted it as genuine, but others thought it more like Ambrose's preaching. In light of Augustine's addresses to wives, masters and clergy in other sermons, I find it likely that this sermon gives a faithful representation of equivalent preaching to children.

6. "Etiam si nondum in animo suo, in animo tamen parentum suorum vel quorumlibet hominum, in quorum manibus nutrienda eius infirmitas iacet, tentari iam potest." *s.* 391.1 (PL 39, 1706).

The child could be damaged by temptation inflicted upon him by parents or caregivers, even though he may not be mature enough to reason and succumb volitionally to sin. Augustine summarized the nature of temptations endured by young children: "And, I may state it briefly, one of that age is being tempted, as soon as he is esteemed by his own in the world, and neglected in Christ."[7] In these reflections, Augustine was guided by his conviction that "certainly [in] every time, also every age, so long as this corruptible flesh is carried, it is not possible to be free from temptations."[8]

Young people in their prime of life have infancy behind them and old age before them. While the former involves temptations being mediated through parents, the latter brings temptation to love possessions and alcohol that must eventually be set aside in death.[9] Augustine's consideration of infancy and old age serve to remind young listeners that their own lives are part of God's temporal order. Life is a journey towards death and each stage brings dealings with God and temptation in forms appropriate to one's age.

Having set a temporal framework for his sermon, Augustine exhorts the young people with regard to interior loves:

> Of course we are prohibiting degrading things from being loved, not love in itself. Do you desire to love? Love wisdom, make it your ambition that you may find her. That the appearance of her might not shock you, order your interior man.[10]

Setting interior love as the focus of change is consistent with Augustine's approach elsewhere. By first alerting the listeners to their temporal situation, the preacher lends urgency to his exhortation. Interior desires need to be reordered because, otherwise, the temptations which are present at every stage of human life will overwhelm them.

Due regard for temporality and interiority enables the preacher to use Scripture to change listeners. The hermeneutic that is focused upon these two concerns both creates a hearing for Scripture, and functions as a method of harnessing Scripture's transformative power. Therefore, Augustine concludes

---

7. "Et, ut brevi complectar, tentatur illa aetas, cum a suis in mundo diligitur, et in Christo negligitur." *s.* 391.1 (PL 39, 1706).

8. "Tempus quidem omne, atque omnis aetas, qua corruptibilis caro illa portatur, vacare a tentationibus non potest." *s.* 391.1 (PL 39, 1706).

9. *s.* 391.2 (PL 39, 1707).

10. "Ab his enim quae turpiter amantur, non ab ipso amore prohibemus. Amare vultis? Amate sapientiam, ambite ut perveniatis ad eam. Ut non vos exhorreat eius aspectus, in homine vos interiore componite." *s.* 391.5 (PL 39, 1708).

the sermon with an appeal that young listeners imitate characters from Scripture who fit their life stage. Boys may consider Daniel;[11] young married girls should ponder the life of Susanna; widows may reflect on Anna, and virgins should think of Mary.[12] All of this is consistent with the assumptions and hermeneutic Augustine utilizes in other sermons, and gives insight as to how his methodology could have been used in addressing young children.

INFANT BAPTISM

Before considering Augustine's preaching on infant baptism, the wider context of the impact of debates with Pelagianism must be outlined, as Augustine's theology of baptism in general was informed by other factors such as Donatism. However, with regard to infant baptism Pelagianism was the most significant factor.[13]

Both Augustine and Pelagius accepted the practice of infant baptism.[14] Further, they agreed that babies had committed no actual sins.[15] Their disagreement centered on whether or not a baby is sinful due to the original sin of Adam. Augustine held that a baby is sinful due to Adam's sin; Pelagius believed that Adam's sin was not inherited by children. In the Pelagian framework, Adam's sin served as an example which could be imitated by children once they were old enough to make rational decisions.[16] It is important to note that the focus of Augustine's thought was original sin, not baptism. As a result of related convictions, he felt committed to defending certain views about babies and baptism. He himself appears to have been uneasy about his pronouncements, for he wrote to Jerome confessing as much and begging for advice.[17] Nonetheless, Augustine felt that the logic of his theology drove him to argue that an infant who died unbaptized would face God's wrath on account of original sin. He conceded that such punishment would be very mild[18] and noted that, similarly, a catechumen who failed to be baptized would also perish.[19]

11. *s.* 391.5 (PL 39, 1709).

12. *s.* 391.6 (PL 39, 1709).

13. David F. Wright, "Augustine and the Transformation of Baptism," in *The Origins of Christendom in the West*, ed. Alan Kreider (Edinburgh: T&T Clark, 2001), 287–310.

14. *s.* 294.2 (PL 38, 1336).

15. *pecc. mer.* 1.22 (CSEL 60, 21).

16. *pecc. mer.* 1.9 (CSEL 60, 10).

17. *Ep.* 166.10 (CSEL 44, 560).

18. *pecc. mer.* 1.21 (CSEL 60, 20).

19. *Jo. eu. tr.* 13.7 (CSEL 36, 134).

Thus, Augustine's views on the necessity of infant baptism and the punishment of unbaptized infants were the consequences of his assumption that the fate of unbaptized infants had to be theologized from a small selection of doctrines he held to unswervingly. Cardinal among these were the conviction that all are born sinful due to Adam's sin, and that baptism is for the remission of sin and therefore essential for salvation. Augustine taught about infant baptism, but when he did so, he was usually seeking to defend or elucidate some basic doctrinal point that was important to him rather than specifically formulate a theology of infant baptism. For example, he describes the perhaps all too common pastoral situation of a mother running to have her sick baby baptized. The minister is waiting to give the sacrament, but the baby dies en route.[20] Augustine traces the situation back to the foundational truth of God's sovereignty, arguing that the parents willed a baptism, the minister willed a baptism, and the child could not have a will either way. In the final analysis, the baby died before baptism because God did not will the child's salvation: "Since so many do not receive salvation, not due to themselves but because God is not willing. This fact is revealed without any mistiness in infants."[21]

Even Augustine's most devoted disciples of subsequent years have distanced themselves from these teachings on infant damnation apart from baptism. As John Calvin wrote, "God declares that he adopts our babies as his own before they are born, when he promises that he will be our God and the God of our descendents after us."[22] But in Augustine's own day, his teaching, understandably, fostered a sense of urgency and despair in congregation members; theirs was, after all, an age of high infant mortality.

When we turn to Augustine's handling of infant baptism in preaching, we find him attempting to address these fears. He emphasized not the damnation of unbaptized infants, but rather the fact that babies in the womb had not sinned,[23] and that Jesus was indeed a savior of infants.[24] So keen was Augustine to reassure his listeners about the possibility of God saving their babies via baptism that he even recounted the story of a baby who had been briefly resurrected by God just long enough to be baptized.[25]

---

20. Ep. 217.19 (CSEL 57, 417).

21. "Cum tam multi salui non fiant, non quia ipsi sed quia deus non uult, quod sine ulla caligine manifestatur in paruulis." Ep. 217.19 (CSEL 57, 417).

22. John Calvin, Inst. 4.15.20: "Infantes nostros, antequam nascantur, se adoptare in suos pronuntiat Deus, quum se nobis in Deum fore promittit, seminique nostro post nos." Library of Christian Classics, trans. Ford Lewis Battles (Philadelphia: Westminster, 1960), 21:1321.

23. s. 165.7–8 (PL 38, 906–7).

24. s. 174.7 (PL 38, 943); 293.11 (PL 38, 1334).

25. s. 324 (PL 38, 1446).

As Augustine tried to reassure his congregation about the salvation of their babies, he sought helpful connections and parallels within the temporal narrative of Scripture. Therefore, he suggested that, as infants were wounded by the sin of another, so they could be saved by the faith of another: "They share a kind if spiritual unity; they believe by another, because they sinned by another."[26] Augustine argued that if Adam's sin can impact people other than Adam, then surely faith is not necessarily an entirely private matter. At a later point in his sermon, he explicitly states that it is parents who offer salvation to infants via their faith.[27]

It is significant for our book that Augustine dwelled upon the temporal connections and development within Scripture's narrative in this way. The sins of the serpent and Adam form the temporal starting point of the narrative which drives Augustine towards his theology of infant baptism and damnation. That he attempted to appeal to it as a parallel ground upon which to base hope of salvation underlines how much the temporal narrative of Scripture formed his doctrinal assumptions. The sin of Adam was the cause of his pastoral problems; Augustine sought to offer pastoral solutions. He did this by means of preaching which involved commitment to using Scripture to change listeners.

PARENTS

Families were of considerable importance to Augustine; in some ways, the family became the paradigm of civic life.[28] He affirmed scriptural teaching that children ought to honor parents while parents should train children with patience.[29] He also drew attention to the humble circumstances of Christ's parents, giving occasion to warn listeners against pride.[30] He realized that parents had considerable influence over the beliefs and prospects of children. That said, part of his instruction concerning parents was a reminder that each individual listener would be responsible for him or herself, and would not be judged on the basis of another family member's behavior.[31] However, the main burden of Augustine's teaching about parents in his preaching was aimed at exhorting listeners to order and moderate their interior love for parents and

26. "Conspiratione quadam communicat spiritus; credit in altero, quia peccauit in altero." s. 294.12 (PL 38, 1342).

27. s. 294.17 (PL 38, 1345).

28. Rowan Williams, "Politics and the Soul: A Reading of the City of God," *Milltown Studies* 19–20 (1987), 64.

29. s. 323.1 (PL 38, 1445); *en. Ps.* 50.24 (CCL 38, 616).

30. s. 4A.1 (RB 84).

31. s. 35.2 (CCL 41, 429).

God appropriately. This focus upon interiority is consistent with the emphasis discerned in other parts of Augustine's preaching.

For example, Augustine could open a sermon by presenting a vision of life as an experience of being drawn by our interior desires:

> Two loves in this life wrestle each other in every temptation—love of the times and love of God. And whichever of these two overcomes, that one drags the lover as if by weight. For it is not by wings or feet, but by affections we come to God.[32]

Elsewhere, he outlines the classical belief that all objects are fixed or moved due to their weight, affirming that love is the weight which draws people to whatever they embrace and do.[33] This vision of competing loves is a fundamental aspect of his grammar of the interior life; it means that no person can reject love and opt for mere rationality. The Stoics desired and pursued happiness and their conception of virtue, no less than the Epicureans did.[34] Since all people desire and love something, the preacher must exhort listeners to love the right objects, in appropriate proportions. Love must be ordered rightly.

In *De Doctrina Christiana*, Augustine made his first attempt to explain his framework for such an ordering of loves. In pursuing his argument that God alone is to be enjoyed and every other thing is to be used, he suggested that people ought to be loved not for their own sake but for the sake of God.[35] *De Doctrina Christiana* was an early outline of these concepts:

> Augustine has not yet achieved a final disposition of these terms in the first book of *De Doctrina Christiana*; it is best to read that book as an exploratory study, in which he is still feeling his way towards a satisfactory conception of the *ordo amoris*.[36]

The ideas explored in *De Doctrina Christiana* remained a mainstay of Augustine's theological framework. While never repudiated, they were applied with more nuance in later sermons, seen in his comments about parents.

---

32. "Amores duo in hac uita secum in omni tentatione luctantur, amor saeculi, et amor dei; et horum duorum qui uicerit, illuc amantem tanquam pondere trahit. Non enim pennis aut pedibus, sed affectibus uenimus ad deum." *s.* 344.1 (PL 39, 1512).

33. *conf.* 13.10 (CCL 27, 246).

34. *s.* 150.3–5 (RE Aug 45, 41–4).

35. *doctr. Chr.* 1.20 (SIM 40).

36. O' Donovan, "Usus and Fruitio in Augustine, De Doctrina Christiana 1," *Journal of Theological Studies* 33, no. 2 (1982): 361–97, 363.

As Augustine affirmed: "He has not destroyed love of parents, wife, children, but ordered them."[37] Augustine did not intend listeners to refrain from loving their parents; he only wanted them to ensure that their love for parents did not exceed their love for God. One way this was applied in preaching was by way of exhorting children to love their parents in Christ.[38] This approach shows that, even when Augustine urged ordering of love, his appeals for due proportion were not crude demands for a mathematical rationing of love. Rather, he was presenting a conceptual vision of relationships in which all is related to God. One can relate to parents in a way that separates them from God, a way that would be worshiping the creation. Alternatively, one can conceptualize parents in relationship to the God who stands behind them; such a vision fosters due ordering of love. As Augustine gained experience in preaching, he learned to apply his insights with greater subtlety. However, the fundamental vision of the universe with which he worked was that for which he contended in *De Doctrina Christiana*. As Rowan Williams has noted:

> The first book of *De Doctrina* therefore offers a definition of moral and spiritual error in terms of confusing means with ends. God alone is the end of desire; and that entails that there is no finality, no "closure", no settled or intrinsic meaning in the world we inhabit.[39]

As Augustine urged people to reorder their interior loves and desires, he appealed to Scripture as his means of effecting change. This was a natural thing to do since his early presentation of use and enjoyment (*De Doctrina*) was intended as a guide for interpreting Scripture.

So Augustine presented the Christ of Scripture as an example of a child who rightly ordered his love of parents and God.[40] Jesus loved his mother, but above that, he set love for God's kingdom,[41] while affirming that the Scriptures commanded children to love their parents.[42] He concluded his sermon on right ordering of love by saying that those who heeded his exhortations would find that it was God's word that they had been hearing.[43]

---

37. "Amorem parentum, uxoris, filiorum, non abstulit, sed ordinauit." *s.* 344.2 (PL 39, 1512).

38. *s.* 65A.5 (RB 86, 44).

39. Williams, "Language, Reality and Desire in Augustine's *De Doctrina*," *Literature and Theology* 3 (1989): 138–50, 140.

40. *s.* 65A.6 (RB 86, 45).

41. *s.* 72A.3 (MA 1, 158).

42. *s.* 65A.7 (RB 86, 45).

43. *s.* 65A.13 (RB 86, 48).

Augustine's focus upon ordering of love, applied to parents in his preaching, is consistent with our book. He focused upon interiority as a means of using Scripture to change people. His instinct when speaking of children appears to have been to emphasize temporality; interiority, however, was in the foreground when preaching about parents. Taken together, Augustine preached about parents and children in a manner which appealed to interiority and temporality using Scripture to change people.

MARRIAGE

The congregation listening to Augustine preach included a number of married people. Humorous comments aimed at them could be dropped into a sermon, such as a reference to the possibility that once married, a man may discover his wife not to be as pretty as he imagined.[44] Couples were addressed by Augustine as a distinct social group, similar to catechumens.[45] His appeals to married people often focused on the danger of adultery, perhaps unsurprisingly since the preacher had confessed that from early days: "Because I was not a lover of marriage but a slave of lust."[46] In order to appreciate Augustine's preaching to married couples, we will first outline the context of his theological views on women more generally.

WOMEN IN AUGUSTINE'S THEOLOGY

Augustine pondered how Genesis 1:27 and 1 Corinthians 11:7–9 could be reconciled.[47] The former insists that both men and women have been made in God's image, while the latter affirms only men. In discussing these passages, Augustine appears to suggest that the woman is in God's image when considered as regards to man, but not when viewed in and of herself.

At least three things here show that Augustine held a higher view of women than is sometimes supposed. First, it has been pointed out that in the context of his argument just cited from *De Trinitate*, Augustine is actually making an allegorical point about the mind, not a literal assessment of human genders.[48] Despite appearances to the contrary, "Augustine was unequivocal on the question of woman's equality with man in her interior being."[49] Second,

44. *s.* 21.1 (CCL 41, 276).

45. *s.* 132.1–2 (PL 38, 734–6).

46. "Quia non amator coniugii sed libidinis seruus eram." *conf.* 6.25 (CCL 27, 90).

47. *De trin.* 12.10 (CCL 50, 364).

48. Maryanne Cline Horowitz, "The Image of God in Man – Is Woman Included?," *Harvard Theological Review* 72, no. 3–4 (1979), 202.

he located the image of God in the mind, as it is able to contemplate God.[50] This capacity to contemplate God was something he viewed as belonging to women as much as men. Thus he wrote to women offering them advice on spiritual matters such as prayer.[51] Third, it may be accepted that Augustine had an "androcentric"[52] view of the world, linking sexual temptation with the female body and accepting the priority of men in social life. Possidius tells us that he would not even have his sister stay in his house and would only see a female visitor with a witness.[53] In holding these views, he was reflecting the society he lived in and, to some degree, the ascetic tradition of Christianity.

The difficulty facing modern interpreters, when confronted by Augustine's views of women, is that on the one hand, he appears almost to question whether women are made in God's image, while on the other hand, he seems to champion the dignity of females. One study captures the disjunction well:

> In his interpretation of Scripture, Augustine is rightly careful to affirm and safeguard woman's equivalence in dignity as a creature made in the image of God. But because of his anthropological theories, this dignity is solely hers by reason of her identification with man in the spiritual level... The novelty of the Gospel lay in introducing the aspect of equivalence which Augustine was at pains to inculcate.[54]

My point is that Augustine strived to emphasize the dignity and worth of women, but he did so from a social and theological starting point which was androcentric; the attempts he made to commend the female gender are, in some ways, all the more remarkable given the assumptions from which he began. When we turn to consider Augustine's preaching to married listeners, we see both his androcentric assumptions and striking commendations of women.

---

49. Kim Power, *Veiled Desire: Augustine's Writings on Women* (London: Darton, Longman and Todd, 1995), 138.

50. *De trin.* 12.4 (CCL 50, 358).

51. *Ep.* 130 (CSEL 44, 40).

52. Tarcisius J. van Bavel, "Augustine's View on Women," *Augustiniana* 39 (1989), 52.

53. Possidius, 26, in C. Mohrmann, vol. 3: *Vita di Cipriano, Vita di Ambrogio, Vita di Agostino,* ed. A. Bastiaensen and Vite dei Santi (Milan: Mondadori, 1975).

54. Kari Elisabeth Børresen, *Subordination and Equivalence: The Nature and Role of Woman in Augustine and Aquinas* (Kampen: Pharos, 1995), 339.

PREACHING TO MARRIED PEOPLE

The concept of romantic love, so central to modern ideals, was entirely absent from Augustine's notion of marriage.[55] His lack of concern for romantic feelings meant that he addressed marriage from the basis, not of sentimentality, but his developed theological framework. Consistent with the wider context of his treatment of women, Augustine made remarkable endeavors to promote women, while still working from within assumptions that were male-centered.

Augustine preached against the tendency of his culture to exonerate husbands from adultery while expecting women to be faithful. He told listeners that they frequently heard of husbands taking their wives to court for adultery, whereas a woman prosecuting her husband was unheard of.[56] Challenging the attitudes of society and secular courts, Augustine preached:

> We have never heard of a man being taken to court because he has been found with his female servant, though it would be an equal sin. In equal sin the man is made to seem innocent, not by divine truth but human perversity.[57]

In preaching to married people, he encouraged a counter-cultural equality between wife and husband. His focus on temporality and interiority fostered this tendency. We see these two emphases fostering mutual responsibility in the following comment: "He fears for your soul, if you both fall into the pit of adultery together: you should be afraid if you fall alone."[58] The arena of interiority—the soul—is endangered by adultery; wife and husband are on a journey together and ought to be concerned for their own and their spouse's souls. The journey theme recurs when Augustine reminds listeners that they are heading towards the heavenly Jerusalem. He urges men that, as the heads of their families, they ought to be leading towards that virtuous place.[59]

We also see the double emphasis on interiority and temporality when Augustine describes the wise woman of Proverbs 31. He argues that the reason charm and beauty are vain is that the wise woman has charity.[60] Introducing

---

55. F. Ellen Weaver and Jean Laporte, "Augustine and Women: Relationships and Teachings," *Augustinian Studies* 12 (1981), 129.

56. *s.* 9.4 (CCL 41, 113).

57. "Adductum uirum ad forum, quia inuentus est cum ancilla sua, numquam audierunt, cum sit par peccatum. In peccato pari innocentiorem facit uideri uirum non diuina ueritas sed humana peruersitas." *s.* 9.4 (CCL 41, 115).

58. "Dolet tibi anima, si in foueam adulterii ambo simul ruatis: doleat tibi, si tu solus ruas." *s.* 392.5 (PL 39, 1712).

59. *s.* 332.4 (PL 38, 1463).

the issue of charity to a description so focused on exterior behavior shows how much Augustine was focused upon interiority. When he enquires as to when such a wise woman will receive the fruit of her labor, he says is found to be at a future temporal point—in the eternal homeland.[61]

Another example may be found in *Sermones* 354. There, Augustine sets a temporal framework in place by emphasizing that the devil fell from heaven due to pride. So serious a sin is pride that its presence in a person destroys the worth of chastity. Augustine's temporal framework looks back to earlier events in God's plans. He preached, "For what benefit is there to someone with chastity if he is dominated by pride? He scorns that from which a person is born and strives after that from which the devil fell."[62] In the above examples of preaching to married people, we discover that Augustine theologizes from his framework, which highlights interiority and temporality. From these twin emphases, he preaches to married people in a manner which both accepted and challenged prevailing attitudes to marriage.

SLAVES

The theological framework from which Augustine addresses the topic of slavery is most clearly delineated in *De Civitate Dei* 19.14–17. He highlights temporality by noting the pilgrim nature of mortal life; he affirms interiority by insisting that Christian masters should give orders from motives free of pride and domination.[63] Thus, interiority and temporality continue to be crucial concepts undergirding his views on slavery.

Augustine utilizes temporality by presenting a view of slavery rooted in his vision of God's past and future dealings with people. Looking back to creation, he affirms, "However nobody by nature, in which God first made man, was slave of a man or sin."[64] Having established that slavery was not part of God's original plan for humanity, Augustine affirms that it was a just punishment for sin: "Of course the situation of slavery, with justice, is understood as imposed upon the sinner."[65] Having looked to the past, Augustine glances towards the future, arguing that when God is all in all, human lordship will cease.[66]

60. *s.* 37.29 (CCL 41, 471).

61. *s.* 37.30 (CCL 41, 472).

62. "Quid enim prodest cui inest continentia, si dominatur superbia? Contempsit unde natus est homo, et appetit unde cecidit diabolus." *s.* 354.9 (PL 39, 1567).

63. *civ. Dei* 19.14 (CCL 48, 680).

64. "Nullus autem natura, in qua prius deus hominem condidit, seruus est hominis aut peccati." *civ. Dei* 19.15.

65. "Condicio quippe seruitutis iure intellegitur inposita peccatori." *civ. Dei* 19.15 (CCL 48, 682).

Augustine views this framework as accounting for both the institution of physical slavery and spiritual slavery to sin. Both are part of God's just punishment of original sin. A person may be enslaved (physically or spiritually) due to their own sin or somebody else's sin. Augustine saw the latter exemplified in Noah's curse.[67] On the other hand, slavery could be part of God's corrective discipline, which Augustine perceived as happening in Daniel's time.[68] In this way, his temporal framework offers him the ability to bemoan the pain and horror of slavery, while simultaneously refraining from taking the step of portraying it as sinful or unjust *per se*. Slavery as an institution is, for the moment, part of the order of the world, but it is a consequence of original sin.

Having utilized temporality to interpret slavery theologically, Augustine focuses upon interiority. Here, he gives a higher priority to interior than physical slavery: "Most certainly it is happier to be a slave of men than of lust, since the most ferocious dominator which can ravage mortal hearts, causing others to be set aside, is the lust for domination itself."[69] Augustine's focus upon interior slavery enabled him to make nuanced judgments and exhortations; the last day would reveal slaves and masters in both the categories of sheep and goats.[70] Social lessons could be learned from captured slaves; Augustine wrote that conversations with African slaves clearly revealed that the Gospel had not penetrated the depths of Africa.[71]

Augustine mentioned slavery on a number of occasions in his preaching. But one would be overly eager to interpret his nuanced interpretation of slavery as giving more dignity to slaves than he offered. It is an exaggeration to say that Augustine preached directly to slaves, addressing them individually. Garnsey claims this occurs in a sermon on Psalm 124.[72] But it would be more accurate to say that Augustine there singled out masters and preached to them about slavery. Usually, such addresses to masters focused upon their interiority, that the master ought to be careful that authority over slaves does not lead to pride.[73]

---

66. *civ. Dei* 19.15 (CCL 48, 682).

67. Gen 9:25.

68. Dan 9:11.

69. "Et utique felicius seruitur homini, quam libidini, cum saeuissimo dominatu uastet corda mortalium, ut alias omittam, libido ipsa dominandi." *civ. Dei* 19.15 (CCL 48, 682).

70. *en. Ps.* 124.8 (CCL 40, 1842).

71. *Ep.* 199.46 (CSEL 57, 284). This letter is referenced by Augustine in *civ. Dei* 20.5 (CCL 48, 703).

72. Peter Garnsey, *Ideas of Slavery from Aristotle to Augustine* (Cambridge: Cambridge University Press, 1997), 210; referring to en. P*s.* 124.8 (CCL 40, 1842).

73. *s.* 114B.12 (DOLBEAU 444).

A master's need of slaves illustrates his human weakness, a weakness the master would be wrong to imagine as being shared by God.[74]

Sometimes when Augustine addressed masters he spoke in a way that would have been reasonably offensive to slaves, such as when he mentioned that many slaves were untrustworthy[75] and served only out of fear,[76] or when his illustration centered upon the differences between an ugly and good looking slave.[77] A certain amount of dignity was afforded to slaves, in a more roundabout manner, when he used them as an illustration of humans in general,[78] though he would still emphasize the great difference in status between slave and master.[79]

While Augustine did not work through all possible social implications, he did preach about slavery, using the Lord's Prayer:

> They should understand that they are brothers, since they have one
> Father. But he that is a master ought not disdain to have a slave as a
> brother, that very one which the master Christ wished to have as a
> brother.[80]

Thus at a foundational level Augustine did affirm the theological equality between master and slave. Exalted positive illustrations could be made from slavery. He described the purchase of a slave at some length, illustrating the point that he viewed a martyr as somebody who was a slave twice over; purchased firstly by creation and secondly by the cross.[81] Augustine preached that all Christians are slaves, bound to obey Christ, their master. He also thought it prudent to mention that one thing that Christ had commanded was that the church obey its bishop.[82]

Numerous members of Augustine's church appear to have made it their habit to release their slaves and provide for their well being as part of their Christian generosity. He mentions the manumission arrangements of sub-deacon Valens[83] and deacon Heraclius.[84] The manumission of slaves was

74. *s.* 306E.4 (DOLBEAU 213).
75. *s.* 345.3 (MA 1, 204).
76. *s.* 198.12 (DOLBEAU 375).
77. *s.* 159.3 (PL 38, 869).
78. *s.* 159B.5 (DOLBEAU 282).
79. *s.* 361.21 (PL 39, 1611).
80. "Intellegant ergo se esse fratres, quando unum habent patrem. sed non dedignetur fratrem habere seruum suum dominus eius, quem fratrem uoluit habere dominus Christus." *s.* 58.2 (PL 38, 393).
81. *s.* 335I.5 (PLS 834).
82. *s.* 359B.9 (DOLBEAU 334).

elsewhere mentioned favourably.[85] However his tendency at such points was to draw theological lessons about the spiritual slavery of sin rather than urge the physical release of slaves by other masters.

We have seen that the theological framework that informed Augustine's approach to slavery was detailed in *De Civitate Dei 19.14–17*. This highlighted both temporality and interiority, conforming to the key concepts we have observed throughout his preaching. In a sermon where Augustine makes extended comments about a slave's manumission we find this same approach developed more fully.

Augustine opens his sermon by setting interiority and temporality before the congregation. Interiority is highlighted by the injunction to delight in the Lord.[86] He draws attention to temporality by urging listeners to make a right use of things as they journey through life to its goal.[87] The centerpiece of the sermon is an extended illustration of a master bringing his slave to church for manumission.[88] Originally, only secular courts had the authority to free slaves, but Constantine had authorized bishops to perform the ceremony of manumission. One assumes from Augustine's references to the practice that Christian masters opted to do this in church as part of their good works.

In this instance, Augustine describes the scene of a master bringing his slave to church for manumission. With an orator's flourish he builds up a sense of tension, saying "You are bringing your slave into church for manumission. Silence falls. Your petition is read; your desires are carried out."[89] Augustine draws out the point that the master values faithfulness in his slave, which is the reason he wishes to reward him with freedom. He then uses this to criticize masters listening to his preaching, rebuking them for valuing faithfulness in slaves, but not offering it to their master in Heaven. Masters have failed to delight in the Lord or use created things aright; this amounts to unfaithfulness for which they would rebuke a slave. He commands earthly masters, saying, "Give to your master, what you praise in your slave."[90]

83. *s.* 356.3 (SPM 1, 134).
84. *s.* 356.7 (SPM 1, 136).
85. *s.* 134.3 (PL 38, 744).
86. *s.* 21.1–2 (CCL 41, 276–8).
87. *s.* 21.3 (CCL 41, 278).
88. *s.* 21.5–7 (CCL 41, 280–3).
89. "Seruum manu mittendum ducis in ecclesiam. Fit silentium. Recitatur libellus tuus, aut fit tui desiderii prosequutio." *s.* 21.6 (CCL 41, 281).
90. "Redde domino tuo, quod laudas in seruo tuo." *s.* 21.6 (CCL 41, 281).

162 | Augustine's Theology of Preaching

Augustine reasons that masters have been bought by God twice over: by creation and redemption. Masters expect obedience from a slave they have purchased, so why they offer God any less? Augustine appears to sense that his illustration has traction with his listeners and proceeds to expand it further. He imagines a scene in which a master is angry with an unfaithful slave; he shouts furiously that the slave had been bought with his own blood and should be ashamed to have been unfaithful. Augustine then supposes a somewhat unlikely response from the slave: "If he dares to answer you, while you inveigh and shout at your slave, will you not blush if he says to you: 'What, I ask you, blood have you given for me?'"[91] One assumes that any slaves listening to this illustration would have felt considerable glee at the unlikely scenario of a slave correcting his master in this way. Augustine draws his own sharp rebuke to masters from this story, arguing that they imagine the money they paid for a slave to be as precious as their blood. However, the blood shed by Christ to purchase them was real, poured out to the point of death.

In this illustration of a slave correcting his master, we find Augustine subverting the normal slave and master relationship. He does so not primarily to advocate social reforms, much less the abolition of slavery. Rather, he is concerned to affect listeners' interior attitudes and desires. The temporal theological framework which Augustine developed, which is outlined above, does not naturally lead him to oppose slavery as an institution: it is a just punishment for original sin and will be ended when Christ returns. Nevertheless, as he urges interior virtue for both masters and slaves, he does on occasion preach so as to subvert the prevailing attitudes of masters and slaves. He continued to use his hermeneutic of interiority and temporality, and he did so with the aim that Scripture would change listeners. He may not have tried to bring about change in every respect with regards to slavery, but he aimed for change nonetheless.

FRIENDS

Since McNamara's seminal study,[92] a number of scholars have focused upon Augustine's view of friendship.[93] The famous comment of Peter Brown testifies

---

91. "Si tibi audeat respondere sic inuehenti et clamanti ipse seruus tuus, non erubesceres si tibi dicat: quem, rogo te, sanguinem pro me dedisti?" s. 21.7 (CCL 41, 282).

92. M.A. McNamara, *Friends and Friendship for Saint Augustine* (New York: Alba House, 1957).

93. Gerald W. Schlabach, "Friendship as Adultery: Social Reality and Sexual Metaphor in Augustine's Doctrine of Original Sin," *Augustinian Studies* 23 (1992): 125–47; Donald Burt, *Friendship and Society: An Introduction to Augustine's Practical Philosophy* (Grand Rapids: Eerdmans, 1999); Paul J. Wadell, *Becoming Friends: Worship, Justice and the Practice of Christian Friendship* (Grand Rapids: Brazos Press, 2002).

to the high value Augustine placed on relationships in general and friendship in particular:

> Augustine will hardly ever spend a moment of his life without some friend... close by him. No thinker in the Early Church was so preoccupied with the nature of human relationships.[94]

Unsurprisingly, the theme of friendship occurs in Augustine's preaching. He could offer extended reflections on the nature of friendship or make unusual passing references to it; an example of the latter would be his warning Christians that the devil desires to become their friend.[95] When the sermons are examined, we find that in the more extended treatments of friendship he utilizes his familiar hermeneutic of appealing to interiority and temporality.

Augustine's theology and experience created a certain tension in his life regarding friendship. On the one hand, he came to believe that a Christian could only experience true friendship with another believer, while on the other he remembered and corresponded with friends from his pre-Christian days. Writing of an early and close friendship he reflected:

> But he was not then my friend, nor indeed afterwards, as true friendship is. For it is not true friendship unless when you join them together, they are clinging to you by that love poured into our hearts by the Holy Spirit, which is given to us.[96]

Augustine developed Cicero's emphasis upon the need of common virtue between friends into a theological view which restricted the true experience of friendship to Christians. That which is held in common between friends is the gift of God's Spirit. Friends bound together by lesser common concerns, such as business, lust, or circumstance, experience something less than true friendship. Yet his own experience of relationships and delight in friendships seems to have created a tension with his theologizing on this point. His attempt to resolve the tension was to link friendship with seeking the conversion of others: "For you truly love that friend, by loving God in your friend. Either because he is in him, or that he might be in him."[97] In his preaching, Augustine softened the theological restrictions he placed on friendship, as his interpretation

---

94. Brown, *Augustine of Hippo*, 20.

95. *s.* 9.4 (CCL 41, 113).

96. "Sed nondum erat sic amicus, quamquam ne tunc quidem sic, uti est uera amicitia, quia non est uera, nisi cum eam tu agglutinas inter haerentes tibi caritate diffusa in cordibus nostris per spiritum sanctum, qui datus est nobis." *conf.* 4.7 (CCL 27, 43).

of friendship became part of the means by which a believer sought to convert his or her friends. We see this worked out in more detail in *Sermon* 105, where Augustine developed the subject via interiority and temporality.

Reflecting upon Luke 11:5–13, Augustine opened his sermon by using Jesus' illustration to stir up listeners' desire to seek God, saying ,"Human sloth should be ashamed: He is more willing to give, than we are to receive."[98] This general observation is then developed. He uses the story from Jesus as the basis for his own meditation—a meditation clearly related to, but an embellishment of, the original image. Augustine invites hearers to imagine that a friend who is travelling stops and asks for food. The mention of a traveler on a road permits Augustine to highlight temporality: all are on a journey through life, as this world is fundamentally a journey-shaped reality.[99] However, in Augustine's story, you do not have any food to offer your friend. He appeals to his congregation, saying that surely everybody must have had this disappointing experience at some time: being unable to provide for a friend who requests help.

Augustine explains what his picture is intended to convey. The travelling friend is saying: "Restore sense to me, make me a Christian."[100] As Augustine develops the scene, the Christian does not know how to answer his or her friend. The friend's question reveals one's own interior poverty: "And he asks and as luck would have it you do not know answers—due to the simplicity of your faith."[101] The question from a friend prompts the other to realize his or her confusion and need. Together, the friends help each other seek after God. As Augustine observed, the one who teaches must learn.

In this way, we see how Augustine portrayed friendship in a slightly more fluid way than his comments in *Confessiones* would have led us to expect.[102] The friendship crosses boundaries between believer and unbeliever and is the stimulus to both seeking God together. When the friends ask where they can go for answers, truth and conversion, Augustine presents the Scriptures as the correct place to turn:

97. "Ille enim ueraciter amat amicum, qui deum amat in amico, aut quia est in illo, aut ut sit in illo." *s.* 336.2 (PL 38, 1471).

98. "Erubescat humana pigritia: plus uult ille dare, quam nos accipere." *s.* 105.1 (PL 38, 618).

99. *s.* 105.2 (PL 38, 619).

100. "Redde mihi rationem, fac me christianum." *s.* 105.2 (PL 38, 619).

101. "Et interrogat quod forte tu per simplicitatem fidei nesciebas." *s.* 105.2 (PL 38, 619).

102. See above, footnote 96.

And where can you search? Where, if not in the Lord's books? Maybe what he asked about is found in a book but is obscure. Maybe the apostle said it in one of his letters. He said it in a manner that you are able to read but not understand it. You are not allowed to pass by.[103]

Augustine's use of the image of friendship in this sermon is all the more striking because he is going beyond and developing the actual story he has in Luke 11. He uses the scriptural text as a departure point to teach the subject in hand. Since, in this instance, he is reasonably free with the text, developing and extrapolating from it, we see where Augustine's theological framework leads him, when he gives it permission to explore. Thus, we get a good insight to that framework as he develops points which are suggested by, but not actually found within, the Scripture on which he preaches.

This example concerning friendship shows that Augustine focused upon temporality and interiority by preaching about the journey we all make through life. Our interior need for God can be revealed by a friend's searching questions.

On another occasion, having read a long passage from *Sirach 22*, Augustine began preaching by explaining that he would speak on only one short saying which appeared to him weighty and significant, selecting *Sirach 22:23*. At least one modern English translation follows the *Clementine Vulgate* (1592) textual tradition, and reads "amico" as making the saying one about friends. Thus, the *New American Standard Translation*:

Make fast friends with a man while he is poor; thus will you enjoy his prosperity with him. In time of trouble remain true to him, so as to share in his inheritance when it comes.

The modern critical *Stuttgart Vulgate* (1969), by contrast, prefers "proximo" to "amico". In this decision, it is closer to the *Septuagint* which spoke of a "πλησιον", a "neighbor" rather than "friend." Most English translations follow this tradition.[104]

---

103. "Et ubi quaeras? ubi, nisi in dominicis libris? Fortassis quod ille interrogauit, in libro positum est, sed obscurum est. Forte dixit hoc apostolus in epistola sua. Sic dixit, ut legere possis, intellegere non possis: transire non permitteris." *s*. 105.3 (PL 38, 619). "Transire" may allude to Luke 10:32, where the Vulgate uses "pertransiit" to describe another needy traveler being neglected.

104. This includes the King James, New Revised Standard and New Jerusalem Bible.

Since we do not have a Hebrew manuscript for this verse of *Sirach* we cannot consult one. Hill suggests that Augustine's focus on friendship may be the explanation for the Clementine tradition rejecting the Septuagint reading.[105] If this is the case, then Augustine's interest in friendship and decision to preach on it from *Sirach* had unforeseen long-term consequences for translation.

Augustine's preaching on friendship in this sermon highlights the need for it to penetrate beyond exterior circumstances and possessions to conjoin people at the most intimate interior level, observing, "For if my friend was a friend when he was rich, and is not a friend when he is poor, then he himself was not a friend to me, but his gold was."[106] Augustine is teaching his listeners to submit to Scripture as the guide for their friendships. Having selected a verse he feels is about friendship, his method is to delve deeper into its possible meaning.

He does so by first noting the temporal development posited by the verse, that a man may be rich and then become poor. The motivation given in the text for keeping up the friendship with a poor man is that temporal changes in circumstances mean he may again in the future become wealthy.[107] Augustine observes that he finds this motivation unacceptable as pastoral advice.[108] Not only do some people remain poor and die in penury, but the ethical implications of loving a friend in the hope he would become rich leaves one in the same situation as the person who spurns a recently bankrupt friend: it is the money that is being befriended.

After briefly reflecting on the parable of Lazarus and the rich man, Augustine suggests an interpretation which centers on Christ. Indeed, he claimed to not only be theologizing an interpretation which focused on Christ, but also that the Lord is himself speaking, explaining the saying more clearly than Augustine could: "Your Lord is speaking to you, your Lord himself—that one who was rich and became poor. He will explain to you better and more reliably this sentence."[109]

This comment reveals much about how Augustine viewed his preaching. He could distinguish his attempts at explanation from God revealing his own

---

105. Augustine, *Sermons*, ed. Rotelle, vol. 2, *The Works of Saint Augustine* (New York: New City Press, 1990), p.232, footnote 3.

106. "Amicus enim meus, si cum diues esset amicus fuit, cum pauper est amicus non est, non ipse mihi amicus, sed aurum eius fuit." *s.* 41.1 (CCL 41, 495).

107. *s.* 41.2 (CCL 41, 496).

108. *s.* 41.3 (CCL 41, 496).

109. "Dicit tibi et dominus tuus, ipse dominus tuus, ipse qui cum diues esset, pauper factus est. Exponet tibi melius et solidius istam sententiam." *s.* 41.7 (CCL 41, 501).

interpretation. Yet while preacher and God are distinguishable, they are inseparable for the preacher still speaks as God teaches. The Lord's explanation is that Jesus set aside his riches to become poor because in his incarnate poverty he was able to draw near to listeners. The various scriptural references cited by Augustine[110] as pointing towards this image of poverty opening the way to divine-human communion legitimized for him the explanation that Christ is the pauper to whom one must remain a friend. In Christ's case, the future riches of inheritance which he shares with his friends are not physical money, but simply being with him.[111]

Sermon 41 is a good example of Augustine taking a verse from Scripture and probing it for understanding. He was attracted to it because it spoke of friendship, a topic of perennial interest to him. His hermeneutic of temporality led him to focus upon seeking a satisfactory solution to the problem posed by the apparent rooting of friendship in the hope of a future change in circumstances. This seemed to militate against his instinctive prioritizing of the interior. His Christological meditation permitted him to conclude the sermon by considering the future temporal riches Christ will share with those who befriended him in his poverty. Such a temporal change may be anticipated and spurs on a generous interior friendship that pays no regard to passing temporal changes in fortune. The great temporal change and the riches that will be brought about by Christ subsume lesser temporal developments. In this way, Augustine urged listeners to set aside lesser temporal concerns, and show friendship which valued the interior reality of a person.

Sermon 385 considers the general topic of love. It opens by affirming the central importance of love in the Old and New Testaments[112] and then proceeds to discuss various levels of love. Love has many degrees, each more or less lawful.[113] Friendship is considered in some detail.[114] That which arises from sharing in a bad conscience is to be repudiated. Friendship that comes about merely from sharing time together or having common interests arises from habit rather than reason. Since animals can enjoy such unreasoning company it is not highly regarded.[115] The highest form of friendship is that which arises

---

110. 2 Cor 8:9, Phil 2:6–8, Ps 34:18, 35:14.

111. *s.* 41.7 (CCL 41, 501).

112. *s.* 385.1 (PL 39, 1690).

113. *s.* 385.2 (PL 39, 1690).

114. *s.* 385.3 (PL 39, 1691).

115. *s.* 385.3 (PL 39, 1691).

from reason and is given with no expectation of reward.[116] Such friendship may only be superseded by the highest of loves—the love of God.

This explanation of friendship certainly has an Augustinian flavor to it. However it reads like a terse summary of the sort of framework which a student could learn from Augustine, rather than the more meditative, reflective questioning which usually characterizes his preaching. The argument that God ought to be loved freely for his own sake, because friends ought to be loved freely for their own sake,[117] appears to be very different from the way Augustine theologized elsewhere about use and enjoyment. All of this suggests that the Maurists may have been correct to attribute parts of this sermon to a preacher other than Augustine himself. That it was included in the Augustinian sermonic corpus testifies mainly to the fact that friendship was a sufficiently prominent topic in his preaching, that those who modeled themselves after him saw fit to attempt a summary of his views on the subject.

Our brief consideration of Augustine's preaching on friendship has shown that as he sought to change people with the Scriptures, he did so by appealing to his foundational hermeneutic of interiority and temporality. On a number of occasions he would develop or extend the issue raised in a reading in the direction of the topic of friendship. When he did so the value of interiority and temporality as hermeneutical tools was all the more clearly displayed.

CONCLUSION

The relationships represented in Augustine's congregation were varied; children, parents, married couples, slaves and friends. We have been concerned to unearth the theological assumptions Augustine brought to the task of preaching to people about the relationships in which they were engaged. Our concern here, as elsewhere, has been with the theological framework which Augustine relied upon in order to preach meaningfully to a congregation.

Augustine has long been recognized as a theologian who gave great weight to the importance of love and relationships, whether in his Trinitarian writings, letters, or *Confessiones*. It is perhaps a mark of how his preaching has been neglected that less has been said of his treatment of distinct relational groups such as parents or slaves. The tendency has been to dwell upon relationships or love in general. The *Sermones* can correct an imbalance in our view of Augustine by exemplifying concrete, specific applications of his

116. *s.* 385.4 (PL 39, 1692).
117. *s.* 385.4 (PL 39, 1692).

theology to distinct relationships. The *Sermones* restore pastoral application and specificity to our appreciation of him.

Once that specificity is seen in various relational contexts we are able to conclude that there is a consistent theological framework from which Augustine preached. His attempts to use Scripture in changing listeners were shaped by an undergirding hermeneutic which focused upon interiority and temporality. As such, his preaching about various relationships was consistent with that discerned in other aspects of his preaching.

8

Conclusion

We began our book by exploring the historical context of Augustine's preaching. Chapter 1 showed that we recognize that, although our study is a doctrinal investigation, doctrine is not formulated in isolation from cultural and historical realities. Following on from that background we considered the challenges faced by pagan oratory in Chapter 2. This presented the issues Augustine was sensitized to through his career as a secular speaker.

The above chapters laid the foundation for exploring how Augustine articulated his approach to interpreting Scripture and preaching in *De Doctrina*. In Chapter 3, we considered the role of interiority, temporality, and Scripture in *De Doctrina*. All of this shaped our in-depth explication in Chapter 4 of our two hermeneutical keys: interiority and temporality.

The value of our terms of investigation as hermeneutical keys was then demonstrated in Chapters 5 to 7. These comprised inductive studies of themes commonly preached about in the *Sermones ad Populum*. Throughout these chapters, we showed that our hermeneutical keys provide a valid reading of Augustine's approach to preaching Scripture. They enabled us to expose the assumed doctrinal framework which Augustine brought to the task of preaching.

Our material has been organized to expose and explore the beliefs developed by Augustine concerning preaching. This has been done in a way which gives readers a sense of what Augustine's preaching was actually like. All of this has been done against the backdrop of relevant historical and rhetorical matters.

TERMS OF INVESTIGATION

The terms *interiority* and *temporality* acted as a hermeneutical guide through the large numbers of *Sermones* which have been explored. Throughout our reading of the *Sermones*, we considered whether the terms provided meaningful hermeneutical keys for reading the *Sermones* and whether they increased understanding of Augustine's assumptions about how he preached. Our conclusion is that our terms are indeed a valid and constructive way of understanding what Augustine believed he was doing while preaching. A reader desiring to understand the *Sermones* and the concerns which were held by Augustine the preacher would benefit from keeping these terms in mind as he or she reads through the *Sermones*.

A guide such as this is helpful when attempting to explore such a vast range of writings. Our claim is not that these terms provide an exhaustive interpretation of the *Sermones*, nor that they are the only valid way of approaching them. However, it would seem reasonable to conclude that they are a valid and meaningful path through what can otherwise appear an insurmountable collection of writings. Their usefulness has been tested across a wide range of the relevant texts.

Scripture played a leading role in our study, as it did in Augustine's preaching. Scripture was, in essence, the reality upon which Augustine continually focused; interiority and temporality were the hermeneutical keys which guided him deeper into Scripture. As he thus ventured deeper into its obscurities and mysteries, Augustine was better able to refigure his congregation's inner longings and destinies around its concerns. The more Augustine explored the interiority and temporality of Scripture, the more listeners' interior desires and temporal lives were drawn into a scriptural view of reality. Augustine's probing of temporality and interiority broke down the walls between congregation and Scripture; lives were refigured by Scripture.

The value of this insight may be seen when it is compared to a recent unpublished interpretation of Augustine's preaching.[1] Boyd-MacMillan's helpful doctoral thesis is concerned with the psychology and spirituality of transformation in preaching, making use of Augustine's *Sermones* and other modern thinkers. Like us, he perceives and makes much of the centrality of Scripture in Augustine's preaching, writing "We have seen Augustine's belief in the power of scripture to reorient desire, albeit over time, which is why he saw his role as bishop to be primarily one of preacher."[2] Boyd-MacMillan seeks to explain how Augustine used the Scriptures to impact listeners:

1. Ronald Boyd-MacMillan, Ronald, "The Transforming Sermon: A Study of the Preaching of St. Augustine, with Special Reference to the Sermones Ad Populum, and the Transformation Theory of James Loder" (PhD diss., University of Aberdeen, 2009).
2. Ibid., 89.

He has a text, and his community is listening. How does he seek to connect the two, consciously, as he preaches? The sermons reveal, at the very least, his aim to issue this essential invitation: *Come with me into the scriptures where the beautiful Christ will enable us to live in the City of God.*[3]

The italicized statement is developed further in his thesis. He describes Augustine's preaching method as personal, scriptural, delightful and theological or world-forming. While this is all very helpful, the crucial point at which our interpretation differs from Boyd-MacMillan's approach is where he posits Scripture as one of several aspects of a transformational program. His thesis goes on to engage with James Loder's theories of transformation and compares them to Augustine's.[4] Boyd-MacMillan's overall aim was to compare Augustine's techniques of transformation to those of the modern day, and thus is a somewhat different approach from our own.

Boyd-MacMillan's dissertation supports our book in that it agrees with our focus upon the transformative and important role played by Scripture in Augustine's preaching. However, in his engagement with James Loder, he considers aspects of Augustine's preaching which are substantively distinct from scriptural interpretation. Our study focuses more narrowly upon the concerns which shaped Augustine's own consideration of Scripture. Our contention is that the very concepts which shaped his interpretation of Scripture, were the means by which he drew others into it. Scripture was then not one of a number of factors in Augustine's approach to transforming people; understanding Scripture was his method.

Comparison with Boyd-MacMillan's study serves to highlight the distinctiveness and value of our two hermeneutical keys for the *Sermones*. Augustine's preaching is relentlessly focused upon Scripture, and it is precisely by focusing on interiority and temporality, in Scripture and listeners' lives, that he unites the experiences of listeners with the Scriptures.

CONTEMPORARY VALUE

Our study of Augustine's preaching has some significant implications for contemporary theology. We shall briefly highlight three areas where this is the case.

---

3. Ibid., 74, italics original.

4. Ibid., 190.

OUR APPROACH TO AUGUSTINE

As we outlined in our preface, Augustinian studies have been dominated by a massive focus upon a small fraction of his corpus. Even when the *Sermones ad Populum* have been mentioned in summary form, it has often been in a dismissive manner. There have been a small number of doctorates which have begun to treat the *Sermones* as a body of theological literature with intrinsic value, and these have been considered in the course of our book.

The general assumption of scholars appears to have been that Augustine's preaching has little to offer our theological understanding which is not already offered in his more philosophical works. Hopefully, our book has demonstrated how unwise it is to overlook Augustine's preaching. There are theological insights to be gleaned which are especially important to our modern setting, where there is considerable interest in the matters of linguistics and communication.

The image we hold of Augustine as bishop, monk, theologian, controversialist and philosopher needs to be supplemented by an aspect of ministry that he himself held in extremely high regard: preaching. The same Augustine who wrote about the nature of time and penned *Confessiones* preached frequently. Our understanding of Augustine is impoverished if we neglect to integrate his preaching ministry with other parts of his life.

Our book has placed considerable emphasis upon the centrality of Scripture in Augustine's preaching. The terms of investigation we have utilized, therefore, were really hermeneutical keys applied to the reading and preaching of Scripture. We create a more faithful portrait of Augustine when his relentless investigation of Scripture through preaching is integrated with other parts of his corpus. For example, it is often observed that *Confessiones* is saturated in Scripture; this needs to be connected with Augustine's preaching. It was the intensity of regular preaching, together with the convictions which led him to preach as he did, which formed the intense concentration upon Scripture which is so artfully utilized in *Confessiones*.

A more historically accurate and vibrant portrait of Augustine is given when preaching is given the important place it held in his own estimation. Much time has been spent by scholars pondering how exactly Augustine developed from Platonism to Christianity. But more effort needs to be expended inquiring how he moved from pagan orator to Christian preacher.

OUR APPROACH TO SCRIPTURE

In today's culture of frenetic activity, and in light of the many demands which press upon ministers, Augustine's preaching urges church leaders to make preaching Scripture central to church life. Augustine had many demands upon his time, but he still prioritized preaching. This general encouragement to take care over preaching responsibilities is one which arises from a relatively basic observation of how devoted Augustine was to preaching.

However, our book has dwelled in some detail upon the undergirding assumptions and convictions which shaped Augustine's preaching. These led us to conclude that he drew people into Scripture by means of his hermeneutic of interiority and temporality. This meant that he drew listeners into a scriptural refiguring of their lives, not by starting with Scripture and then moving on to other issues, but rather by retaining an ever deepening focus upon Scripture.

This surely has lessons for our modern approach to Scripture. It is possible for a minister or Christian to hold Scripture in high regard and, consequentially, to devote time and energy to reading it. Such a person is likely to have a number of reliable insights about principles of interpretation which they will utilize. The problem is that in such a person it is all too easy to cultivate an attitude whereby one manages and controls Scripture. A high regard for Scripture and devotion to it can turn into a situation where the reader sets him or herself over Scripture in judgment. It becomes assumed that Scripture could not challenge or surprise the reader, for the interpreter has such a reliable understanding of interpretation that genuine challenge is precluded. It is, of course, deeply ironic that such a management of Scripture should be prevalent amongst those who hold it in the highest regard. Augustine challenges such a culture; he is the model of a preacher and a Christian who approached Scripture expecting that God would, first of all, address him. He did not restrict his studies only to the places where he thought he knew what God's message would be. Rather, he sought out the mysteries and obscurities, in the hope that God's surprising voice would warm his heart and motivate him to draw others into the experience of hearing God speak.

In our modern age, where we have benefited from increasingly nuanced insights about interpretation and hermeneutics, Augustine is refreshing, as a preacher who held to a hermeneutic that drew him and others deeper into Scripture. It is surely a more healthy approach than that which manages and controls Scripture by means of clichés or favorite texts.

OUR APPROACH TO PREACHING

It is often thought that, in our day, preaching is a dying art and people do not have the facility to listen to protracted monologue preaching. Much could be said to challenge the assumptions which lie behind such beliefs. But we shall restrict ourselves to a few brief comments arising from our study of Augustine's preaching.

First, Augustine's preaching was not a simple matter of a preacher speaking monologues. There was more going on during the preaching event. Not only was it common for Augustine to be interrupted, he elicited interaction from listeners and spoke in a way that integrated dialogical modes of communication. He acted out short role-plays, answered questions he put in the mouths of listeners, and made observations about the daily lives of his congregation. Since Augustine's preaching arose out of prayer and meditation upon a text, he was in effect welcoming listeners into the stream of a conversation he had already been enjoying between himself and God. Modern assumptions about the monologue style of speaking fail to do justice to the Augustinian praxis of preaching.

Second, Augustine's approach of delving ever more deeply into Scripture is an encouragement to remain with the passage of Scripture, rather than beginning with it only to launch off into other topics of interest. Augustine's method of persuasion involved going ever more deeply into the temporality and interiority of a passage; he did not take a simple lesson from the passage, and then consider ways listeners could make behavioral changes on the basis of that insight. Augustine's preaching modeled a profound confidence in God's ability to use Scripture to draw people into relationship with himself.

Third, Augustine's preaching utilized the full reality of the preacher's experiences—his prayers, meditation on Scripture, rhetorical ability, and relationships with listeners. These were all subsumed under the power of Scripture to transform desires and expectations, but they were important aspects of what it meant to preach. This is a reminder that preaching involves more than simply learning rules for communication; the hermeneutical concerns which Augustine utilized provided an interpretive framework for his prayers, pastoral care, and meditations before a service. All these were done in a manner aimed at drawing listeners into the temporality and interiority of Scripture.

FURTHER AREAS FOR INVESTIGATION

There is much more that could be said about the preaching of Augustine. Our book has drawn attention to an aspect of Augustine's ministry which is full of significance for today and has to date been underappreciated in the scholarly literature.[5] We have not been able to investigate specific ways in which the preaching ministry of Augustine impacted upon areas of doctrine and ministry with which we are more familiar. We have noted that it is likely there was a significant impact upon the *Confessiones*, but it remains to be seen how Augustine's preaching affected, for example, his doctrine of the church or his ethics of love. If preaching was as important to Augustine as we have concluded it was, an account of his ecclesiology or ethics which neglects to consider his preaching is surely deficient.

All the signs are that Augustine will continue to figure as the subject of a multitude of books and journal articles. He may yet be a key protagonist in the revival of Christianity and preaching—a role he has played before on more than one occasion. It may be hoped that other scholars will take note of the importance preaching held for Augustine and integrate it into their account of him, and the doctrine he taught. Preachers on the other hand might benefit from reflection on the doctrinal convictions about interiority and temporality which informed Augustine's attempts to use scripture to change listeners. As we journey through this short life, we all need to be more deeply changed. Augustine's method of hearing scripture preached remains God's most loving and gracious means for accomplishing that.

---

5. As has been mentioned, there are two notable exceptions: Gowans, *The Identity of the True Believer.* Boyd-MacMillan, "The Transforming Sermon: A Study of the Preaching of St. Augustine, with Special Reference to the Sermones Ad Populum, and the Transformation Theory of James Loder". We also note a helpful thesis on Enarrationes in Psalmos: Dowler, "Songs of Love: A Pastoral Reading of St Augustine of Hippo's Enarrationes in Psalmos".

Bibliography

Adams, Miriam Annunciata. *The Latinity of the Letters of Saint Ambrose*. Whitefish: Kessinger Publishing, 2007.

Alexander, James, "Donatism." In *The Early Christian World*, vol.2. Edited by Philip F. Esler, 953–61. London: Routledge, 2000.

Alexander, William M. "Sex and Philosophy in Augustine." *Augustinian Studies* 5 (1974): 197–208.

Alfeche, M. "The Rising of the Dead in the Works of St. Augustine." *Augustiniana* 39 (1989): 54–98.

Alflatt, Malcolm. "The Development of the Idea of Involuntary Sin in St. Augustine." *Revue des Etudes Augustiniennes* 20, no. 1 (1974): 113–34.

Ando, Clifford. "Christian Literature." In *The Edinburgh Companion to Ancient Greece and Rome*, edited by Edward Bispham, Thomas Harrison and Brian A. Sparkes, 402–06. Edinburgh: Edinburgh University Press, 2006.

Annas, Julia. *Plato: A Very Short Introduction*. Oxford: Oxford University Press, 2003.

Arnold, Duane W.H., and Pamela Bright, ed. *De Doctrina Christiana, a Classic of Western Culture*. Notre Dame: University of Notre Dame Press, 1995.

Auerbach, Erich. "Figura." In *Scenes from the Drama of European Literature: Six Essays*, edited by E. Auerbach,11–76. New York: Meridian Books, 1973.

———. *Mimesis: The Representation of Reality in Western Literature*. Princeton: Princeton University Press, 1953.

Ayres, Lewis. "Augustine on the Rule of Faith: Rhetoric, Christology, and the Foundation of Christian Thinking," *Augustinian Studies* 36, no. 1 (2005): 33–49.

———. "The Grammar of Augustine's Trinitarian Theology." In *Nicea and Its Legacy, an Approach to Fourth Century Trinitarian Theology*, edited by L. Ayres, 364–83. Oxford: Oxford University Press, 2004.

Babcock, William S. "Augustine and the Spirituality of Desire." *Augustinian Studies* 25 (1994): 179–99.

Barilli, Renato. *Rhetoric. Theory and History of Literature*, vol. 63, edited by Wlad Godzich and Jochen Schulte-Sasse. Minneapolis: University of Minnesota Press, 1989.

Barnes, M.R. "The Arians of Book V, and the Genre of De Trinitate." *Journal of Theological Studies* 44 (1993): 185–95.

———. "Rereading Augustine's Theology of the Trinity." In *The Trinity*, edited by Stephen T. Davis, Daniel Kendall, and Gerald O'Collins, 145–76. Oxford: Oxford University Press, 2001.

———. "The Use of Augustine in Contemporary Trinitarian Theology." *Theological Studies* 56 (1995): 237–51.

Barry, M.I. *St. Augustine, the Orator: A Study of the Rhetorical Qualities of St. Augustine's Sermones Ad Populum.* Washington: The Catholic University of America, 1924.

Bavel, Tarcisius J. van. "Augustine's View on Women." *Augustiniana* 39 (1989): 5–53.

———. "The Cult of the Martys in St. Augustine: Theology Versus Popular Religion?" In *Martyrium in Multidisciplinary Perspective*, edited by M. Lamberigts and P. Van Deun, 351–62. Leuvan: Leuvan University Press, 1995.

Bearsley, P. "Augustine and Wittgenstein on Language." *Philosophy* 58 (1983): 229–36.

Beckwith, Carl L. *Hilary of Poitiers on the Trinity: From De Fide to De Trinitate.* Oxford: Oxford University Press, 2008.

Benardete, Seth. *The Rhetoric of Morality and Philosophy: Plato's Gorgias and Phaedrus.* London: University of Chicago Press, 1991.

Berardino, Angelo Di, and Basil Studer, eds. *History of Theology: The Patristic Period.* Collegeville: Liturgical Press, 1996.

Bernard, R.W. "The Rhetoric of God in the Figurative Exegesis of Augustine." In *Biblical Hermeneutics in Historical Perspective: Studies in Honor of Karlfried Froelich on His Sixtieth Birthday*, edited by M.S. Burrows and P. Rorem, 88–99. Grand Rapids: Eerdmans, 1991.

Bernardin, Joseph B. "St. Augustine as Pastor." In *A Companion to the Study of St. Augustine*, edited by Roy W. Battenhouse, 57–89. New York: Oxford University Press, 1955.

Beversluis, John. *Cross-Examining Socrates: A Defense of the Interlocutors in Plato's Early Dialogues.* Cambridge: Cambridge University Press, 2000.

Blanshard, Alastair. "Rhetoric." In *The Edinburgh Companion to Ancient Greece and Rome*, edited by Edward Bispham, Thomas Harrison, and Brian A. Sparkes, 339-50. Edinburgh: Edinburgh University Press, 2006.

Boa, Kenneth. *Augustine to Freud, What Theologians and Psychologists Tell Us About Human Nature.* Nashville: Broadman & Holman, 2004.

Bochet, Isabelle, *'Le Firmament de l'Écriture': L'hermeneutique augustinienne*. Collection des Études Augustiniennes, Série Antiquité, 172. Paris: Institut d'Études Augustiniennes, 2004.

Bonnardière, Anne-Marie la. "Augustine: Minister of the Word of God." In *Augustine and the Bible*, edited by Pamela Bright, 245-251. Indiana: Notre Dame Press, 1999.

———. "La Bible" "Liturgique" "De Saint Augustin." In *Jean Chrysostome et Augustin*, 147–60. Paris: Actes du colloque de Chantilly, 1975.

Bonner, Gerald. "Augustine's Conception of Deification." *Journal of Theological Studies* 37, no. 2 (1986): 369–86.

———. "Augustine as Biblical Scholar." In *Cambridge History of the Bible*, edited by P.R. Ackroyd and C.F. Evans, 541–63. Cambridge: Cambridge University Press, 1970.

———. "Pelagianism and Augustine." *Augustinian Studies* 23 (1992): 33–52.

Bons, Jeroen A.E. "Gorgias the Sophist and Early Rhetoric." In *A Companion to Greek Rhetoric*, edited by Ian Worthington, 37–46. Oxford: Blackwell Publishing, 2007.

Booth, Edward. *Saint Augustine and the Western Tradition of Self-Knowing, Saint Augustine Lectures*. Villanova: Villanova University Press, 1986.

Børresen, Kari Elisabeth. *Subordination and Equivalence: The Nature and Role of Woman in Augustine and Aquinas*. Kampen: Pharos, 1995.

Bourke, V.J. *Joy in Augustine's Ethics, Saint Augustine Lectures*. Villanova: Villanova University Press, 1978.

Bowersock, G.W. *Martydom and Rome*. Cambridge: Cambridge University Press, 1995.

Boyarin, Daniel. *Dying for God: Martyrdom and the Making of Christianity and Judaism*. Stanford: Stanford University Press, 1999.

Boyd-MacMillan, Ronald. "The Transforming Sermon: A Study of the Preaching of St. Augustine, with Special Reference to the Sermones Ad Populum, and the Transformation Theory of James Loder." PhD diss., University of Aberdeen, 2009.

Braun, Willi. "Rhetoric, Rhetoricality, and Discourse Performances." In *Rhetoric and Reality in Early Christianities*, edited by Willi Braun, 1–26. Waterloo, Ontario: Wilfrid Laurier University Press, 2005.

Bray, Gerald. *Holiness and the Will of God: Perspectives on the Theology of Tertullian*. London: Marshall, Morgan & Scott, 1979.

Brennan, Brian. "Augustine's 'De Musica'." *Vigiliae Christianae* 42, no. 3 (1988): 267–81.

Bretherton, Luke. *Hospitality as Holiness: Christian Witness Amid Moral Diversity*. Aldershot: Ashgate, 2006.

Bright, Pamela. "Augustine: The Hermeneutics of Conversion." In *Handbook of Patrisic Exegesis: The Bible in Ancient Christianity*, edited by Charles Kannengiesser, 1219–33. Leiden: Brill, 2004.

———. "Biblical Ambiguity in African Exegesis." In *De Doctrina Christiana: A Classic of Western Culture*, edited by Duane W.H. Arnold and Pamela Bright, 25–32. Notre Dame: University of Notre Dame Press, 1995.

———. *The Book of Rules of Tyconius: Its Purpose and Inner Logic*. Notre Dame: University of Notre Dame Press, 1988.

———. "North African Church." In *Augustine through the Ages*, edited by Allan Fitzgerald, 185–90. Grand Rapids: Eerdmans, 1999.

Brown, P. "Augustine and a Crisis of Wealth in Late Antiquity." *Augustinian Studies* 36, no. 1 (2005): 33–50.

Brown, Peter. *Augustine of Hippo*. London: Faber & Faber, 2000.

———. *The Cult of the Saints*. London: SCM Press, 1981.

———. *Power and Persuasion in Late Antiquity: Towards a Christian Ethic*. Wisconsin: University of Wisconsin Press, 1992.

———. "St. Augustine's Attitude to Religious Coercion." *Journal of Roman Studies* 54 (1964): 107–16.

Bruyn, Theodore S. de. "Philosophical Counsel Versus Customary Lament in Fourth-Century Responses to Death." In *Rhetoric and Reality in Early Christianities*, edited by Willi Braun, 161–86. Waterloo, Ontario: Wilfrid Laurier University Press, 2005.

Bubacz, Bruce S. "Augustine's Illumination Theory and Epistemic Structuring." *Augustinian Studies* 11 (1980): 35–48.

Burke, Kenneth. *The Rhetoric of Religion: Studies in Logology*. Berkeley: University of California Press, 1970.

Burns, J. Patout. *Cyprian the Bishop*. London: Routledge, 2002.

———. "From Persuasion to Predestination: Augustine on Freedom in Rational Creatures." In *In Dominico Elquio, in Lordly Eloquence: Essays on Patristic Exegesis in Honour of Robert Louis Wilken*, edited by Paul M. Blowers, Angela Russell Christman, David G. Hunter and Robin Darling Young, 294–316. Cambridge: Eerdmans, 2002.

Burnyeat, M.F., "Wittgenstein and Augustine De Magistro." In *The Augustinian Tradition*, edited by G.B. Matthews, 286–303. London: University of California Press, 1999.

Burt, Donald. *Friendship and Society: An Introduction to Augustine's Practical Philosophy*. Grand Rapids: Eerdmans, 1999.

Burton, Philip. *Language in the Confessions of Augustine*. Oxford: Oxford University Press, 2007.

———. "The Vocabulary of the Liberal Arts in Augusine's Confessions." In *Augustine and the Disciplines, from Cassiciacum to Confessions*, edited by K. Pollmann and Mark Vessey, 141–64. Oxford: Oxford University Press, 2005.

Byassee, Jason. *Praise Seeking Understanding: Reading the Psalms with Augustine*. Grand Rapids: Eerdmans, 2007.

Cahall, Perry J. "The Trinitarian Structure of St. Augustine's Good of Marriage." *Augustinian Studies* 34, no. 2 (2003): 223–32.

Calvin, John. *Institutes of the Christian Religion*, 2 vols. Edited by John T. McNeill. Philadelphia: Westminster Press, 2001.

Cameron, Averil. *Christianity and the Rhetoric of Empire: The Development of Christian Discourse*. Berkely: University of California Press, 1991.

Cameron, Michael. "The Christological Substructure of Augustine's Figurative Exegesis." In *Augustine and the Bible*, edited by Pamela Bright, 74–103. Notre Dame, IN: Notre Dame Press, 1999.

———. "Totus Christus and the Psychagogy of Augustine's Sermons." *Augustinian Studies* 36, no. 1 (2005): 59–70.

Campbell, Gordon, ed. *The Grove Encyclopedia of Classical Art and Architecture*. Oxford: Oxford University Press, 2007.

Canning, Raymond. *The Unity of Love for God and Neighbour in St. Augustine*. Leuven: Augustinian Historical Institute, 1993.

———. "Uti/Frui." In *Augustine through the Ages*, edited by Allan Fitzgerald, 859–61. Grand Rapids: Eerdmans, 1999.

Caputo, John D., and Michael J. Scanlon, eds. *Augustine and Postmodernism. Philosophy of Religion*. Bloomington: Indiana University Press, 2005.

Cary, Phillip. *Augustine's Invention of the Inner Self: The Legacy of a Christian Platonist*. Oxford: Oxford University Press, 2000.

———. *Inner Grace: Augustine in the Traditions of Plato and Paul*. Oxford: Oxford University Press, 2008.

———. "Interiority." In *Augustine through the Ages*, edited by Allan Fitzgerald, 454–56. Grand Rapids: Eerdmans, 1999.

———. *Outward Things: The Powerlessness of External Things in Augustine's Thought*. Oxford: Oxford University Press, 2008.

Cavadini, John. "Feeling Right: Augustine on the Passions and Sexual Desire." *Augustinian Studies* 36 (2005): 195–217.

———. "The Structure and Intention of Augustine's De Trinitate." *Augustinian Studies* 23 (1992): 103–24.

Chadwick, Henry. "Augustine." In *The Cambridge History of Early Christian Literature*, edited by Frances Young, Lewis Ayres, ad Andrew Louth, 328–41. Cambridge: Cambridge University Press, 2004.

———. *Augustine, a Very Short Introduction.* Oxford: Oxford University Press, 1986.

———. "Frui – Uti." In *Augustinus-Lexikon*, edited by Cornelius Mayer, 71–75. Basel: Schwabe, 2004.

———. "New Letters of St. Augustine." *Journal of Theological Studies* 34, no. 2 (1983): 425–52.

———. "New Sermons of Augustine." *Journal of Theological Studies* 47, no. 1 (1996): 69–91.

———. "Philosophical Tradition and the Self." In *Late Antiquity: A Guide to the Postclassical World*, edited by G.W. Bowersock, P. Brown and Oleg Grabar, 60–81. London: The Belknap Press, 1999.

Chang, Curtis. *Engaging Unbelief: A Captivating Strategy from Augustine and Aquinas.* Downers Grove: Intervarsity Press, 2000.

Chapman, Emmanuel. "Some Aspects of St. Augustine's Philosophy of Beauty." *The Journal of Aesthetics and Art Criticism* 1, no. 1 (1941): 46–51.

Chappell, T.D.J. *Aristotle and Augustine on Freedom: Two Theories of Freedom, Voluntary Action and Akrasia.* London: Macmillan, 1995.

Chin, Catherine M. "The Grammarian's Spoils: De Doctrina Christiana and the Contexts of Literary Education." In *Augustine and the Disciplines, from Cassiciacum to Confessions*, edited by K. Pollmann and Mark Vessey, 167–83. Oxford: Oxford University Press, 2005.

Clark, Donald Lemen. *Rhetoric in Greco-Roman Education.* New York: Columbia University Press, 1957.

Clark, Elizabeth. "Adam's Only Companion: Augustine and the Early Christian Debate on Marriage." *Recherches Augustiniennes* XXI (1986): 139–62.

Clark, Gillian, *Augustine: The Confessions.* Exeter: Bristol Phoenix Press, 2004.

Clark, Mary, "De Trinitate." In *The Cambridge Companion to Augustine*, edited by Eleonore Stump and Norman Kretzmann, 91–102. Cambridge: Cambridge University Press, 2001.

Clarke, M.L. *Rhetoric at Rome: A Historical Survey.* London: Routledge, 1996.

Classen, C.J. "Ciceros Kunst Der Überredung." In *Rhétorique et Éloquence Chez Cicéron*, edited by W. Ludwig. Genève: Fondation Hardt Entretiens, Vol. 28, 1982.

Clifford, Gay. *The Transformations of Allegory, Concepts of Literature*. London: Routledge & Keegan Paul Ltd, 1974.

Colish, Marcia L. "St. Augustine's Rhetoric of Silence Revisited." *Augustinian Studies* 9 (1978): 15–24.

Comeau, M. *Saint Augustin: Exégète Du Quatrième Évangile*. Paris: Beauchesne, 1930.

Connerton, Paul. *How Societies Remember*. Cambridge: Cambridge University Press, 1989.

Consigny, Scott Porter. *Gorgias, Sophist and Artist*. Columbia: University of South Carolina Press, 2001.

Constantinidou, Soteroula. *Logos into Mythos: The Case of Gorgias' Encomium of Helen*. Athens: Institut Du Livre, 2008.

Conybeare, Catherine. "The Duty of a Teacher: Liminality and Disciplina in Augustine's De Ordine." In *Augustine and the Disciplines, from Cassiciacum to Confessions*, edited by K. Pollmann and Mark Vessey, 49–65. Oxford: Oxford University Press, 2005.

Cooper, Kate. "Ventriloquism and the Miraculous: Conversions, Preaching, and the Martyr Exemplum in Late Antiquity." In *Signs, Wonders, Miracles: Representations of Divine Power in the Life of the Church*, edited by Kate Cooper and Jeremy Gregory, 22–45. Gateshead: Boydell & Brewer, 2005.

Corbeill, Anthony. "Rhetorical Education in Cicero's Youth." In *Brill's Companion to Cicero: Oratory and Rhetoric*, edited by James M. May, 23–48. Leiden: Brill, 2002.

Costello, Charles Joseph. "St. Augustine's Doctrine on the Inspiration and Canonicity of Scripture." Ph.D., diss. The Catholic University of America, 1930.

Couenhoven, Jesse. "St. Augustine's Doctrine of Original Sin." *Augustinian Studies* 36, no. 2 (2005): 359–96.

Courcelle, Pierre. *Les Confessions De Saint Augustin Dans La Tradition Littéraire: Antécédents et Postérité*. Paris: Études Augustiniennes, 1950.

Coward, H.G. "Memory and Scripture in the Conversion of St. Augustine." In *Grace, Politics and Desire: Essays on Augustine*, edited by H. Meynell, 19–30. Calgary: University of Calgary Press, 1990.

Craig, Christopher P. *Form as Argument in Cicero's Speeches: A Study of Dilemma, American Classical Studies*. Atlanta: Scholar's Press, 1993.

Cranz, F. Edward. "Quintilian as Ancient Thinker." *Rhetorica* XIII, no. 3 (1995): 219–30.

Crowe, Brian. "'To Receive in a Becoming Manner the Testimony of the Divine Writings': Augustine on Exegesis and Formation in Understanding the Doctrine of Original Sin." Senior Sophister Dissertation, supervised by Lewis Ayres (Dublin: Trinity College, 1998).

Cunningham, Mary B. and Allen, Pauline, eds. *Preacher and Audience: Studies in Early Christian and Byzantine Homiletics, A New History of the Sermon*, vol. 1. Leiden: Brill, 1998.

Curley, Augustine J. *Augustine's Critique of Skepticism*. New York: Peter Lang, 1996.

Daley, B.E. *The Hope of the Early Church: A Handbook of Patristic Eschatology*. Cambridge: Cambridge University Press, 1991.

———. "Position and Patronage in the Early Church." *Journal of Theological Studies* 44, no. 2 (1993): 529–53.

Dam, Raymond Van. *Becoming Christian: The Conversion of Roman Cappadocia*. Philadelphia: University of Pennsylvania Press, 2003.

Daniels, Donald E. "The Argument of De Trinitate and Augustine's Theory of Signs." *Augustinian Studies* 8 (1977): 33–54.

Dawson, John David. *Christian Figural Reading and the Fashioning of Identity*. Berkely: University of California Press, 2002.

———. "Figure, Allegory." In *Augustine through the Ages*, edited by Allan Fitzgerald, 365–68. Grand Rapids: Eerdmans, 1999.

———. "Sign Theory, Allegorical Reading, and the Motions of the Soul in De Doctrina." In *De Doctrina Christiana: A Classic of Western Culture*, edited by Duane W.H. Arnold and Pamela Bright, 123–44. Notre Dame: University of Notre Dame Press, 1995.

De Plinval, G. *La Technique Du Dialogue Chez Saint Augustin et Saint Jerome, Actes Du Premier Congrès De La Fédération Internationales Des Associations D'études Classiques*. Paris, 1950.

De Ste. Croix, G.E.M. *Christian Persecution, Martyrdom & Orthodoxy*. Oxford: Oxford University, 2006.

Decret, François. *Early Christianity in North Africa*. Eugene: Cascade Books, 2009.

Deems, Mervin Monroe. "Augustine's Use of Scripture." *American Society of Church History* 14, no. 3 (1945): 188–200.

Deferrari, Roy Joseph. "St. Augustine's Method of Composing and Delivering Sermons." *The American Journal of Philology* 43, no. 2 (1922): 97–123.

———. "Verbatim Reports of Augustine's Unwritten Sermons." *American Philological Association* 46 (1915): 35–45.

Dickinson, G.L. *Plato and His Dialogues.* London: Unwin Brothers Ltd, 1931.

Dixon, Peter. *Rhetoric. The Critical Idiom,* vol. 19; London: Methuen & Co Ltd, 1971.

Dodaro, R.J. *Christ and the Just Society in the Thought of Augustine.* Cambridge: Cambridge University Press, 2004.

———. "Eloquent Lies, Just Wars and the Politics of Persuasion: Reading Augustine's City of God in a 'Postmodern' World." *Augustinian Studies* 25 (1994): 77–138.

Dombrowski, Daniel A. "Starnes on Augustine's Theory of Infancy: A Piagetian Critique." *Augustinian Studies* 11 (1980): 125–33.

Donelly, Dorothy F., ed. *The City of God: A Collection of Critical Essays.* New York: Peter Lang, 1995.

Dowden, Ken. "Rhetoric and Religion." In *A Companion to Greek Rhetoric,* edited by Ian Worthington, 320-35. Oxford: Blackwell Publishing, 2007.

Dowler, Robert. "Songs of Love: A Pastoral Reading of St Augustine of Hippo's Enarrationes in Psalmos." PhD diss., Durham University, 2006.

Doyle, G. Wright. "Augustine's Sermonic Method." *Westminster Theological Journal* 39 (1977): 213–83.

Dreyfus, François. "Du Texte À La Vie." *Revue Biblique* (1979): 5–58.

Drobner, Hubertus R. "The Chronology of Augustine's Sermones Ad Populum 3: On Christmas Day." *Augustinian Studies* 35, no. 1 (2004): 43–53.

———. "The Chronology of St. Augustine's Sermones Ad Populum." *Augustinian Studies* 31, no. 2 (2000): 211–18.

———. "The Chronology of St. Augustine's Sermones Ad Populum 2: Sermons 5 to 8." *Augustinian Studies* 34, no. 1 (2003): 49–66.

———. "Psalm 21 in Augustine's Sermones Ad Populum: Catecheses on Christus Totus and Rules of Interpretation." *Augustinian Studies* 37, no. 2 (2006): 145–69.

———. "Studying Augustine, an Overview of Recent Research." In *Augustine and His Critics,* ed. Robert Dodaro and George Lawless, 18–34. London: Routlege, 2000.

Duddy, Thomas. *Mind, Self and Interiority.* Aldershot: Avebury, 1995.

Dunn, Geoffrey D. *Tertullian, The Early Church Fathers.* London: Routledge, 2004.

Edwards, Mark Julian. *Origen against Plato.* Aldershot: Ashgate, 2002.

English, E.D., ed. *Reading and Wisdom: The De Doctrina Christiana of Augustine in the Middle Ages.* Notre Dame: Notre Dame Press, 1995.

Eno, Robert B. "Doctrinal Authority in Saint Augustine." *Augustinian Studies* 12 (1981): 133–72.

Enos, Richard Leo, and Thompson, R., eds. *The Rhetoric of St. Augustine of Hippo: De Doctrina Christiana and the Search for a Distinctly Christian Rhetoric.* Waco: Baylor University Press, 2008.

Eskridge, James Burnette. *The Influence of Cicero Upon Augustine in the Development of His Oratorical Theory for the Training of the Ecclesiastical Orator.* Menasha: George Banta Publishing, 1912.

Fahey, Michael Andrew. *Cyprian and the Bible: A Study in Third-Century Exegesis.* Tübingen: J.C.B. Mohr, 1971.

Fairbairn, Donald. *Life in the Trinity.* Downers Grove: Intervaristy Press, 2009.

———. "Patristic Exegesis and Theology: The Cart and the Horse." *Westminster Theological Journal* 69, no. 1 (2007): 1–19.

———. "Patristic Soteriology: Three Trajectories." *Journal of Evangelical Theological Society* 50, no. 2 (2007): 289–310.

Fantham, Elaine. *The Roman World of Cicero's De Oratore.* Oxford: Oxford University Press, 2004.

Fergusson, Everett. *Baptism in the Early Church: History, Theology, and Liturgy in the First Five Centuries.* Grand Rapids: Eerdmans, 2009.

Finaert, J. *Saint Augustin Rhéteur.* Paris: Société d'édition "Les Belles Lettres", 1939.

Finn, Richard. *Almsgiving in the Later Roman Empire: Christian Promotion and Practice (313–450).* Oxford Classical Monograph Series. Oxford: Oxford University Press, 2006.

Finn, Thomas M. "Ritual and Conversion: The Case of Augustine." In *Nova & Vetera: Patristic Studies in Honor of Thomas Patrick Halton,* edited by John Petruccione, 148–61. Washington: The Catholic University of America Press, 1998.

Fitzgerald, Allan. "Habit." In *Augustine through the Ages,* edited by Allan Fitzgerald, 409–11. Grand Rapids: Eerdmans, 1999.

——— , ed. *Augustine through the Ages: An Encyclopaedia.* Grand Rapids: Eerdmans, 1999.

Ford, David F. *Christian Wisdom: Desiring God and Learning in Love.* Cambridge Studies in Christian Doctrine. Cambridge: Cambridge University Press, 2007.

Forman, R.J. *Augustine and the Making of a Christian Literature: Classical Tradition and Augustinian Aesthetics, Text and Studies in Religion.* Vol. 65. New York: Edwin Mellen Press, 1995.

Fortin, Ernest L. "Augustine and the Problem of Christian Rhetoric." *Augustinian Studies* 5 (1974): 85–100.

Fredriksen, Paula. "Paul and Augustine: Conversion Narratives, Orthodox Traditions, and the Retrospective Self." *Journal of Theological Studies* 37, no. 1 (1986): 3–34.

Frend, W.H.C. *The Donatist Church.* Oxford: Clarendon Press, 1952.

———. *Martyrdom and Persecution in the Early Church: A Study of a Conflict from the Maccabees to Donatus.* Oxford: Blackwell, 1965.

———. "Town and Countryside in Early Christianity." In *The Church and Town and Countryside,* edited by Derek Baker, 25–42. Oxford: Blackwell, 1979.

Fulmer, Burt. "Augustine's Theology as a Solution to the Problem of Identity in Consumer Society." *Augustinian Studies* 37, no. 1 (2006): 111–29.

Gaddis, Michael. *There Is No Crime for Those Who Have Christ: Religious Violence in the Christian Roman Empire.* London: University of California Press, 2005.

Gagarin, Michael. "Probability and Persuasion: Plato and Early Greek Rhetoric." In *Persuasion: Greek Rhetoric in Action,* edited by Ian Worthington, 46–68. London: Routledge, 1994.

Gaisser, Julia Haig. *The Fortunes of Apuleius and the Golden Ass.* Princeton: Princeton University Press, 2008.

Garnsey, Peter. *Ideas of Slavery from Aristotle to Augustine.* Cambridge: Cambridge University Press, 1997.

Gaskell, Philip, ed. *Landmarks in Classical Literature.* Edinburgh: Edinburgh University Press, 1999.

Gerson, Lloyd P. *Knowing Persons: A Study in Plato.* Oxford: Oxford University Press, 2003.

Gilman, James E. *Fidelity of Heart: An Ethic of Christian Virtue.* Oxford: Oxford University Press, 2001.

Gleason, Maud W. *Making Men: Sophists and Self-Presentation in Ancient Rome.* Princeton: Princeton University Press, 1995.

Goodchild, Philip. *Theology of Money.* London: SCM Press, 2007.

Gorday, Peter. *Principles of Patristic Exegesis: Romans 9–11 in Origen, John Chrysostom, and Augustine.* Studies in the Bible and Early Christianity, vol. 4. New York: Edwin Mellen Press, 1983.

Gorman, M.M. "The Early Manuscript Tradition of St. Augustine's Confessiones." *Journal of Theological Studies* 34, no. 1 (1983): 114–45.

Gowans, Coleen Hoffman. *The Identity of the True Believer in the Sermons of Augustine of Hippo, a Dimension of His Christian Anthropology.* New York: Edwin Mellen Press, 1998.

Grech, Prosper. "Hermeneutical Principles of Saint Augustine in Teaching Christianity," In *Teaching Christianity*, 80–94. New York: New City Press, 1996.

Griffiths, Paul J. *Lying: An Augustinian Theology of Duplicity.* Grand Rapids: Brazos Press, 2004.

———. "The Nature of Desire." *First Things*, Vol. 198, December 2009, 27–30.

Gross, Abraham. *Spirituality and Law; Courting Martyrdom in Christianity and Judaism.* New York: University Press of America, 2005.

Gross, Nicolas P. *Amatory Persuasion in Antiquity.* London: Associated University Presses, 1985.

Grudem, Wayne. "Why It Is Never Right to Lie: An Example of John Frame's Influence on My Approach to Ethics." In *Speaking the Truth in Love: The Theology of John Frame*, edited by John J. Hughes, 778–801. Phillipsburg: P&R Publishing, 2009.

Hadot, Pierre. *Philosophy as a Way of Life: Spiritual Exercises from Socrates to Foucault*, edited by Arnold Davidson. Oxford: Blackwell, 1995.

Hagendahl, Harold. *Augustine and the Latin Classics,* 2 vols, vol. 2, *Studia Graeca et Latina*; Göteborg: Acta Universitatis Gothoburgensis, 1967).

Hall, Robert G. "Ancient Historical Method and the Training of an Orator." In *The Rhetorical Analysis of Scripture: Essays from the 1995 London Conference*, edited by Stanley E. Porter and Thomas H. Olbricht, 103–18. London: Continuum International Publishing Group, 1997.

Hanby, Michael, *Augustine and Modernity.* London: Routledge, 2003.

———. "These Three Abide: Augustine and the Eschatological Non-Obsolescence of Faith." *Pro Ecclesia*, vol. 16.3 (2005): 340–60.

Hanson, Victor Davis. "Holding the Line: Frontier Defense and the Later Roman Empire." In *Makers of Ancient Strategy: From the Persian Wars to the Fall of Rome*, 227–46. Princeton: Princeton University Press, 2010.

Harmless, William. *Augustine and the Catechumenate.* Collegeville: Pueblo, 1995.

———. "The Identity of the True Believer in the Sermons of Augustine of Hippo: A Dimension of His Christian Anthropology." *Journal of Early Christian Studies* 7, no. 2 (1999): 330–31.

Harris, W.V., ed. *The Spread of Christianity in the First Four Centuries: Essays in Explanation, Columbia Studies in the Classical Tradition.* Columbia: Brill, 2005.

Harrison, Carol. *Beauty and Revelation in the Thought of Saint Augustine, Oxford Theological Monographs.* Oxford: Clarendon Press, 1992.

———. "De Doctrina Christiana." *New Blackfriars* 87, no. 1008 (2006): 121–31.

———. "Delactatio Victrix: Grace and Freedom in Saint Augustine," in *Studia Patristica,* edited by Elizabeth A. Livingstone. Louvain: Peter's Press, 1993.

———. *Rethinking Augustine's Early Theology, an Argument for Continuity.* Oxford: Oxford University Press, 2006.

———, "The Rhetoric of Scripture and Preaching: Classical Decadence or Christian Aesthetic?" In *Augustine and His Critics,* edited by Robert Dodaro/ George Lawless, 214–30. London: Routlege, 2000.

Harrison, E.L. "Was Gorgias a Sophist?" *Phoenix* 18, no. 3 (1964): 183–92.

Harrison, S.J. *Apuleius: A Latin Sophist.* Oxford: Oxford University Press, 2000.

Harrison, Simon. *Augustine's Way into the Will: The Theological and Philosophical Significance of De Libero Arbitrio, Oxford Early Christian Studies.* Oxford: Oxford University Press, 2006.

Hart, David Bentley. *The Beauty of the Infinite: The Aesthetics of Christian Truth.* Grand Rapids: Eerdmans, 2003.

———. *The Story of Christianity.* London: Quercus, 2010.

Hebrüggen-Walter, Stefan. "Augustine's Critique of Dialectic: Between Ambrose and the Arians." In *Augustine and the Disciplines, from Cassiciacum to Confessions,* edited by K. Pollmann and Mark Vessey, 184–205. Oxford: Oxford University Press, 2005.

Higgins, Colin. "Gorgias." In *The Sophists: An Introduction,* edited by Patricia O'Grady, 45–55. London: Duckworth, 2008.

Hill, Edmund. "St. Augustine's Theory and Practice of Preaching." *Clergy Review* 45 (1960): 589–97.

———. "Unless You Believe, You Shall Not Understand." *Augustinian Studies* 25 (1994): 51–64.

Holtzen, Thomas L. "The Therapeutic Nature of Grace in St. Augustine's De Gratia et Libero Arbitrio." *Augustinian Studies* 31, no. 1 (2000): 93–118.

Hornblower, Simon and Spawforth, Anthony, eds. *The Oxford Companion to Classical Civilization.* Oxford: Oxford University Press, 1998.

Horowitz, Maryanne Cline. "The Image of God in Man—Is Woman Included?" *Harvard Theological Review* 72, no. 3–4 (1979): 175–206.

Hunter, David G. "Augustinian Pessimism? A New Look at Augustine's Teaching on Sex, Marriage and Celibacy." *Augustinian Studies* 25 (1994): 153–78.

———. "The Date and Purpose of Augustine's De Continentia." *Augustinian Studies* 26 (1995): 7–24.

———. "Reclaiming Biblical Morality: Sex and Salvation History in Augustine's Treatment of the Hebrew Saints." In *In Dominico Elquio, in Lordly Eloquence: Essays on Patristic Exegesis in Honour of Robert Louis Wilken*, edited by Paul M. Blowers, Angela Russell Christman, David G. Hunter, and Robin Darling Young, 317–35. Cambridge: Eerdmans, 2002.

———. "Sex, Sin and Salvation: What Augustine Really Said." *Washington Theological Union*, 2002. Available at http://www.wtu.edu/news/lectures/Augustine_Lec1_text.htm

Jackson, B.D. *Augustine's De Dialectica*. Dordrecht: D. Reidel Publishing Company, 1975.

———. "The Theory of Signs in De Doctrina Christiana." *Revue des Etudes Augustiniennes* 15 (1972): 9–49.

Jackson, Timothy P. *The Priority of Love: Christian Charity and Social Justice*. Princeton: Princeton University Press, 2003.

Jeanrond, Werne G. *A Theology of Love*. London: T&T Clark, 2010.

Jensen, Michael. "I Wish to Be What I Am: Martyrdom and the Self in Theological Perspective." DPhil. diss., Oxford University, 2008.

Jones, A.H.M. *The Later Roman Empire*, vol. 2. Oxford: Blackwell, 1973.

Kahlos, Maijastina. *Debate and Dialogue: Christian and Pagan Cultures C.360–430*. Aldershot: Ashgate, 2008.

———. *Forbearance and Compulsion: The Rhetoric of Religious Tolerance and Intolerance in Late Antiquity*. London: Duckworth, 2009.

Kahn, Charles H. *Plato and the Socratic Dialogue: The Philosophical Use of a Literary Form*. Cambridge: Cambridge University Press, 1996.

Kannengiesser, Charles. *Handbook of Patristic Exegesis: The Bible in Ancient Christianity*, vol. 2. Leiden: Brill, 2004.

———. "Interrupted De Doctrina Christiana." In *De Doctrina Christiana: A Classic of Western Culture*, edited by Duane W.H. Arnold and Pamela Bright, 3–13. Notre Dame: University of Notre Dame Press, 1995.

———. "A Key for the Future of Patristics: The 'Senses' of Scripture." In *In Dominico Elquio, in Lordly Eloquence: Essays on Patristic Exegesis in Honour of Robert Louis Wilken*, edited by Paul M. Blowers, Angela Russell Christman,

David G. Hunter, and Robin Darling Young, 90–106. Cambridge: Eerdmans, 2002.

———. "Local Setting and Motivation of De Doctrina Christiana." In *Augustine, Presbyter Factus Sum*, edited by J.T. Lienhard, E.C. Muller, and R.J. Teske, 331-9. New York: Peter Lang, 1993.

Kärkkäinen, Veli-Matti. "The Christian as Christ to the Neighbour: On Luther's Theology of Love." *International Journal of Systematic Theology* 6, no. 2 (2004): 101–17.

Kastely, James L. "In Defence of Plato's Gorgias." *PMLA* 106, no. 1 (1991): 96–109.

Kelly, J.N.D. *Early Christian Doctrines*. Bedford: A & C Black, 1977.

Kelsey, David H. *Eccentric Existence: A Theological Anthropology*, vol. 1. Louisville: Westminster John Knox Press, 2009.

———. *The Uses of Scripture in Recent Theology*. London: SCM Press, 1975.

Kennedy, George. *The Art of Rhetoric in the Roman World 300 B.C.– A.D. 300*. Princeton: Princeton University Press, 1972.

———. *Classical Rhetoric and Its Christian and Secular Tradition from Ancient to Modern Times*. London: Croom Helm, 1980.

———. *Quintilian*. New York: Twayne Publishers, 1969.

Kenney, John Peter. *The Mysticism of Augustine: Rereading the Confessions*. New York: Routledge, 2005.

Ker, John. *History of Preaching*. London: Hodder & Stoughton, 1887.

Keresztes, Paul. *Imperial Rome and the Christians: From the Severi to Constantine the Great*, vol. 2. Lanham: University Press of America, 1989).

Kevane, Eugene. "The Prooemium of St. Augustine's De Doctrina Christiana." *Augustinian Studies* 1 (1970): 153–80.

Kile, Chad. "Feeling Persuaded: Christianization as Social Formation." In Willi Braun (ed.), *Rhetoric and Reality in Early Christianities* (Waterloo, Ontario: Wilfrid Laurier University Press, 2005), 219–48.

Kirwan, Christopher. *Augustine: The Arguments of the Philosophers*. London: Routledge, 1991.

Klauck, Hans-Josef. *The Religious Context of Early Christianity: A Guide to Graeco-Roman Religions, Studies of the New Testament and Its World*. Edinburgh: T&T Clark, 2000.

Kleinberg, A.M. "De Agone Christiano: The Preacher and His Audience." *Journal of Theological Studies* 38, no. 1 (1987): 16–33.

Klingshirn, William E. "Divination and the Disciplines of Knowledge According to Augustine." In *Augustine and the Disciplines, from Cassiciacum to Confessions*, edited by K. Pollmann and Mark Vessey, 113–40. Oxford: Oxford University Press, 2005.

Klosko, George. "The Insufficiency of Reason in Plato's Gorgias." *The Western Political Quarterly* 36, no. 4 (1983): 579–95.

———. "The Refutation of Callicles in Plato's 'Gorgias'." *Greece & Rome* 31, no. 2 (1984): 126–39.

Konstan, David. *The Emotions of the Ancient Greeks: Studies in Aristotle and Classical Literature*. Toronto: University of Toronto, 2006.

Koterski, Joseph W. "St. Augustine on the Moral Law." *Augustinian Studies* 11 (1980): 65–77.

Kraut, Richard, ed. *The Cambridge Companion to Plato, Cambridge Companions*. Cambridge: Cambridge University Press, 1992.

Laird, Andrew. "Figures of Allegory from Homer to Latin Epic." In *Metaphor, Allegory and the Classical Tradition*, edited by G.R. Boys-Stones, 151–75. Oxford: Oxford University Press, 2003.

Lancel, Serge. *St Augustine*. London: SCM Press, 2002.

Langan, John P. "Augustine on the Unity and Interconnection of the Virtues." *Harvard Theological Review* 72, no. 1–2 (1979): 81–95.

Langford, Wendy. *Revolutions of the Heart: Gender, Power and the Delusions of Love*. London: Routledge, 1999.

Lavallee, L. "Augustine on the Creation-Days." *Journal of Evangelical Theological Society* 32 (1989): 457–64.

Lawless, George. "Augusine's Use of Rhetoric in His Interpretation of John, 21:19–23." *Augustinian Studies* 23 (1992): 53–67.

———. "The Monastery as Model of the Church: Augustine's Commentary on Psalm 132." *Angelicum* 60 (1983): 258–74.

———. "Psalm 132 and Augustine's Monastic Ideal." *Angelicum* 59 (1982): 526–39.

Leone, Anna. "Christianity and Paganism in North Africa." In *The Cambridge History of Christianity: Constantine to C. 600*, edited by Augustine Casiday and Frederick W. Norris, 231–47. Cambridge: Cambridge University Press, 2007.

Lepelley, Claude. "The Survival and Fall of the Classical City in Late Roman Africa." In *The City in Late Antiquity*, edited by John Rich, 50-76. London: Routledge, 1992.

Lienhard, J.T. "Augustine: Sermon 51: St. Joseph in Early Christianity." In *In Dominico Elquio, in Lordly Eloquence: Essays on Patristic Exegesis in Honour of Robert Louis Wilken*, edited by Paul M. Blowers, Angela Russell Christman,

David G. Hunter, and Robin Darling Young, 336–47. Cambridge: Eerdmans, 2002.

———. "Reading the Bible and Learning to Read: The Influence of Education on St. Augustine's Exegesis." *Augustinian Studies* 27, no. 1 (1996): 7–25.

Litfin, Duane. "The Perils of Persuasive Preaching." *Cultic Studies Journal* 2, no. 2 (1985): 267–73.

———. *St. Paul's Theology of Proclamation: 1 Corinthians 1–4 and Graeco-Roman Rhetoric.* Cambridge: Cambridge University Press, 1994.

———. "St. Paul's Theology of Proclamation: An Investigation of 1 Corinthians 1–4 in the Light of Graeco-Roman Rhetoric." PhD, diss., Cambridge University, 1983.

López, Fernández. "The Concept of Authority in the Institutio Oratoria Book One." In *Quintilian and the Law: The Art of Persuasion in Law and Politics,* edited by Olga Eveline Tellegen-Couperus, 29–36. Leuvan: Leuvan University Press, 2003.

Lubac, Henri de. *Augustinianism and Modern Theology.* London: Geoffrey Chapman, 1969.

———. *Medieval Exegesis: The Four Senses of Scripture, vol. 1: Retrieval and Renewal in Catholic Thought.* Edinburgh: T&T Clark, 1998.

———. *Paradoxes of Faith.* San Francisco: Ignatius Press, 1987.

———. *Scripture in the Tradition.* New York: Crossroad Publishing, 2000.

MacIntyre, Alasdair. *After Virtue: A Study in Moral Theory.* London: Duckworth, 1981.

MacMullen, Ramsay. *Christianity and Paganism in the Fourth to Eighth Centuries.* New Haven: Yale University Press, 1997.

———. "The Preacher's Audience (AD 350–400)." *Journal of Theological Studies* 40 (1989): 503–11.

Mallard, William. *Language and Love: Introducing Augustine's Religious Thought through the Confessions Story.* Pennsylvania State: Pennsylvania State University Press, 1994.

Manville, Brook. "Donatism and St. Augustine: The Confessions of a Fourth Century Bishop." *Augustinian Studies* 9 (1977): 125–39.

Marback, Richard. *Plato's Dream of Sophistry.* Columbia: University of South Carolina, 1999.

Marcel, Pierre. *The Biblical Doctrine of Infant Baptism, Sacrament of the Covenant of Grace.* London: James Clarke, 1950.

Marec, Erwan. *Monuments Chrétiens D'hippone Ville Épiscopale De Saint Augustin.* Paris: Arts et Métiers Graphiques, 1958.

Markus, R.A. "Augustine: In Defense of Christian Mediocrity." In *The End of Ancient Christianity*, 45–62. Cambridge: Cambridge University Press, 1998.

———. *Signs and Meanings: World and Text in Ancient Christianity*. Liverpool: Liverpool University Press, 1996.

———. "Signs, Communication and Communities." In *De Doctrina Christiana: A Classic of Western Culture*, edited by Duane W.H. Arnold and Pamela Bright, 97–108. Notre Dame: University of Notre Dame Press, 1995.

———. "St. Augustine on Signs," *Phronesis* 2 (1957): 60–83.

——— (ed.). *Augustine: A Collection of Critical Essays* (Garden City: Anchor, 1972).

Matthews, G.B. *Augustine. Blackwell Great Minds*, ed. Steven Nadler. Oxford: Blackwell, 2005.

Maxwell, Jaclyn L. *Christianization and Communication in Late Antiquity: John Chrysostom and His Congregation in Antioch*. Cambridge: Cambridge University, 2006.

May, James M. "Ciceronian Oratory in Context." In *Brill's Companion to Cicero: Oratory and Rhetoric*, edited by James M. May, 49–70. Leiden: Brill, 2002.

———. *Trials of Character: The Eloquence of Ciceronian Ethos*. London: University of North Carolina Press, 1988.

Mazzeo, Joseph Anthony. "The Augustinian Conception of Beauty and Dante's Convivio." *The Journal of Aesthetics and Art Criticism* 15, no. 4 (1957): 435–48.

McComiskey, Bruce. *Gorgias and the New Sophistic Rhetoric*. Rhetorical Philosophy and Theory. Carbondale/Edwardsville: Southern Illinois University Press, 2002.

McLynn, Neil B. *Ambrose of Milan: Church and Court in a Christian Capital*. Berkeley: University of California Press, 1994.

McNamara, M.A. *Friends and Friendship for Saint Augustine*. New York: Alba House, 1957.

McWilliam, Joanne, ed. *Augustine: From Rhetor to Theologian*. Waterloo: Wilfrid Laurier University Press, 1992.

Meconi, David Vincent. "St. Augustine's Early Theory of Participation." *Augustinian Studies* 27, no. 2 (1996): 79–96.

Mercer, Nick. *Words and Minds: How We Use Language to Think Together*. Oxford: Routledge, 2000.

Merdinger, J.E. *Rome and the African Church in the Time of Augustine*. London: Yale University Press, 1997.

Miles, Margaret. *Augustine on the Body*. American Academy of Religion Dissertation Series, vol. 31. Missoula: The American Academy of Religion, 1979.

———. "Vision: The Eye of the Body and the Eye of the Mind in Saint Augustine's De Trinitate and Confessions." *The Journal of Religion* 63, no. 2 (1983): 125–42.

Miller, Fred D. "Plato on the Parts of the Soul." In *Plato and Platonism*, edited by Johannes M. Ophuijsen, 84–101. Washington D.C.: The Catholic University of America Press, 1999.

Mohler, James A. *Late Have I Loved You: An Interpretation of Saint Augustine on Human and Divine Relationships*. New York: New City Press, 1991.

Morgan, Teresa. *Popular Morality in the Early Roman Empire*. Cambridge: Cambridge University Press, 2007.

Morstein-Marx, Robert. *Mass Oratory and Political Power in the Late Roman Republic*. Cambridge: Cambridge University Press, 2004.

Mothersill, Mary. *Beauty Restored*. Oxford: Oxford University Press, 1984.

Mouw, Richard J. "Violence and the Atonement." In *Must Christianity Be Violent? Reflections on History, Practice and Theology*, edited by Kenneth R. Chase and Alan Jacobs, 159–82. Grand Rapids: Brazos, 2003.

Muller, Earl. "The Dynamic of Augustine's De Trinitate, a Response to a Recent Characterization." *Augustinian Studies* 26, no. 1 (1994): 65–92.

Murphy, James J. *Quintilian on the Teaching of Speaking and Writing*. Carbondale: Southern Illinois University Press, 2003.

Naddaff, Ramona A. *Exiling the Poets: The Production of Censorship in Plato's Republic*. Chicago: University of Chicago Press, 2002.

Narducci, Emanuele. "Orator and the Definition of the Ideal Orator." In *Brill's Companion to Cicero: Oratory and Rhetoric*, edited by James M. May, 427–44. Leiden: Brill, 2002.

Norman, Naomi. "Carthage," in *Augustine through the Ages*, edited by Allan Fitzgerald, 132–33. Grand Rapids: Eerdmans, 1999.

O' Connell, M.J. "De Doctrina." In *Augustine through the Ages*, edited by Allan Fitzgerald, 278–80. Grand Rapids: Eerdmans, 1999.

O' Connell, Robert. *Art and the Christian Intelligence in St Augustine*. Oxford: Blackwell, 1978.

———. *Soundings in St. Augustine's Imagination*. New York: Fordham University Press, 1994.

O' Conner, W.R. "The Uti-Frui Distinction in Augustine's Ethics." *Augustinian Studies* 14 (1983): 45–62.

O' Donnell, James. "Augustine's Idea of God." *Augustinian Studies* 25 (1994): 25–36.

———. "Augustine's Unconfessions." In *Augustine and Postmodernism*, edited by John D. Caputo and Michael J. Scanlon, 212–21. Bloomington: Indiana University Press, 2005.

———. *Augustine, Sinner & Saint: A New Biography*. London: Profile Books, 2005.

———. "Augustine: His Time and Lives." In *The Cambridge Companion to Augustine*, edited by Eleonore Stump and Norman Kretzmann, 8–25. Cambridge: Cambridge University Press, 2001.

———. *Confessions: Commentary on Books 8–13, vol. 3*. Oxford: Clarendon Press, 1992.

———. "De Doctrina Christiana." In *Augustine through the Ages*, edited by Allan Fitzgerald, 278–80. Grand Rapids: Eerdmans, 1999.

O' Donovan, Oliver. *Common Objects of Love: Moral Reflection and the Shaping of Community*. Grand Rapids: Eerdmans, 2002.

———. *The Problem of Self-Love in St. Augustine*. New Haven/London: Yale University Press, 1980.

———. "Usus and Fruitio in Augustine, De Doctrina Christiana 1," *Journal of Theological Studies* 33, no. 2 (1982): 361–97.

O' Meara, J.J. "The Immaterial and the Material in Augustine's Thought." In *Nova & Vetera: Patristic Studies in Honor of Thomas Patrick Halton*, edited by John Petruccione, 181–95. Washington: The Catholic University of America Press, 1998.

———. *Studies in Augustine and Eriugena*. Washington: The Catholic University of America Press, 1992.

O' Neill, J.C. "How Early Is the Doctrine of Creatio Ex Nihilo?" *Journal of Theological Studies* 53, no. 2 (2002): 449–65.

Oberhelman, Steven M. *Rhetoric and Homiletics in Fourth-Century Christian Literature: Prose Rhythm, Oratical Style, and Preaching in the Works of Ambrose, Jerome and Augustine*. American Philological Association American Classical Studies. Atlanta: Scholars Press, 1991.

Oden, Thomas C. *Justification Reader*. Grand Rapids: Eerdmans, 2002.

———. *Life in the Spirit: Systematic Theology*, vol. 3. San Francisco: Harper San Francisco, 1992.

Old, Hughes Oliphant. *The Reading and Preaching of the Scriptures in the Worship of the Christian Church: The Patristic Age*, 7 vols. Grand Rapids; Cambridge: Eerdmans, 1996–2010.

Olkowski, Dorothea, and Morley, James, eds. *Merleau-Ponty: Interiority and Exteriority, Psychic Life and the World*. New York: State University of New York Press, 1999.

Osborn, Eric. "Tertullian." In *The First Christian Theologians*, 143–49. Oxford: Blackwell, 2004.

———. *Tertullian: First Theologian of the West*. Cambridge: Cambridge University Press, 1997.

Palardy, William B. "Peter Chrysologus' Interpretation of the Raising of Lazarus." In *Studia Patristica*, edited by Elizabeth A. Livingstone, 129–33. Leuvan: Peeters, 1991.

Parmentier, M. "The Gifts of the Spirit in Early Christianity." In *The Impact of Scripture in Early Christianity*, edited by J.D. Boeft and M.L. Van Poll-Van De Lisdonk, 58–78. Leiden: Brill, 1999.

Pasquarello III, Michael. *Sacred Rhetoric: Preaching as a Theological and Pastoral Practice of the Church*. Grand Rapids: Eerdmans, 2005.

Paulsell, Stephanie. *Honoring the Body: Meditations on a Christian Practice*. The Practices of Faith Series. San Francisco: Jossey-Bass, 2002.

Peace, J. "St. Augustine on the Education of a Preacher." *Evangelical Review of Theology* 3, no. 2 (1981): 287–93.

Pellegrino, Michele. "General Introduction to Augustine's Sermons." In *Sermons*, edited by John Rottelle, 13–137. New York: New City Press, 1990.

Peterson, R.L. "To Behold and Inhabit the Blessed Country: Revelation, Inspiration, Scripture and Infallibility. An Introductory Guide to Reflections Upon Augustine, 1945–80." In *Biblical Authority and Conservative Perspectives: Viewpoints from Trinity Journal*, edited by Douglas Moo, 65–100. Grand Rapids: Kregal Publications, 1997.

Pickstock, Catherine. *After Writing, on the Liturgical Consummation of Philosophy. Challenges in Contemporary Theology*. Oxford: Blackwell, 1998.

———. "Eros and Emergence." *Telos* 127 (2004): 97–118.

———. "Justice and Prudence: Principles of Order in the Platonic City." *The Heythrop Journal* 42, no. 3 (2001): 269–82.

———. "Music: Soul, City and Cosmos after Augustine." In *Radical Orthodoxy*, edited by John Millbank, Catherine Pickstock, and Graham Ward, 243–77. London: Routledge, 1999.

———. "Reply to David Ford and Guy Collins." *Scottish Journal of Theology* 54 (2001): 405–22.

Pollmann, K., "Augustine's Hermeneutics as a Universal Discipline?" In *Augustine and the Disciplines, from Cassiciacum to Confessions*, edited by K.

Pollmann and Mark Vessey, 206–31. Oxford: Oxford University Press, 2005.

———. *Doctrina Christiana*. Freiburg: Switz, 1996.

Polman, A.D.R. *The Word of God According to St Augustine*. London: Hodder & Stoughton, 1961.

Pope, Hugh. *St. Augustine of Hippo: Essays Dealing with His Life and Times and Some Features of His Work*. Garden City, New York: Image Books, 1961.

Power, Kim. *Veiled Desire: Augustine's Writings on Women*. London: Darton, Longman and Todd, 1995.

Press, G.A. "The Content and Argument of Augustine's De Doctrina Christiana." *Augustiniana* 31 (1981): 165–82.

———. "Doctrina in Augustine's De Doctrina Christiana." *Philosophy and Rhetoric* 17 (1984): 98–120.

———. "The Subject and Structure of Augustine's De Doctrina Christiana." *Augustinian Studies* 11 (1980): 99–124.

Preus, J.S. *From Shadow to Promise; Old Testament Interpretation from Augustine to the Young Luther*. Cambridge: Belknap Press of Harvard University Press, 1969.

Przywara, Erich. *An Augustine Synthesis, Spiritual Masters*. London: Sheed and Ward, 1936.

Quinn, John M. *A Companion to the Confessions of Augustine*. New York: Peter Lang, 2002.

Quinn, Patrick. *Aquinas, Platonism and the Knowledge of God*. Avebury Series in Philosophy. Aldershot: Avebury, 1996.

Race, William H. "Shame in Plato's Gorgias." *The Classical Journal* 74, no. 3 (1979): 197–202.

Rackett, Michael R. "Anti-Pelagian Polemic in Augustine's De Continentia." *Augustinian Studies* 26 (1995): 25–50.

Ramirez, J. Roland. "Demythologizing Augustine as Great Sinner." *Augustinian Studies* 12 (1981): 61–88.

Ramsey, Boniface O.P., "Ambrose." In *The First Christian Theologians*, edited by G.R. Evans, 225–33. Oxford: Blackwell, 2004.

———. "Wealth." In *Augustine through the Ages*, edited by Allan Fitzgerald, 876–81. Grand Rapids: Eerdmans, 1999.

Ramsey, P. "Human Sexuality in the History of Redemption." *Journal of Religious Ethics* 16 (1988): 56–88.

Rapp, Claudia. *Holy Bishops in Late Antiquity: The Nature of Leadership in an Age of Transition*. The Transformation of the Classical Heritage. London: University of California Press, 2005.

Rashkover, Randi, and Pecknold, C.C. Pecknold. *Liturgy, Time, and the Politics of Redemption*. Grand Rapids: Eerdmans, 2006.

Raven, Susan. *Rome in Africa*. London: Routledge, 1993.

Rebillard, Eric. "Interaction between the Preacher and His Audience: The Case- Study of Augustine's Preaching on Death." In *Preaching, Second Century, Tertullian to Arnobius, Egypt before Nicaea*, edited by Elizabeth A. Livingstone, 86–96.. Leuven: Peeters, 1997.

———. "Sermones." In *Augustine through the Ages*, ed. Allan Fitzgerald, 773–92. Grand Rapids: Eerdmans, 1999.

Ricoeur, Paul. *Memory, History, Forgetting*. Chicago: University of Chicago Press, 2004.

———. "Philosophical Hermeneutics and Biblical Hermeneutics." In *From Text to Action*, edited by Kathleen Blamey and John Thompson, 89–101. London: Athlone Press, 1991.

———. "Preface to Bultmann." In *The Conflict of Interpretations: Essays in Hermeneutics*, edited by Don Ihde, 377–96. London: Routledge, 2004.

———. *Temps et Récit*. vol. 1, *L'ordre Philosophique*, Paris, 1983.

———. *Temps et Récit*. vol. 2, *L'ordre Philosophique*, Paris, 1984.

———. *Temps et Récit*. vol. 3, *L'ordre Philosophique*, Paris, 1985.

Rist, J.M. "Augustine on Free Will and Predestination." *Journal of Theological Studies* 20 (1969): 420–47.

———. *Augustine: Ancient Thought Baptized*. Cambridge: Cambridge University Press, 1994.

———. "A Note on Eros and Agape in Pseudo-Dionysius." *Vigiliae Christianae* 20, no. 4 (1966): 235–43.

Rogers, Jack Bartlett, and McKim, Donald K. *The Authority and Interpretation of the Bible: An Historical Approach*. London: Harper & Row, 1979.

Roldanus, Johannes. *The Church in the Age of Constantine: The Theological Challenges*. London: Routledge, 2006.

Rollinson, Philip. *Classical Theories of Allegory and Christian Culture. Language and Literature Series*, vol. 3. Pittsburgh: Duquesne University Press, 1981.

Rosenberg, Stanley, "Interpreting Atonement in Augustine's Preaching." In *The Glory of the Atonement*, edited by Charles Hill and Frank James III, 221–38. Downers Grove: InterVaristy Press, 2004.

Rowe, C.J. *Plato*. London: Bristol Classical Press, 2003.

Russell, Robert P. "The Augustinian Roots of Calvin's Eucharistic Thought." *Augustinian Studies* 7 (1976): 69–98.

Rylaarsdam, David, "Theological Reflection and Augustine's Confessions." In *For God So Loved the World*, edited by Arie Leder, 199–209. Belleville: Essence, 2006.

Salzman, Michele Renee. *The Making of a Christian Aristocracy: Social and Religious Change in the Western Roman Empire*. Cambridge: Harvard University Press, 2002.

Sandbach, F.H. *The Stoics*. London: Chatto & Windus, 1975.

Sanlon, Peter. "An Augustinian Mindset." *Themelios* 33, no. 1 (2008): 39–45.

———. "Depth and Weight: Augustine's Sermon Illustration," *Churchman* 122, no. 1 (2008): 61–76.

———. "The Rhetoric of Allegory in the Old Testament Sermons of Augustine." MPhil diss., Cambridge University, 2007.

Satterlee, Craig A. *Ambrose of Milan's Method of Mystagogical Preaching*. Collegeville: Liturgical Press, 2002.

Scanlon, Michael J. "Augustine and Theology as Rhetoric." *Augustinian Studies* 25 (1994): 37–50.

Schäublin, Christoph, "De Doctrina Christiana: A Classic of Western Culture?" In *De Doctrina Christiana: A Classic of Western Culture*, edited by Duane W.H. Arnold and Pamela Bright, 47–67. Notre Dame: University of Notre Dame Press, 1995.

Schiappa, Edward. *The Beginnings of Rhetorical Theory in Classical Greece*. New Haven: Yale University Press, 1999.

Schindler, D.C. "Freedom Beyond Our Choosing: Augustine on the Will and Its Objects." *Communio* 29 (2002): 618–53.

Schlabach, Gerald W. "Friendship as Adultery: Social Reality and Sexual Metaphor in Augustine's Doctrine of Original Sin." *Augustinian Studies* 23 (1992): 125–48.

Shanzer, Danuta R., "Augustine's Disciplines: Silent Diutius Musae Varronis?" In *Augustine and the Disciplines, from Cassiciacum to Confessions*, edited by K. Pollmann and Mark Vessey, 69–112. Oxford: Oxford University Press, 2005.

Sheerin, Daniel, "Rhetorical and Hermeneutical Synkrisis in Patristic Typology." In *Nova & Vetera: Patristic Studies in Honor of Thomas Patrick Halton*, edited by John Petruccione, 22–39. Washington: The Catholic University of America Press, 1998.

Shipley, Graham, et al., eds. *The Cambridge Dictionary of Classical Civilization.* Cambridge: Cambridge University Press, 2006.

Shults, F. LeRon. *Reforming the Doctrine of God.* Grand Rapids: Eerdmans, 2005.

Siebach, James. "Rhetorical Strategies in Book One of St. Augustine's Confessions." *Augustinian Studies* 26, no. 1 (1994): 93–108.

Sluiter, I. "Communication, Eloquence and Entertainment in Augustine's De Doctrina Christiana." In *The Impact of Scripture in Early Christianity*, edited by J.D. Boeft and M.L. Van Poll-Van De Lisdonk, 245–67. Leiden: Brill, 1999.

Sorabji, Richard. *Emotion and Peace of Mind: From Stoic Agitation to Christian Temptation.* Oxford: Oxford University Press, 2000.

Soskice, Janet Martin. "Monica's Tears: Augustine on Words and Speech." *New Blackfriars* 83, no. 980 (2002): 448–58.

Starnes, C., "St. Augustine and the Vision of Truth," *Dionysius* 1 (1977): 85–126.

Stauffer, Devin. "Socrates and Callicles: A Reading of Plato's Gorgias." *The Review of Politics* 64, no. 4 (2002): 627–57.

———. *The Unity of Plato's Gorgias: Rhetoric, Justice and the Philosophic Life.* New York: Cambridge University Press, 2006.

Steel, C.E.W. *Cicero, Rhetoric, and Empire, Oxford Classical Monographs.* Oxford: Oxford University Press, 2001.

Sterk, Andrea. *Renouncing the World yet Leading the Church: The Monk-Bishop in Late Antiquity.* London: Harvard University Press, 2004.

Stock, Brian. *After Augustine: The Meditative Reader and the Text.* Philadelphia: University of Pennsylvania Press, 2001.

———. *Augustine the Reader: Meditation, Self-Knowledge and the Ethics of Interpretation.* Cambridge: Harvard University Press, 1996.

Straw, Carol E. "Augustine as Pastoral Theologian: The Exegesis of the Parables of the Field and Threshing Floor." *Augustinian Studies* 14 (1983): 129–51.

Studer, Basil. *Trinity and Incarnation; the Faith of the Early Church.* Edinburgh: T&T Clark, 1993.

Stump, Eleonore, and Kretzmann, Norman, eds. *The Cambridge Companion to Augustine.* Cambridge Companions. Cambridge: Cambridge University Press, 2001.

Sullivan, Thérèse. "S. Aureli Augustini Hipponiensis Episcopi De Doctrina Christiana Liber Quartus: A Commentary, with a Revised Text, Introduction and Translation." PhD. diss., The Catholic University of America, 1930.

Sutherland, Christine Mason. "Augustine, Ethos and the Integrative Nature of Christian Rhetoric." *Rhetor* 1 (2004): 1–18.

Swift, Louis J. "Augustine on Fama: The Case of Pinianus." In *Nova & Vetera: Patristic Studies in Honor of Thomas Patrick Halton*, edited by John Petruccione, 196–205. Washington: The Catholic University of America Press, 1998.

Tarnas, Richard. *The Passion of the Western Mind*. New York: Harmony Books, 1991.

Tatarkiewicz, Wladyslaw. "The Great Theory of Beauty and Its Decline." *The Journal of Aesthetics and Art Criticism* 31, no. 2 (1972): 165–80.

Taylor, Charles. *A Secular Age*. Cambridge: Belknap Press, 2007.

———. *Sources of the Self: The Making of the Modern Identity*. Cambridge: Cambridge University Press, 1989.

Tertullian. *Treatises on Penance: On Penitence and on Purity*, vol. 28. London: Longmans, Green and Co, 1959.

TeSelle, Eugene. "Serpent, Eve, and Adam: Augustine and the Exegetical Tradition." In *Augustine, Presbyter Factus Sum*, edited by J.T. Lienhard, E.C. Muller, and R.J. Teske, 341–61. New York: Peter Lang, 1993.

———. "Some Reflections on Augustine's Use of Scripture." *Augustinian Studies* 7 (1976): 165–78.

Teske, R.J. *Paradoxes of Time in Saint Augustine: The Aquinas Lecture*. Milwaukee: Marquette University Press, 1996.

———. *To Know God and the Soul: Essays on the Thought of Augustine*. Washington: Catholic University of America Press, 2008.

Thielicke, Helmut. *The Evangelical Faith*, vol. 1. Edinburgh: T&T Clark, 1974.

Thomas, Carol G./Edward Kent Webb, "From Orality to Rhetoric: An Intellectual Transformation." In *Persuasion: Greek Rhetoric in Action*, edited by Ian Worthington, 3–25. London: Routledge, 1994.

Thorsteinsson, Runar M. *Roman Christianity & Roman Stoicism: A Comparative Study of Ancient Morality*. Oxford: Oxford University Press, 2010.

Tiley, Maureen A. *The Bible in Christian North Africa: The Donatist World*. Minneapolis: Fortress Press, 1997.

Tissot, Gabriel, ed. *Ambrose of Milan: Traité Sur L'évangile De S. Luc*, vols. 45 & 52. Paris: Les Éditions du Cerf, 1956, 1958.

Toom, Tarmo. *Thought Clothed with Sound: Augustine's Christological Hermeneutics in De Doctrina Christiana*. International Theological Studies. Oxford: Peter Lang, 2002.

Tourneau, Roger le. "North Africa to the Sixteenth Century." In *The Cambridge History of Islam: The Indian Sub-Continent, South-East Asia, Africa and the Muslim West*, edited by P.M. Holt, Ann K.S. Lambton, and Bernard Lewis, 211–37. Cambridge: Cambridge University Press, 1970.

Tournier, Paul. *Guilt and Grace: A Psychological Study*. London: Hodder & Stoughton, 1962.

Trapé, A. St. *Augustine: Man, Pastor, Mystic*. New York: Catholic Book Publishing Company, 1986.

Trembath, Kern Robert. *Evangelical Theories of Inspiration: A Review and Proposal*. Oxford: Oxford University Press, 1987.

Troup, Calvin L. *Temporality, Eternity and Wisdom: The Rhetoric of Augustine's Confessions*. Columbia: University of South Carolina Press, 1999.

Uhalde, Kevin. *Expectations of Justice in the Age of Augustine*. Philadelphia: University of Pennsylvania Press, 2007.

Van Der Meer, F. *Augustine the Bishop: The Life and Work of a Father of the Church*. London: Sheed and Ward, 1961.

Van Fleteren, Frederick. "Augustine, Neoplatonism, and the Liberal Arts: The Background to De Doctrina Christiana. " In *De* Doctrina Christiana: A Classic of Western Culture, edited by Duane W.H. Arnold and Pamela Bright, 14–24. Notre Dame: University of Notre Dame Press, 1995.

———. "Authority and Reason, Faith and Understanding in the Thought of Saint Augustine." *Augustinian Studies* 4 (1973): 33–71.

———. "Comments on a Recent Edition of De Doctrina Christiana." *Augustinian Studies* 34, no. 1 (2003): 126–37.

———. "De Doctrina Christiana Aside: Miscellaneous Observations." *Augustinian Studies* 27, no. 2 (1996): 107–28.

———, "De Utilitate Credendi." In *Augustine through the Ages*, edited by Allan Fitzgerald, 861–62. Grand Rapids: Eerdmans, 1999.

———. "Per Speculum et in Aenigmate: The Use of 1 Corinthians 13:12 in the Writings of Augustine." *Augustinian Studies* 23 (1992): 69–102.

Van Fleteren, Frederick, and Schnaubelt, Joseph C., eds. *Augustine: Biblical Exegete*. New York: Peter Lang, 2001.

Van Neer, J. "Some Observations on Augustine on Laughter." *Augustiniana* 56, no. 1–2 (2006): 81–92.

Vanhoozer, Kevin J. "The Love of God: Its Place, Meaning and Function in Systematic Theology." In *First Theology: God, Scripture and Hermeneutics*, 71–95. Apollos: Leicester, 2002.

Verbraken, Pierre-Patrick. *Etudes Critiques Sur Les Sermons Authentiques De Saint Augustin*. Instrumenta Patristica, vol. 12, Steenbrugis, 1976.

Vickers, Brian. *In Defence of Rhetoric*. Oxford: Clarendon Press, 1988.

Von Balthasar, Hans Urs. *The Glory of the Lord: A Theological Aesthetics*. Edinburgh: T&T Clark, 1982.

Wadell, Paul J. *Becoming Friends: Worship, Justice and the Practice of Christian Friendship*. Grand Rapids: Brazos Press, 2002.

Walker, G.S. Murdoch. *The Churchmanship of St. Cyprian*. Cambridge: James Clarke, 2003.

Walter, Otis M. "Plato's Idea of Rhetoric for Contemporary Students: Theory and Composition Assignments." *College Composition and Communication* 35, no. 1 (1984): 20–30.

Wardy, Robert. *The Birth of Rhetoric: Gorgias, Plato and Their Successors*. Issues in Ancient Philosophy. London: Routledge, 1996.

Weaver, F. Ellen, and Laporte, Jean. "Augustine and Women: Relationships and Teachings." *Augustinian Studies* 12 (1981): 115–31.

Webb, Ruth, "Imagination and the Arousal of the Emotions in Greco-Roman Rhetoric." In *The Passions in Roman Thought and Literature*, edited by Susanna Morton Braund and Christopher Gill, 112–27. Cambridge: Cambridge University Press, 1997.

Weinandy, Thomas G. *Athanasius: A Theological Introduction, Great Theologians*. Aldershot: Ashgate, 2007.

———. *Does God Suffer?* Edinburgh: T&T Clark, 2000.

Weiss, Roslyn, "Socrates: Seeker or Preacher?" In *A Companion to Socrates*, edited by Sara Ahbel-Rappe and Rachana Kamtekar, 243–53. Oxford: Blackwells, 2006.

Wetzel, James. "Augustine." In *The Oxford Handbook of Religion and Emotion*, edited by John Corrigan, 349–63. Oxford: Oxford University Press, 2007.

———. *Augustine and the Limits of Virtue*. Cambridge: Cambridge University Press, 1992.

White, Peter, "Bookshops in the Literary Culture of Rome." In *Ancient Literacies: Culture of Reading in Greece and Rome*, edited by William A. Johnson and Holt N. Parker, 268–87. Oxford: Oxford University Press, 2009.

Wilder, Amos Niven. *Early Christian Rhetoric: The Language of the Gospel*. Peabody: Hendrickson Publishers, 1999.

Williams, A.N. *The Divine Sense: The Intellect in Patristic Theology*. Cambridge: Cambridge University Press, 2007.

Williams, D.H. *Ambrose of Milan and the End of the Arian-Nicene Conflicts,* Oxford Early Christian Studies. Oxford: Clarendon Press, 1995.

———. *Evangelicals and Tradition: The Formative Influences of the Early Church, Deep Church.* Milton Keynes: Paternoster Press, 2005.

———. *Tradition, Scripture and Interpretation: A Sourcebook of the Ancient Church.* Grand Rapids: Baker Books, 2006.

Williams, Rowan. "The Bible." In *Early Christianity: Origins and Evolution to A.D. 600,* edited by Ian Hazlett, 81–91. London: SPCK, 1991.

———. "De Trinitate." In *Augustine through the Ages,* edited by Allan Fitzgerald, 845–51. Grand Rapids: Eerdmans, 1999.

———. "'Good for Nothing'?" *Augustinian Studies* 25 (1994): 9–24.

———. "Insubstantial Evil." In *Augustine and His Critics,* edited by Robert Dodaro and George Lawless, 105–23. London: Routlege, 2000.

———. "Language, Reality and Desire in Augustine's De Doctrina." *Literature and Theology* 3 (1989): 138–50.

———. "Politics and the Soul: A Reading of the City of God." *Milltown Studies* 19–20 (1987): 55–72.

———. *Why Study the Past? The Quest for the Historical Church.* London: Darton, Longman and Todd, 2005.

Williams, Thomas. "Biblical Interpretation." In *The Cambridge Companion to Augustine,* edited by Eleonore Stump and Norman Kretzmann, 59–70. Cambridge: Cambridge University Press, 2001.

Willis, G.C. *St. Augustine's Lectionary.* London: Alcuin Club Collections, 1962.

Wilson-Kastner, Patricia. "Grace as Participation in the Divine Life in the Theology of Augustine of Hippo." *Augustinian Studies* 7 (1976): 135–54.

Woodbridge, John D. *Biblical Authority: A Critique of the Rogers/McKim Proposal.* Grand Rapids: Zondervan, 1982.

Woodruff, Paul. "Socrates among the Sophists." In *A Companion to Socrates,* edited by Sara Ahbel-Rappe/Rachana Kamtekar, 36–47. Oxford: Blackwell, 2006.

Worthington, Ian, ed. *Persuasion: Greek Rhetoric in Action,* 1994.

Wright, David F., "Augustine and the Transformation of Baptism." In *The Origins of Christendom in the West,* ed. Alan Kreider, 287–310. Edinburgh: T&T Clark, 2001.

Yates, Jonathan, "Augustine's Appropriation of Cyprian the Martyr-Bishop against the Pelagians." In *More Than a Memory: The Discourse of Martyrdom and the Construction of Christian Identity in the History of Christianity,* edited by Johan Leemans, 119–35. Leuvan: Peeters, 2005.

Young, Frances. *Biblical Exegesis and the Formation of Christian Culture*. Cambridge: Cambridge University Press, 1997.

Young, Frances. Ayres, Lewis, and Louth, Andrew, eds. *The Cambridge History of Early Christian Literature*. Cambridge: Cambridge University Press, 2004.

Yunis, Harvey. "Plato's Rhetoric." In *A Companion to Greek Rhetoric*, edited by Ian Worthington, 75–89. Oxford: Blackwell Publishing, 2007.

Zizioulas, John D. *Communion and Otherness*. London: T&T Clark, 2006.

Index